David Hume

Updated Edition

Twayne's English Authors Series

Bertram H. Davis, Editor

Florida State University

TEAS 77

DAVID HUME
Portrait by Sir Joshua Reynolds.

David Hume
Updated Edition

John Valdimir Price

University of Edinburgh

Twayne Publishers • Boston
A Division of G. K. Hall & Co.

David Hume, Updated Edition
John Valdimir Price

Copyright 1991 by G. K. Hall & Co.
All rights reserved.
Published by Twayne Publishers
A division of G. K. Hall & Co.
70 Lincoln Street
Boston, Massachusetts 02111

Copyediting supervised by Pauline Chin.
Book production by Janet Z. Reynolds.
Book design by Barbara Anderson.
Typeset by Graphic Sciences Corp., Cedar Rapids, Iowa.

10 9 8 7 6 5 4 3 2 1

Library of Congress Cataloging-in-Publication Data

Price, John Valdimir.
     David Hume / John Valdimir Price. — Updated ed.
        p.   cm. — (Twayne's English authors series ; TEAS 77)
     Includes bibliographical references and index.
     ISBN 0-8057-7004-6
     1. Hume, David, 1711-1776.   I. Title.   II. Series.
   B1498.P73   1991
     192—dc20
                                                    91-8717
                                                      CIP

In Memoriam

A. W. C.
(1923–1987)

F. J. H.
(1909–1967)

E. C. M.
(1907–1986)

Contents

Preface
Chronology

> *Chapter One*
> Hume's Life and Publications: A Study in
> Controversy   1

> *Chapter Two*
> Youth and Energy: The Remembered *Treatise*   24

> *Chapter Three*
> The Moral Sciences: Ideas in Search of a Form   39

> *Chapter Four*
> Courage and Perseverance: The Two *Enquiries*   62

> *Chapter Five*
> Hume as Historian   83

> *Chapter Six*
> Hume and Religious Skepticism   106

> *Chapter Seven*
> David Hume: Man of Letters   127

Notes and References   139
Selected Bibliography   156
Index   160

Preface

Since the first edition of this book was published in 1968, studies on David Hume and the Scottish Enlightenment have expanded exponentially. We now have a Hume Society, a journal called *Hume Studies,* and scholarly conferences on Hume. Most of the new emphasis is on Hume the philosopher. This is still the only book in English, so far as I know, that is not a biography yet considers Hume's career as philosopher, moralist, essayist, economist, historian, theologian, and man of letters. Commentaries on aspects of Hume's career as historian and man of letters have begun to appear, however, and doubtless others will follow.

In this second edition, I have taken into account some of the more interesting and significant works that have been published about Hume in the past 25 years. Much of this new material is biographical. I have expanded the references and the bibliography to direct the reader's attention to some of this material. The remainder of the text is organized chronologically to present a discussion of Hume's career as man of letters rather than as philosopher, economist, or historian. A book that tries to cover so much must inevitably give only a taste of what is on the menu for the hungry reader, but I hope the curious reader, who is perhaps reading Hume for the first time, will go on to dine more heartily.

I was fortunate to have the assistance of Ernest Mossner, John MacQueen, David Norton, Richard Popkin, Sylvia Price, and Kathleen Williams in preparing the first edition. In the intervening years a number of friends, colleagues, and other scholars have drawn my attention to new material about Hume, and I must give them a general acknowledgment for their help and interest. Carson Bergstrom, Wojciech Nowicki, and J. Martin Stafford, as well as several of my former students, gave me specific help with several points, and I hope they will be pleased with the result. It is also a pleasure to thank the University of Edinburgh for various grants to cover preparation costs. I am especially grateful to Katharine Wilkinson for reading various portions of the revised typescript and for her constant encouragement. For this second edition, I have amended the dedication to record my debts to, and admiration for, three colleagues whose lives made a difference to mine: Wayne Colver, Fred Hoffman, and Ernest Mossner. As Hume wrote to one of his friends, "One would little regret Life, were it not the Experience of such good Friends."

Chronology

1711   David Hume born 26 April (O.S.) in Edinburgh; the second son of Joseph, proprietor of Ninewells, in the parish of Chirnside, in Berwickshire.

1723–1725   Attends Edinburgh University.

1725–1726   *Treatise* "projected."

1725–1734   Pursues self-education at Ninewells and Edinburgh.

1726   Leaves college.

1729–1733   Pursues education so intently as to damage health.

1734   Writes famous letter about health to Dr. John Arbuthnot; goes to London, then to Bristol, where he works in a merchant's office.

1734–1737   Tours France (Paris, Reims, La Flèche). Writes most of *Treatise* in La Flèche.

1737–1739   Moves to London; arranges publication of *Treatise*, the first two volumes of which appear in January 1739.

1739   Returns to Edinburgh and Ninewells.

1740   *Abstract of Treatise* (first two volumes) appears in March; volume 3 of *Treatise* appears in November.

1741   First volume of *Essays, Moral and Political* published.

1742   Second volume of *Essays, Moral and Political* published.

1744–1745   Candidate (unsuccessful) for chair of Ethics and Pneumatical Philosophy at University of Edinburgh.

1745–1746   Lives in London; tutor to Marquess of Annandale.

1746–1747   Secretary to General St. Clair.

1747   Visits Cork and Ninewells.

1748   *Three Essays, Moral and Political* published. *Account of Stewart* published. New Edition of *Essays, Moral and Political* appears. *Philosophical Essays concerning Human Understanding* published in April (title changed in 1758 to *Enquiry concerning Human Understanding*).

1749–1751 Lives in London and Ninewells.

     1751 Returns to Edinburgh; candidate (unsuccessful) for chair of Logic at University of Glasgow. *Bellmen's Petition* published. *Enquiry concerning Principles of Morals* appears in December.

     1752 *Political Discourses* published in February.

1752–1757 Keeper of Advocates' Library (now the National Library of Scotland).

1753–1756 *Essays and Treatise on Several Subjects,* a collected four volume edition of Hume's works, excluding *Treatise,* published.

     1754 First volume of *The History of Great Britain* published in November.

     1756 *The History of Great Britain* (1649–1689) published in November or December. (Imprint reads 1757, but volume appeared before then.)

     1757 *Four Dissertations* published in February.

1758–1759 Lives in London.

     1759 *The History of England* (1485–1603), two volumes, published in March.

     1759 Returns to Edinburgh.

     1762 *The History of England* (55 B.C.–1485), two volumes published. First volume reviewed in December 1761; second in February 1762. Andrew Millar brings out "a new edition corrected" entitled *The History of England* (six volumes).

1763–1766 Secretary to Lord Hertford in His Britannic Majesty's Embassy, Paris; meets Comtesse de Boufflers in late 1763; corresponds with Jean-Jacques Rousseau.

     1766 Returns to London bringing Rousseau with him; quarrels with Rousseau; publishes *Exposé succinct de la contestation . . . entre M. Hume et M. Rousseau,* translated later the same year as *A Concise and Genuine Account of the Dispute between Mr. Hume and Mr. Rousseau.*

1767–1768 Under-Secretary of State, Northern Department, until January.

1769–1776 Retires to Edinburgh.

     1776 Visits London and Bath. Dies in Edinburgh on 25 August.

1777 Posthumous edition of *Essays and Treatises*. Autobiography, *The Life of David Hume, Esq., written by himself,* published.

1779 *Dialogues concerning Natural Religion* edited by his nephew, David Hume, published.

Chapter One
Hume's Life and Publications: A Study in Controversy

If the boyhood of David Hume did not give evidence of the subtleties and discriminations that were to become his philosophical hallmark (his mother had, in a story that is probably apocryphal, described him as a "fine good-natured crater, but uncommon wake-minded"), an early account by one of his oldest friends indicates that his philosophical abilities were already beginning to appear. Writing on 5 June 1740, to his sister Agnes, William Mure of Caldwell described Hume as "extreamly curious in most parts of learning and how much soever he has shown himself a Sceptick upon subjects of speculation and enquiry, he is as far from it as any man with regard to the qualities of a well natured friendly disposition, and an honest heart."[1] Hume's autobiography, *My Own Life,* relates that he was "seized very early with a passion for Literature which has been the ruling Passion of my Life . . ."; and, in a letter written at the age of 23, Hume comments "that from my earliest Infancy, I found alwise a strong Inclination to Books & Letters."[2] He attempted to study law but gave up because of his profound interest in philosophy and literature. Matriculating at Edinburgh University in 1723, Hume pursued his education with ordinary success. While at Edinburgh, Hume wrote one of his earliest surviving literary works, a school exercise entitled "An Historical Essay on Chivalry and modern Honour."[3] His unfavorable opinion of the Dark Ages, typical though it was of the eighteenth century, was to alter in no important respects: in an appendix to the first volume of the *History of England,* Hume repeats the same conclusions—about the feudal and Anglo-Norman governments and their manners—that he had reached at the age of fourteen.[4]

Early Aspirations

Hume's first interest was not history but philosophy, as his private and public observations about *A Treatise of Human Nature* reveal. In a 1751 letter to his friend and philosophical debater, Gilbert Elliot of Minto,

Hume said the *Treatise* had been "plan'd before I was one and twenty, & compos'd before twenty five," adding that he had repented his "Hast a hundred, & a hundred times" (*HL*, 1, 158). For some time, Hume did not publicly acknowledge the *Treatise*. When he finally devised both an acknowledgment and simultaneous repudiation of the work, he seems, at the last minute, to have changed his mind about the matter. A unique copy of the 1770 edition of his *Essays and Treatise on Several Subjects* contains the earliest known publication of his "Advertisement," in which he describes the *Treatise* as a "Work, which the Author had projected before he left College, and which he wrote and published not long after."[5] About a year after Hume's death, the posthumous 1777 edition of *Essays and Treatises on Several Subjects* reprinted this "Advertisement." Nevertheless, the *Treatise* contains some of Hume's most important philosophical discussions, and modern commentators have ignored his plea to disregard it. While he altered some of his views in revising the *Treatise* for presentation in other forms, Hume did not radically renounce his basic principles.

Hume's assertions about the early, juvenilian design of the *Treatise* may be taken almost literally, and it is conceivable that the work could have been planned before Hume was 21. He led a quiet, reflective life during that period and was preoccupied with the revolutionary quality of his first philosophical work. Writing to his good friend Henry Home (later Lord Kames) in February 1739, Hume remarked:

Tis now a fortnight since my Book was publish'd; & besides many other considerations, I thought it wou'd contribute very much to my Tranquillity, & might spare me many Mortifications, to be in the Countrey, while the Success of the Work was doubtful. I am afraid twill remain so very long. Those, who are accustom'd to reflect on such abstract Subjects, are commonly full of Prejudices; & those, who are unprejudiz'd, are unacquainted with metaphysical Reasonings. My Principles are also so remote from all the vulgar Sentiments on this Subject, that were they to take place, they wou'd produce almost a total Alteration in Philosophy; & you know Revolutions of this kind are not easily brought about. I am young enough to see what will come of the Matter; but am apprehensive lest the chief Reward I shall have for some time will be the Pleasure of studying on such important Subjects, & the Approbation of a few Judges.[6]

Perhaps the most interesting point about this observation is Hume's use of the phrase "metaphysical Reasonings" to describe the *Treatise*; his dismissive description of metaphysics in the *Enquiry concerning Human Understanding* (see chapter 4) suggests that one may take his later repudiation of the principles in the *Treatise* seriously. Nevertheless, his sanguine remarks in the letter to Henry Home would not lead one to suspect some of the great difficulties Hume experienced in composing his work, difficulties that acutely affected his health. Late in 1729, he was afflicted with lassitude, ptyalism, scurvy, and loss of appetite, which he attributed to the intensity of his studies. For over five years, Hume's ill health continued and was the occasion of one of his most interesting letters.[7] In it, Hume gives a full description of the disorders to which both his mind and body were subject. One of his concluding questions—"Whether I can ever hope for a Recovery?"—is almost plaintive in the suffering it reflects. Whatever the cause of the afflictions, Hume did recover, apparently while spending three years in a Jesuit retreat in France, during which the *Treatise* was completed.[8] Hume left for France in 1734 by way of Bristol, going first to Paris, then to Rheims, and finally to La Flèche in Anjou.

While working on the *Treatise* at La Flèche, Hume remained in touch with his friends in Britain, though few letters from this period survive. Writing to James Birch, whom he had met in Bristol in 1734 and to whom he had written from Rheims, Hume found time in La Flèche to answer a query from Birch:

As to a celebrated Professor, I do not know, if there is such to be met with at present in any part of France, especially for the Sciences, in which generally speaking the French are much inferiour to our own Countrymen. But as you know there is nothing to be learnt from a Professor, which is not to be met with in Books, & there is nothing requir'd in order to reap all possible Advantages from them, but an Order & Choice in reading them; in which besides the small Assistance I can give you, your own Judgement wou'd alone be sufficient; I see no reason why we shou'd either go to an University, more than to any other place, or ever trouble ourselves about the Learning or Capacity of the Professor.

Hume's observation perhaps accurately reflects the poor quality of English university education and the only slightly better facilities of Scotland in the early part of the eighteenth century; but only the most intrepid (or stupid) "Professor" would be likely, in the last part of the twentieth century, to dispute Hume's claim.

A Treatise of Human Nature

In spite of his health and his doubts about the likely success of the work, Hume sold, for £50, the copyright for the first two volumes of the *Treatise* to John Noone, of Cheapside, London, on 26 September 1738; they appeared anonymously in January 1739. The third volume, which Francis Hutcheson, then professor of Moral Philosophy at the University of Glasgow, read, appeared in November 1740. Dissatisfaction with John Noone led Hume, with the aid of Hutcheson, to find another publisher (Thomas Longman) for the third volume. The financial arrangements are unknown. One thousand copies of each volume were printed.

Hume's high expectations for the success of the three volumes, expressed in letters to his friends, were to be denied. In his autobiography, he remarked that the *Treatise* had fallen "*dead-born from the Press.*"[9] This is an exaggeration, but flat contradiction would also exaggerate its reception. The *Treatise* did not go unnoticed; it simply was not a popular success, which is not a surprise since few philosophical treatises are. Hume said in his "Advertisement" to the first two volumes, "If I have the good fortune to meet with success, I shall proceed to the examination of Morals, Politics, and Criticism; which will compleat this Treatise of Human Nature. The approbation of the public I consider as the greatest reward of my labours; but am determin'd to regard its judgment, whatever it be, as my best instruction." This was a rash promise. Despite the hostile reviews given to the first two volumes, the last volume was published 21 months later; but Hume never wrote, or at least never published, the promised volume on criticism.

The interval between publication was both exciting and frustrating. The first notice of the *Treatise* appeared on the Continent in the *Neuen Zeitungen von gelehrten Sachen.* Some seven lines long, the review remarked that "The author's intentions are sufficiently betrayed in the subtitle of the work, taken from Tacitus, *Rara temporum felicitas, ubi sentire, quae velis, & quae sentias, dicere, licet.*"[10] Other articles in learned journals on the Continent drew attention to the *Treatise,* but the review that Hume most wanted to see appeared in the *History of the Works of the Learned.* When it was published in two parts in the November and December 1739 issues, Hume might just as well have wished that the two volumes had been ignored. The reviewer makes fun of Hume's ideas and methodology and ridicules the claims for the book. The first part of the review (devoted only to book 1 of the *Treatise*) abuses Hume with rather limp sarcasm, referring to him as "this extraordinary Philosopher" and "so profound a Genius." The second part is somewhat restrained and seems to have been written by another person. The author cites Hume's abilities without resort to sarcasm and suggests that "Time and Reason may ripen these Qualities [of 'Prudence, Tenderness, and Delicacy']" necessary to compose a "treatise" of human nature. Professor Ernest Mossner has conjectured that the reviewer in the November issue may have been the Reverend William Warburton, who could always manage a fine line in abuse; however, this identification appears unlikely.[11] Regardless of reviewer, the reception of the *Treatise* was not what Hume had hoped for; therefore he carried out a plan made prior to the review—that of publishing, in the strictest anonymity, an abstract of the *Treatise*.

Before the review of the *Treatise* appeared in the *History of the Works of the Learned*, Hume had planned to send to that journal an anonymous letter in which he would explain the argument of the *Treatise*. Instead, he decided to publish the abstract as a pamphlet. The *Daily Advertiser* of 11 March 1740 announced the publication of a pamphlet entitled *An Abstract of a late Philosophical Performance, entitled A Treatise of Human Nature, &c. Wherein the chief Argument and Design of that Book, which has met with such Opposition, and been represented in so terrifying a Light, is further illustrated and explain'd*. When the pamphlet was actually published, the title was not quite so melodramatic: *An Abstract of a Book lately Published: entituled, A Treatise of Human Nature, &c. Wherein the Chief Argument of that Book is farther Illustrated and Explained*. One would like to think that a copy with the title announced in the *Daily Advertiser* did in fact appear, but all known copies of the *Abstract* have the latter and less emotional title.

This extraordinary effort by Hume to call attention to his work might be thought egoistic, and Hume had been accused by reviewers of having too many egoisms in his work. It was not uncommon, however, in the eighteenth century for an author to puff his or her own writing. Early reviews of the *Treatise* sufficiently, if not abundantly, indicate that reviewers simply did not understand Hume's argument; and if a restatement of it, in abbreviated form, could bring about a proper appreciation of what he did, Hume could easily risk other charges of egoism in explicating his work. For many years, the author of the *Abstract* was thought to be Adam Smith, but the republication of the work in 1938 put an end to that legend.[12] The *Abstract* is still one of the best, if not the best, introduction to Hume's most important ideas in the *Treatise*.

Unfortunately, the fate of the *Abstract* was not much better than that of the first two volumes of the *Treatise*; reviewers ignored it in passing judgment upon the *Treatise*. Indeed, very few copies of the work have survived into the twentieth century. After such an effort, Hume could not expect book 3 of the *Treatise* to enjoy a better reception, and in fact it suffered a worse fate, attracting only one review. A French journal, published in Amsterdam, *Bibliotheque raisonée des ouvrages des savans de l'Europe,* had identified Hume as the author of the *Treatise* in a short notice in its issue for the second quarter of 1739. Later the journal devoted 49 pages to a review of the first two volumes in its April–May–June 1740 issue; and, finally, in the April–May–June 1741 issue, 17 pages were devoted to the third volume of the *Treatise*. Hume could not, however, take comfort from either review despite the friendly assistance of the editor, Pierre Desmaizeaux. Hume had apparently hoped to have enough success with the third volume in order to write his fourth, "On Criticism." He gave up the idea after the tepid reception of the *Treatise* and redirected his efforts.[13]

Essays, Moral and Political

In spite of this adversity, perhaps because of it, Hume, as he recorded in his autobiography, "very soon recovered the Blow, and prosecuted with great Ardour my Studies in the Country." He began work on a group of essays called *Essays, Moral and Political,* sometimes incorrectly thought to be a recasting of the *Treatise* in a more popular literary form.[14] Hume was probably working on the *Essays* as early as 1739, the year the *Treatise* was published, and the result was the *Essays, Moral and Political* of 1741 and 1742. After the disappointment with the *Treatise*, Hume was not seeking easy popularity so much as he was clarity and accessibility for his ideas. Some of the subjects—"Of the Delicacy of Taste and Passion," "Of Impudence and Modesty," "Of Simplicity and Refinement"—are more acceptable as essays than as parts of a lengthy philosophical treatise. Equally, if the 1740s could be said to have a dominant literary form, it was the essay. The first volume of *Essays, Moral and Political* appeared in late 1741, printed by R. Fleming and A. Alison for Edinburgh's leading publisher, Alexander Kincaid; the second volume, again by the same printer and publisher, appeared in January 1742. The success of the work led to a second edition of volume one in mid–1742.

The reading public's ready acceptance of this new form into which Hume had cast his ideas emerges—not without a little modest pride—in a letter to his friend Henry Home, on 13 June 1742: "The Essays are all sold in London . . . I am also told that Dr [Joseph] Butler has every where recommended them" (*NHL*, 10). The mention of Bishop Butler is interesting: Butler's intellectual landmark, *The Analogy of Religion,* had appeared in 1736, some six years before Hume's *Essays*. Hume's "experimental method of reasoning" is in marked contrast to Butler's often tortuous analogical method of reasoning.[15] Some 33 years later, when Hume was writing his autobiography, he recalled with pleasure his early feelings about the success of the *Essays*: "The Work was favourably received, and soon made me entirely forget my former Disappointment."

The literary milieu into which Hume thrust his *Essays* was looking pretty barren in 1741. The great days of Jonathan Swift and Alexander Pope were behind, and both men were a few years from death. Samuel Johnson's much admired poem "London" had been published in 1738, but his *Life of Savage* was not to appear until 1744. Oliver Goldsmith was only twelve years old at the time. James Thomson's poems were well-known, but no essayist of any significance had brought his or her wares to an eager market. To suggest that Hume had produced a "best-seller" would be a gross distortion of a modern metaphor, but the clarity of his style was immediately attractive: eighteenth-century readers liked difficult subjects and topics but wanted them in shipshape sentences. Hume's *Essays* appeared at a propitious time and helped to sustain the essay as a significant literary genre.

One success gave hopes of another—this time for the chair of ethics and pneumatical philosophy (now the chair of moral philosophy) at the University of Edinburgh. The chair had been vacated by Dr. John Pringle upon his appointment as Physician-General to H. M. Forces in Flanders, and the Lord Provost of Edinburgh, John Coutts, suggested his young friend David Hume apply for the chair. Hume did, but to be a philosopher is one thing: to become a professor of philosophy is another. A major campaign to prevent him from being considered for the chair was mounted, and the *Treatise* was again cited in evidence against Hume. He produced a pamphlet in his defense that he sent to Henry Home, who promptly published it, apparently without Hume's consent (*NHL*, 15). Only one copy of this work has apparently survived into the twentieth century, and even it did not emerge until 1966, when it was acquired by the National Library of Scotland. Entitled *A Letter from a Gentleman to His Friend in Edinburgh: containing Some Observations on A Specimen of the Principles concerning Religion and Morality, said to be maintain'd in a Book lately publish'd, intituled, A Treatise of Human Nature, &c.*, it further defends and explains the ideas in the *Treatise,* but to no avail: William Cleghorn was appointed to the chair.[16] Perhaps it was just as well Hume did not receive the appointment. Cleghorn died at the age of thirty-five without having published a single work.[17]

Unsuccessful in this attempt, Hume managed, later in 1745, to land a job of some pecuniary value, but one with a slight drawback. As tutor to the Marquess of Annandale, he had as his pupil a young man mad as a March hare. Hume spent a year with his unfortunate charge and then accepted a position with General James St. Clair as secretary to a proposed Canadian expedition, one which ended with an incursion into France.[18] After that, he again served with General St. Clair on military embassies to Vienna and Turin.

The period that Hume spent with General St. Clair may be considered the least interesting for anyone wishing to know more about the philosopher as man of letters. Hume remarked, noncommittally, in *My Own Life* that "These two Years were almost the only Interruptions which my Studies have received in the Course of my Life"; but he immediately added, "I passed them agreeably and in good Company." The implied values—studies, agreeability, good humor—continued as features throughout his life, with the latter two prevailing towards the end of his life.

The Two *Enquiries* and "Of Miracles"

In 1748, the fever of publishing returned; and Hume produced not only a third edition of the *Essays, Moral and Political* but also what is more accurately called a recasting of the *Treatise* than his *Essays, Moral and Political*: the *Philosophical Essays concerning Human Understanding* (25 April 1748, published in London by Andrew Millar, thus inaugurating Hume's long association with this publisher and his printer, William Strahan). By this time, Hume was achieving financial independence as well as a reputation as a man of letters. In 1750, a second edition of the *Philosophical Essays concerning Human Understanding* appeared, along with the first edition of his *An Enquiry into the Principles of Morals*, which clarified and reworked part of book 3 of the *Treatise*. Two years later, Hume brought forth his *Political Discourses*, containing the essays: "Of Commerce," "Of Luxury," "Of Money," "Of Interest," "Of the Balance of Trade," "Of the Balance of Power," "Of Taxes," "Of Public Credit," "Of Some Remarkable Customs," "Of the Populousness of Antient Nations," "Of the Protestant Succession," and "Idea of a Perfect Commonwealth." These productive and active years set a pattern and a pace for his literary endeavors over the next ten years.

Total success was not, however, immediately at hand. In *My Own Life*, Hume remarks that the initial reception of the *Philosophical Essays concerning Human Understanding* was not all that he might have wished: "On my return from Italy, I had the Mortification to find all England in a Ferment on account of Dr. Middletons Free enquiry; while my Performance was entirely overlooked and neglected."[19] This unhappy state of affairs did not persist. For one thing, the *Philosophical Essays concerning Human Under-*

standing (henceforth called the first *Enquiry,* since Hume changed its title in 1753 to match *An Enquiry concerning the Principles of Morals*) contained the essay "Of Miracles," which even thirty-five years ago could still excite captious dismissal as "the one thoroughly silly production of his pen."[20] Hume had omitted an early version of the essay on miracles from the *Treatise,* and most of his friends advised him to omit it from *An Enquiry concerning Human Understanding.*

Hume had hoped to have Bishop Butler read the *Treatise,* and he wrote to Henry Home in December 1737, that "Your Thoughts & mine agree with Respect to Dr Butler, & I wou'd be glad to be introduc'd to him. I am at present castrating my Work, that is, cutting off its noble Parts, that is, endeavouring it shall give as little Offence as possible" (*NHL,* 2–3). Hume was, of course, referring to his discussion of miracles, which, along with another essay in the first *Enquiry,* "Of a Particular Providence and of a Future State" (changed from the first edition's title, "Of the Sceptical or Academical Philosophy"), attracted as much attention, rejection, and attempted refutation as the rest of his previous works combined. A clue to religious thought in the mid-1750s and to Hume's reputation can be seen in an examination of some of the responses to "Of Miracles."[21]

The first notice came from an obscure, but gifted, Irish clergyman, the Reverend Philip Skelton, in his two volumes of dialogues, *Ophiomaches: Or, Deism Revealed.*[22] Skelton's work is an intelligent Christian's attempt to refute deism on philosophical grounds. The book is cast in a series of eight dialogues, a form which Hume had already experimented with in section 11 of *An Enquiry concerning Human Understanding* and later adopted in "A Dialogue" at the end of *An Enquiry concerning the Principles of Morals* and in his last work. The discussions involve three Deists— Messrs. Dechaine, Tempton, and Cunningham—and one free-spoken defender of the miraculous in Christianity, the Reverend Shepherd (the names are fictitious, though Reverend Shepherd's clearly has some symbolic connotations). The treatment of Hume's "Of Miracles" is gentlemanly and scholarly, perhaps because Skelton mistakenly considered Hume a Deist. In the fifth dialogue, Shepherd answers Dechaine, who, quoting Hume's first *Enquiry,* had put forward an empirical argument against miracles—and, implicitly, Hume—by combining an empirical argument with revelation:

To conclude, we cannot conceive it possible, that so many thousands of people should, in so short a time, croud into the church of *Christ,* in the teeth of all their inveterate prejudices, and of the most outrageous persecutions, had not miracles

been everywhere wrought for their conviction; nor can we, without horrible blas-
phemy against the wisdom of God, suppose, that he should have wrought so many
miracles to propagate a religion, which was to depend on the genuineness of its records, and yet not provide sufficiently, whether by Divine or human means, against
the charge or corruption of those records. If the ordinary methods of his providence
had not been sufficient for this purpose, we cannot help concluding, that he would
have vouchsafed a series of miracles, to ascertain the genuineness of the Scriptures,
as well as to prove the doctrines, contained in them, to be Divine: for our conviction
must have been a part of his intention, as well as that of the Christians in the Apos-
tolic age.[23]

Skelton's tautologies and rhetorical certainties, weak though they are as argument and philosophy, do not disguise a genuine attempt to establish the
validity of miracles.[24]

One of the more popular books on religion in the mid-eighteenth century was John Leland's *View of the Principal Deistical Writers*.[25] Leland attempts disinterest but is openly hostile to Hume. Employing the popular
convention of a "letter to a friend," he argues that testimony is part of experience, and that Hume "cannot therefore make his argument properly bear,
except he can prove, that miracles are absolutely impossible" (*View,* 2:65).
Leland accuses Hume of identifying the "*miraculous nature* of an event"
with the "*absolute impossibility* of it" (*View,* 2:65–66) and of ignoring the
intervention of God in the processes of nature: "The only case therefore in
which they [miracles] are never to be believed, is when they are pretended to
be wrought in favour of religion" (*View,* 2:98). Leland had prepared his
readers to accept that he was not taking Hume seriously, having asserted in
his opening remarks that Hume's "writings seem, for the most part, to be
calculated rather to amuse, or even confound, than to instruct and enlighten
the understanding: And there are not a few things in them, that strike at the
foundation of natural, as well as the proofs and evidences of revealed religion" (*View,* 2:2). Leland, like many of his contemporaries, felt that discussion or analysis of certain subjects, particularly the "truth" of religious
propositions, was not to be countenanced. Hume would be amused to discover that human nature is much the same in the last part of the twentieth
century.

The maelstrom surrounding "Of Miracles" began to calm down when
Hume began, in 1754, to publish his *History of England,* which he
completed in 1760. In 1762, however, Dr. George Campbell stirred the
waters vigorously in what was the most comprehensive examination of
miracles to appear in the eighteenth century: *A Dissertation on Miracles:*

Containing an Examination of the Principles advanced by David Hume, Esq. In an Essay on Miracles. Hume read the work in manuscript, which was sent to him by a clerical friend, the Reverend Hugh Blair. Writing to Blair in 1761, Hume states that he perused the "ingenious performance" attentively, but perhaps without the seriousness and gravity that Blair would have expected. He observes that the faults of the manuscript lie not so much in the composition but in the subject and anticipates Blair's comment: "I know you will say, it lies in neither, but in myself alone. If that be so, I am sorry to say that I believe it is incurable" (*HL,* 1:348–49). He then offers several criticisms of Campbell's discourse. When the work appeared on 7 June 1762, Hume wrote him a very friendly letter; and Campbell replied in kind.[26]

The "Advertisement" prefixed to Campbell's book is disarming:

The *Essay on Miracles* deserves to be consider'd, as one of the most dangerous attacks that have been made on our religion. The danger results not solely from the merit of THE PIECE; it results much more from that of THE AUTHOR. *The piece* itself, like every other work of Mr Hume, is ingenious; but its merit is more of the oratorial kind than of the philosophical. The merit of *the author,* I acknowledge, is great. The many useful volumes he has published of *history,* and on *criticism, politics,* and *trade,* have justly procur'd him, with all persons of taste and discernment, the highest reputation as a writer. What pity is it, that this reputation should have been sullied by attempts to undermine the foundations both of *natural religion,* and of *reveal'd!*[27]

This attitude toward Hume reflects, in general, the attitude of the moderate clergy—men like Robert Wallace and William Robertson—and it was perhaps encouraged by Hume's unfailing good nature.[28] Briefly stated, Campbell's argument posits that "regular" miracles and "religious" ones are not the same, but both are capable of proof from testimony. Hume's whole argument is built on a false hypothesis: he incorrectly assumes that the "evidence of testimony is derived solely from experience" (*DM* 14). Instead, Campbell suggests, "testimony hath a natural and original influence on belief, antecedent to experience" (*DM* 14). He then cites some of the ways in which testimony could be advanced in favor of religion. His conclusion reminds one of Bishop Butler's method of analogical reasoning. Campbell affirms that we have no presumption against religious miracles, but, in fact, experience a peculiar presumption in favor of miracles as evidence for religion. Why? Because of man's expectations of an afterlife, he tends to be scrupulous in his acceptance of miracles. The evidence advanced for religious miracles, therefore, is valid.

These various responses are indicative of the ambivalent attitude that Hume's critics exhibited. Except for those who attacked him hysterically for alleged heresy or atheism, criticism of Hume's ideas was divided, as in the preceding examples, into two kinds: (1) those who apparently understood Hume but refused to take him seriously; and (2) those who understood him but were more intent upon preserving the sanctity of religion than in answering him. And even this breakdown is not so facile as it seems, for the most sympathetic readers did not always understand Hume's arguments. When they did, they frequently refused to believe that he was serious. Yet the impact that Hume's first *Enquiry* had upon religious and philosophical thought is beyond question. In forming skeptical doubts about the truth-value of the a priori propositions that were the foundations for much philosophical and religious thought, Hume not only led thinkers away from the pitfalls of unsupported generalizations, but also led them into a new methodology for the exegesis of epistemological propositions. He called into question the usefulness of "testimony" as evidence in decision procedure, and he suggested the proper distinction between "faith" and "knowledge."

Amid all this hullabaloo over Hume's atheism, deism, or whatever brand of religious heterodoxy that fitted the purposes of his antagonists, *An Enquiry concerning the Principles of Morals* appeared in December 1751, published by Andrew Millar. In his autobiography, Hume said of it: "In the same Year was published at London my Enquiry concerning the Principles of Morals, which, in my own opinion (who ought not to judge on that subject) is of all my writings, historical, philosophical, or literary, incomparably the best: It came unnoticed and unobserved into the World." Again, this comment should not be taken at face value, for the second *Enquiry* went into a second edition in 1753, in the first set of Hume's collected works, *Essays and Treatises on several Subjects.*[29]

Although Hume thought the second *Enquiry* was his best work, he did reorganize and revise it more than any of his other works, and it would not be unthinkable for an author to like best the work on which he had expended much time and labor. One of the reasons, perhaps the major reason, that the second *Enquiry* did not enjoy instant acclaim is attributable to the number of responses the first *Enquiry,* with "Of Miracles," was evoking. Most commentators in the mid-eighteenth century were often more eager to defend the sanctity of religion—natural religion, revealed religion, religion in any form—than they were to assess a work on its own terms. Hume's arguments in "Of Miracles" and "Of a Particular Providence and of a Future State" led most writers, to judge from the attacks on Hume, to reinstate the miraculous in religion. Not even the enlightened eighteenth century was willing to forego miracles and marvels in order to discuss or to analyze a new system of ethics. I think it is likely that Hume's second *Enquiry* attracted only scattered attention because of the preponderant inclination of other writers to reject his skeptical dismantling of the miraculous.

Political Discourses

Hume's analysis of ethics did not go totally unnoticed. It was reviewed along with his *Political Discourses,* which appeared in February 1752, in the January 1752 issue of the *Monthly Review,* a periodical that began in 1749.[30] The comments about Hume are cordial; of the second *Enquiry,* William Rose, the reviewer, said in his opening paragraph:

> The reputation this ingenious author has acquir'd as a fine and elegant writer, renders it unnecessary for us to say any thing in his praise. We shall only observe in general, that clearness and precision of ideas on abstracted and metaphysical subjects, and at the same time propriety, elegance and spirit, are seldom found united in any writings in a more eminent degree than in those of Mr. *Hume.* The work now before us will, as far as we are able to judge, considerably raise his reputation; and, being free from that sceptical turn which appears in his other pieces, will be more agreeable to the generality of Readers. His subject is important and interesting, and the manner of treating it easy and natural.

Of the *Political Discourses,* Rose said:

> Few writers are better qualified, either to instruct or entertain their readers, than Mr. *Hume.* On whatever subject he employs his pen, he presents us with something new; nor is this his only merit, his writings (as we observed in the preceding article) receive a farther recommendation from that elegance and spirit which appears in them, and that clearness of reasoning, which distinguishes them from most others. The discourses now before us, are upon curious and interesting subjects; abound with solid reflections; and shew the author's great knowledge of ancient and modern history, and his comprehensive views of things.[31]

Like most eighteenth-century reviewers, Rose devotes almost all his review to summary and quotation; his use of the word "curious" to describe Hume's ideas is, of course, to be taken in its eighteenth–century meaning of "inquisitive; desirous of information; addicted to enquiry."[32] His sympathetic attitude undoubtedly was music to Hume's ears.

Hume was most encouraged by the reception of *Political Discourses,* "the only work of mine, that was successful on the first Publication: It was well received abroad and at home."[33] One of the essays, "Of the Populousness of Antient Nations," involved Hume in a friendly dispute with an important Scottish clergyman, the Reverend Robert Wallace, with whom he exchanged many letters. Hume had also read in manuscript a composition by Wallace entitled *A Dissertation on the Numbers of Mankind in Antient and Modern Times.* In publishing his *Political Discourses,* Hume asked Wallace for permission to refer to his manuscript in a footnote to the essay "Of the Populousness of Antient Nations." Wallace gave the permission, and Hume's essay then helped to stimulate publication of Wallace's *Dissertation* in 1753. Although they disagreed, Hume helped Wallace with the redaction of his manuscript, making several suggestions for stylistic changes, particularly in the omission of Scotticisms.[34]

Wallace had argued in his book that the ancient world was more populous, while Hume had taken the position that modern world (i.e., the eighteenth century) was. Hume was right, of course, but in the eighteenth century the matter was still something of a burning issue. Hume rejected the idea of decline, so popular until the close of the seventeenth century; he also rejected, with equal skepticism, the popular eighteenth-century idea of progress. Wallace had on his side something often better than being right: powerful supporters. Two members of the University of Edinburgh faculty—Kenneth Mackenzie, professor of civil law, and Charles Mackie, professor of history—supported Wallace, certainly not the first instance in scholarship and argument when professors have been on the wrong side. Altogether, the dispute between Hume and Wallace may well serve as a paradigm for friendly disagreement.

The *Political Discourses* introduced Hume's thought to a wider audience than he had previously enjoyed. Of the twelve discourses, eight would belong today to the study of economics; the remainder, including the "Populousness" essay, to politics or social history. Hume's approach to all the problems presented in his discussion is always philosophical; he discards any preconceived notions that might hinder him from arriving at an exact estimate, say, of the principles of public credit in "Of Public Credit." I do not mean to imply that Hume brought no preconceived notions at all; but he did bring to economic and political questions certain preconditions, typical of his thought, that produced lucid analyses. These preconditions were a belief in the power of reason to settle disputes, a refusal to accept a priori conditions in empirical matters, and an inclination to look to history for guidelines. Of more than incidental interest is the impact Hume's thought had on his friend Adam Smith, whose ideas on economics were in part derived from and anticipated by Hume.[35]

The History of England

After the publication of *Political Discourses,* Hume began several projects, but his next publication was the one that made him rich and famous: a history of England. He wrote to his friend John Clephane on 5 January 1753: "As there is no happiness without occupation, I have begun a work which will employ me several years, and which yields me much satisfaction. Tis a History of Britain, from the Union of the Crowns to the present time. I have already finished the reign of King James" (*HL,* 1:170). On the importance of history, he adds, "You know that there is no post of honour in the English Parnassus more vacant than that of History. Style, judgement, impartiality, care—everything is wanting to our historians; and even Rapin, during this latter period, is extremely deficient."

Hume's remark about the inadequacy of previous historians is well taken. The reference to the history of Paul de Rapin, styled Rapin-Thoyras, is a clear indication that Hume was dissatisfied with attempts to write a history of England. Rapin, a French Protestant, had written a history of England in French, which was translated by Nicholas Tindal in fifteen volumes (1725–31). Other histories of England, all less distinguished than Rapin's, which appeared before Hume's, include the following: Thomas Carte, *A General History of England* (1747–55; four volumes); Laurence Echard, *The History of England, From the First Entrance of Julius Caesar and the Romans, To the End of the reign of King James the First* (1707, with two additional volumes in 1718, appendix in 1720); William Guthrie, *A General History of England, from the Invasion of Julius Caesar, to the revolution in 1689* (1744–51, two volumes); James Ralph, *History of England during the Reigns of K. William, O. Anne, and K. George I* (1744–46, two volumes); and James Tyrell, *The General History of England* (1696–1704). Despite Hume's comment to Clephane that he was writing a history "to the present time," his history, like that of Guthrie, stops in 1689. Hume's only real rival as a historian of England was his fellow Scot, Tobias Smollett, whose *Complete History of England* (1757–60), does cover "the present time." Initially, it outsold Hume's history, but by the time Hume completed his history in 1762, his work dom-

inated the market, and Smollett's continuation from 1689 was often published with Hume's work.[36]

Hume's contract for the first volume of his history, devoted to the reigns
of James I and Charles I, was remarkable: he did not have Millar publish
the first volume because of an astonishing offer from the Edinburgh publishers, Hamilton, Balfour, and Neill. Gavin Hamilton offered to pay
Hume twelve hundred pounds sterling for the copyright to the first edition
of his work; he was to print two thousand copies and no more, or so he
wrote to William Strahan in 1754 (*Life*, 302–303). This rather extravagant commitment evolved into something more practical: Hume did not
contract for more than one volume at a time; he accepted four hundred
pounds for a first edition of the first volume of two thousand copies, and
would entertain a proposal for six hundred pounds for a second edition
(*HL*, 1:193, 234–345, *Life*, 303).

The hopes that Hamilton had for the success of the volume were not,
however, realized when it appeared in November 1754. Hume recorded
Hamilton's disappointment in his autobiography: "I was assailed by one
Cry of Reproach, Disapprobation, and even Detestation: English, Scotch,
and Irish; Whig and Tory; Churchman and Sectary, Free-thinker and Reli-
gionist; Patriot and Courtier united in their Rage against the Man, who had
presumed to shed a generous Tear for the Fate of Charles I, and the Earl of
Strafford." The "Religionists" did indeed accuse Hume of not making the
proper genuflections before the citadel of Christianity: Hume did not regard the activities of the church, particularly those activities which affected
secular life, as "off limits" in his discussion (*see Life*, 305–12, for a summary of some of the criticism).

The second volume, devoted to the Commonwealth and the Restoration, appeared in late 1756 (dated 1757) and was more favorably received
than the first volume. Much of the initial failure of that first volume could
have been attributed to Gavin Hamilton's ineptitude as a businessman.
The second volume was published in London by Andrew Millar. Yet
Hume was still suspicious of the handling of the publication and noted in
his autobiography that the "Conspiracy of the Booksellers contributed
very much to retard the Sale." The evidence for this assertion is ambivalent, but it does seem to support Hume.[37] Hume was not discouraged.
Renewing his negotiations with Millar, he carried on with the work and
produced another four volumes between 1759 and 1762. They comprised
a complete history of England from the invasion of Julius Caesar to the
end of 1689.

This was the last of Hume's major works to appear during his lifetime, and its success leaves him still listed in some library catalogues as "David Hume, the Historian." While the success of the *History of England* made Hume financially independent, even wealthy by eighteenth-century standards, he enjoyed the work's eventual popularity more than he relished the financial rewards. In a slightly inaccurate anecdote, Sylas Nevil records in his diary, on 22 May 1773, that "Baker and I supped with Dr Home by invitation. The Dr told us a remarkable anecdote of David Hume. When the Dr returned home in 1758 David was so poor that he said he would give all expectations in life for £30 a year. What a change of times."[38] Hume was neither opulent nor poor in 1758, though he might very well have articulated this sentiment some years earlier.

Four Dissertations

During the time that Hume was writing the *History of England,* he also planned to publish several long essays, or "dissertations," as he called them. The publication of "dissertations" probably caused him as much difficulty as any composition he published during his lifetime, and their complicated publishing history can only be hinted at.[39] Originally, the "four short Dissertations" were to contain "The Natural History of Religion," "Of the Passions," "Of Tragedy," and one Hume designated as "some Considerations previous, to Geometry & Natural Philosophy" (*HL*, 1:223). After an exchange of several letters, Hume and Millar planned to bring out a volume entitled *Five Dissertations,* omitting "some Considerations previous, to Geometry & Natural Philosophy," and adding "Of Suicide" and "Of the Immortality of the Soul." This volume was printed, but at Hume's request was not published. Then the "five" were again reduced to "three," and the essays on suicide and immortality were deleted. Hume added another, an able and elegant excursion into the psychology of aesthetics, "On the Standard of Taste," and the completed work, *Four Dissertations,* appeared on 7 February 1757. The two self-suppressed dissertations, already printed, did manage to get into private circulation, through the offices of Millar. They were published in French in 1770, and in English in London in 1777, just after Hume's death. Both as intellectual documents and as items in publishing history, the problems that these two essays caused Hume seem disproportionate to their quality, especially when compared to the other four dissertations. However, Hume still managed to leave a stick for religious bigots to beat him with: the excellent scholarly analysis "Of the Natural History of Religion" was promptly assaulted by the zealots.

Rousseau and Beattie

Except for an attempt to remove him from the Church of Scotland, life was especially pleasant for Hume from 1764 until his death in 1776. He visited France again from 1763 to 1766, serving as personal secretary for Francis Seymour Conway, Earl of Hertford, who had been appointed as ambassador to the Court of France. Returning to France after a long absence, Hume had the opportunity to extend his previous acquaintance by correspondence with the Comtesse de Boufflers. He thought at one time "of settling there for Life." There he also met Jean-Jacques Rousseau, whom he instinctively liked. France, however, was not all pleasure for him. Rousseau was never at ease with Hume. As a result of Rousseau's vanity and paranoia, Hume was involved in an embarrassing and silly contretemps with him, when Rousseau came with Hume to England in 1766 (*Life*, 507–32).[40] Although Rousseau gave Hume a great deal of misery during 1765–66, Hume's last years were spent in contemplation and peace—with one other exception. James Beattie, author of *An Essay on the Nature and Immutability of Truth; in opposition to Sophistry and Scepticism* (1770), decided to attack not only Hume's writing but his personality as well. The book gave Beattie a reputation as a defender of the faith, upholder of orthodoxy, and protector of young minds, a role in which Beattie cast himself: "Being honoured with the care of a part of the British youth; and considering it as my indispensable duty (from which I trust I shall never deviate) to guard their minds against impiety and error, I endeavoured, among other studies that belong to my office, to form a right estimate of Mr Hume's philosophy, so as not only to understand his peculiar tenets, but also to perceive their *connection* and *consequences*."[41] Beattie's attitude towards Hume both as philosopher and human being and his capabilities for understanding Hume can be fairly gauged from this sample from the introduction to *An Essay on Truth*:

There is a writer now alive, of whose philosophy I have much to say. By his philosophy, I mean the sentiments he has published in a book called, *A Treatise of Human Nature,* in three volumes, printed in the year 1739; the principal doctrines of which he has since republished again and again . . . why is this author's character so replete with inconsistency! why should his principles and his talents extort at once our esteem and detestation, our applause and contempt! That he, whose manners in private life are said to be so agreeable, should yet, in the public capacity of an author, have given so much cause of just offence to all the friends of virtue and mankind, is to me matter of astonishment and sorrow, as well as of indignation. That he, who succeeds so well in describing the fates of nations, should yet have failed so egregiously in explaining the operations of the mind, is one of those incongruities in human genius, for which philosophy will never be able fully to account . . . His philosophy has done great harm. Its admirers, I know, are numerous; but I have not as yet met with one person, who both admired and understood it.[42]

Beattie fails to explain how it is possible to admire Hume without understanding him, and one does wonder how Hume's philosophy could have done great harm if no one could understand it. As readers, we can share Hume's perplexity when he wrote to a friend about "that bigotted silly Fellow, Beattie" (*HL,* 2:301). Of those who attempted to disturb the philosopher's "autumnal serenity," Beattie was undoubtedly the most vociferous and to posterity the most foolish (see *Life,* 577–88, for other attacks).

Dialogues concerning Natural Religion

While the quotation from Beattie serves as an example of both the insensitivity and the intellectual impoverishment of some of Hume's opponents, its rancor was repeated after Hume's death, particularly upon the posthumously published *Dialogues concerning Natural Religion.* Had Hume published this work during his lifetime, it undoubtedly would have produced replies which would have made all previous accounts of his religious inclinations seem like panegyrics in comparison. In fact, the *Dialogues* raised very few hostile eyebrows, perhaps because a dead man does not pose a threat to an established order in religion.

The *Dialogues* was composed between 1751 and 1755 and revised thereafter.[43] The first mention of the work appears in a letter of 10 March 1751, to Sir Gilbert Elliot, who was asked to make some suggestions for the arguments of one of the speakers, Cleanthes, the empirical theist (see *HL,* 1:153–57). It is likely that Hume was working on the *Dialogues* at the same time he wrote his "Natural History of Religion." There are verbal parallels in the two works. When Hume had asked Elliot, among others, including Adam Smith, about the advisability of publishing the *Dialogues,* he was firmly advised not to do so. In a letter dated 6 October 1763, Hume ironically threatened to dedicate the *Dialogues* to the Reverend Hugh Blair, another friend who had read a draft of the work: "I have no present thoughts of publishing the work you mention: but when I do, I hope you have no objection of my dedicating it to you" (*NHL,* 72).

Blair had said of the work, in a context mentioning Hume's relations with the *philosophes* of Paris: "But had you gone one step farther—I am well informed, in several Poker Clubs in Paris your Statue would have been erected. If you will show them the MSS of certain Dialogues perhaps that honour may still be done you. But for Gods sake let that be a posthumous work, if ever it shall see the light: Tho' I think it had better not" (*NHL*, 72–73n.). In spite of this opposition—or perhaps because of it—Hume undertook some elaborate measures to insure at least the posthumous publication of the *Dialogues*. In a letter of 8 June 1776, to his printer William Strahan, Hume asked to have five hundred copies of the *Dialogues* printed when he returned to Edinburgh; and he would have given the "literary Property of the whole" to Strahan to use as he wished after these copies were printed (see *HL*, 2:323–324).

Hume's increasingly poor health prevented publication of the *Dialogues* during his lifetime, and in a codicil to his will, dated 7 August 1776, he revoked a passage authorizing Adam Smith to publish the work. In his will, he had, in fact, left all his manuscripts to Smith, "Desiring him to publish my Dialogues concerning Natural Religion." In the codicil, he left the manuscript first to Strahan to publish, stating that, if the *Dialogues* were not published within two and a half years of his death, it was to be published by his nephew, also named David Hume. Hume left two, possibly three, copies of the manuscript; and he gave one to Smith in case an accident should prevent either Strahan or his nephew from publishing the work. As it happened, William Strahan apparently permitted the nephew, who was only nineteen when his uncle died, to publish the *Dialogues*. The book appeared in 1779, first published in Edinburgh, with a second edition shortly thereafter in London. Contemporary notices give Robinson of London as the bookseller. The work was advertised in the *Weekly Magazine*, Edinburgh, October 1779, and also in the *Monthly Review*, London, December 1779. A French translation, purporting to be published in Edinburgh, appeared in the same year, and a German one followed in 1781.

The *Dialogues concerning Natural Religion* was accorded at least two extensive notices in Great Britain, the first being that of Thomas Hayter, *Remarks on Mr. Hume's Dialogues, concerning Natural Religion*, published in 1780. This sixty-five page pamphlet is devoted exclusively to a consideration of the *Dialogues*. Hayter, described on the title page as a "Fellow of King's College, Cambridge; and one of the Preachers at his Majesty's Chapel in Whitehall," has the distinction of being one of those who was not fooled by Hume's apparently pious disclaimers and by the ostensible "victory" of Cleanthes over Philo in the work. While numerous commentators have tried to explain Hume's disinterested stance on religion, Hayter recognized Humean thought when he saw it: "Let us consider however that Mr.

Hume, after the great nominal superiority attributed to Cleanthes, could not possibly, without appearance of vanity, have appointed Cleanthes his representative. The fact indeed indisputably is, that Philo, not Cleanthes, personates Mr. Hume."[44]

Hayter's analysis of Hume is a familiar kind: with people like Hume for its "friends," religion needs no enemies. He is scrupulously fair to Hume, but he understands fully neither Hume's method nor his principles. Philo's theological mistakes are the result, Hayter argues, of his lack of familiarity with the truth of the gospels. Like many eighteenth-century commentators, Hayter equated religion with Christianity, in the manner of Fielding's Thwackum in *Tom Jones* (1749): "When I mention Religion, I mean the Christian Religion; and not only the Protestant Religion, but the Church of *England*." Hume was challenging not only the conclusions drawn from age-old precepts but the validity of those precepts as well; and this intent Hayter failed to see.

Hayter is clever in his answer to Hume: wherever possible, he uses Hume's own texts against him; and he reads the text closely. He quotes from Hume frequently (about one-fourth of the pamphlet is quotation) and tries to demonstrate logical errors in Hume's thought. Quoting from the second edition of the *Dialogues,* Hayter says:

Philo . . . maintains religion to be the parent of evil, rather than of good: more a friend to vice, than virtue—The instance of the bad tendency of religion, produced by Philo at p. 249, carries a very striking air. "Many religious exercises are entered into with seeming fervour, where the heart at the time, feels cold and languid: a habit of dissimulation is by degrees contracted: and fraud and falsehood become the predominant principle." Concise piece of demonstration! A man performs certain religious offices negligently—is rendered by that means a hypocrite—quickly after a complete rogue! when such unbounded licentiousness of inference is freely and unblushingly practised, there seems to be no reason why one man, as well as another, may not presume to draw conclusions.[45]

It is likely that Hume, in the passage Hayter quotes, is remarking upon some of the social necessities of piety; but Hayter has cogently suggested that the activities Philo mentions do not necessarily follow one from another. In context, however, Hume seems to refer to a psychological, not a logical, progression. Hayter's answer at least deals with the issue, not with the man.

A second reply to Hume's *Dialogues* appeared in 1781 in Joseph Milner's *Gibbon's Account of Christianity considered: Together with some*

Strictures on Hume's Dialogues concerning Natural Religion. Milner, "Master of the Grammar-School of Kingston upon Hull," is considerably more zealous in his promotion of Christianity than Hayter; and his method is simple to the point of being narrow-minded: "I speak seriously, I never knew a man who gave probable evidence of an honest, careful, insight into himself, and of a just cultivation of all proper means of informing himself concerning God, his duty and the value of his soul, and the evidences of Christianity, but he would ingenuously confess he was thus corrupt and sinful: And, as far as I can judge from observation, the direct contrary was the case of all who were of a different opinion" (*Gibbon's Account,* 104). In other words, neither Hume nor Gibbon gave a careful, serious consideration to the evidence of Christianity; if they had, they could not have failed to be aware of their corruption and sinfulness, as well as of the truth of Christianity. In fact, Milner, several times, verges upon an identification of Christianity with an awareness of one's own sinfulness.

Now that Milner has established Hume's gross inattention to the evidence of salvation, he introduces the ad hominem argument. Quoting Hume's view of a future state, as expressed in the *Dialogues,* Milner observes that "the tendency of these passages is still more poisonous, to teach us that what Christianity offers in a future life is not worth the having, and that the belief of it is an enemy to all true virtue in this" (*Gibbon's Account* 120). Milner continues, occasionally breaking into apostrophes to the "force of Scripture-truth," or denigrating Hume and Gibbon for their failure to accept the validity of the gospels when such acceptance was so easy. All Hume's suggestions or observations are challenged on the grounds of being either inimical to Christianity or violations of divine law because Hume thinks the way he does. Like Hayter, Milner was not fooled by the declaration in favor of Cleanthes that closes the *Dialogues:* "it is evident from the whole tenour of the book, and still more so from the entire scepticism of his former publications, that Philois [*sic*] is his favourite. Sincerity constitutes no part of a philosopher's virtue" (*Gibbon's Account* 199). Milner finally concludes that Hume is beyond the reach of salvation (he was, after all, dead), but Gibbon was not (he was still alive); and that Hume will be severely dealt with on Judgment Day.

Posthumous controversy over Hume's irreligion or skepticism was often vitriolic, and the publication of the *Dialogues concerning Natural Religion* may have sparked some of the denunciations of Hume. James Boswell, for example, found the publication so offensive that he extended his disapproval to Hume's nephew: "Mr. David Hume, advocate, had come in. Though I was offended by his publishing his uncle's posthumous poison, I liked the sedateness of his manner."[46] Had Hume lived longer, he probably would have been less perturbed by the attacks than his attackers were at his seeming indifference to their extravagances and to their alleged concern for his soul.[47]

When Hume died on 25 August 1776, Adam Smith said of his life and death, in a famous letter:

> Thus died our most excellent, and never-to-be-forgotten friend; concerning whose philosophical opinions men will no doubt judge variously, every one approving or condemning them as they happen to coincide, or disagree with his own; but concerning whose character and conduct there can scarce be a difference of opinion. His temper, indeed, seemed to be more happily balanced, if I may be allowed such an expression, than that perhaps of any other man I have ever known. . . . The extreme gentleness of his nature never weakened either the firmness of his mind, or the steadiness of his resolutions. . . . Upon the whole, I have always considered him, both in his lifetime, and since his death, as approaching as nearly to the idea of a perfectly wise and virtuous man, as perhaps the nature of human frailty will admit. (Reprinted in *HL,* 2:452)

Chapter Two

Youth and Energy: The Remembered *Treatise*

Major Ideas in the *Treatise*

A Treatise of Human Nature: Being an Attempt to introduce the experimental Method of Reasoning into MORAL SUBJECTS is in many ways a conventional dissertation in philosophy. For example, the first book, *Of the Understanding,* seems to be an exposition on the same subjects as John Locke's *Essay concerning Human Understanding* (1690). Despite the emphasis on Newtonian reasoning in both Hume and Locke, *Treatise* in no way ignores the traditional problems of philosophy. Yet in a century more appreciative of Hume than the nineteenth, one commentator has said about the *Treatise,* and many have agreed, that "His work is, and will remain, the inevitable starting-point for all further investigation of these subjects ['Necessary Connection' and 'Problem of Induction']."[1]

Unfortunately we know little about the composition of the *Treatise,* although an interesting letter to Michael Ramsay, an early friend, has surfaced in the Czartoryski Museum in Cracow, Poland. Hume recommends that his friend read certain works of Nicolas Malebranche, George Berkeley, and Pierre Bayle, in order that he may read a draft of Hume's *Treatise* with greater profit, and will make, Hume hopes, useful criticisms. He also mentions Michael's cousin, Andrew Michael Ramsay, better known as the Chevalier Ramsay, who had extended much kindness to Hume. Hume's opinion of the Chevalier's philosophical abilities made him reluctant to let the Chevalier read his *Treatise:* "I shall be oblig'd to put all my Papers into the Chevalier Ramsay's hands when I come to Paris; which I am really sorry for. For tho' he be Free-thinker enough not to be shockt with my Liberty, yet he is so wedded to whymsical Systems, & is so little of a Philosopher, that I expect nothing but Cavilling from him. I even fortify myself against his Disapprobation & am resolv'd not to be in the least discourag'd by it, if I should chance to meet with it."[2] This letter, written 31 August 1737, indicates that the principles of the *Treatise* were almost completely formed and that Hume was ready to present his philosophy to the world.

In the introduction to his *Treatise,* Hume disavows the "tedious lingering method" of past thinkers as unlikely to lead to a comprehension of human nature; in a striking metaphor, he likens human nature to a citadel whose outskirts have occasionally been ambushed or captured but whose center has never been taken. The problem for the philosopher using the "experimental Method of Reasoning" is to master human nature, admitting ignorance when necessary rather than claiming certitude or infallibility.

Writing "Of the Origin of our Ideas," Hume divides all perceptions of the mind into ideas and impressions; the latter group includes the impressions of sensation (the special bodily senses) and the impressions of reflection (the passions, desires and emotions).[3] These perceptions and their assuming forms are further divided into simple and complex. Hume, in fact, gives the term "idea" a broader range of meaning—than it has in Locke, since it includes concepts, notions, fancies, conjectures and so forth—than Locke does. We repeat impressions in our memories, where an impression is recollected with most of its original force, or in the imagination, where an impression is recollected with little of its original force, "a perfect idea." The imagination has the ability to synthesize and recombine all the ideas at its command.

We might be tempted to think that this distinction between "impressions" and "ideas" was simply a repetition of Locke's view and Berkeley's additions.[4] On the contrary, Hume's *Treatise* is more a criticism of Locke and Berkeley than a supplement to them. This distinction Hume counts as his "first principle," and he will admit nothing into the contents of the mind except impressions and ideas. Hume's epistemology also gives impressions precedence over ideas, so that impressions actually create ideas. When an idea is ambiguous, a person may seek the impression which was the occasion of it. Finding no impression for the "idea," one can conclude "that the term is altogether insignificant" (*Abstract,* 11). Hume uses his distinction between ideas and impressions as an empirical measure by which he assesses what he considers a widespread tendency to discourse on ideas not occasioned by an impression or collection of impressions.

This simple but subtle arrangement of the activity of the understanding leads Hume, by equally simple logic, into some startling pronouncements about cause and effect. When Locke noted in his discussion "Of the Association of Ideas" in his *Essay concerning Human Understanding,* that ideas not allied by nature could combine because of custom, he also noticed the peculiar associations of ideas that sometimes arise, only to suggest the damaging moral or emotional effects such associations could produce. Hume writes of the "kind of Attraction" that certain ideas have for each other, but he suggests that the causes of this attraction are unknown "and must be resolv'd into *original* qualities of human nature" (*Treatise*, 1:i, 4; 13). Hume's definition of certain traditional philosophical terms now becomes more subjective than philosophers like Descartes would have wished: "substance," for example, is defined as nothing more than a "collection of simple ideas" united by the imagination and associated with specific phenomena. The suggestiveness of complex ideas becomes so great, Hume says, that we create associations that have no corollaries in nature. After much preliminary analysis of our ideas of space and time, of cause and effect, of knowledge and probability, Hume affirms that subjective, individually-experienced custom is the power or agent which unites cause and effect, that the contiguity and the constant conjunction of two events impose upon our minds so strong a sense of permanent relation that we cannot disassociate them.

This mind-imposed relationship between two events is a product of experience. We experience X prior to and contiguous to Y, and we infer that X causes Y; Hume states that this inference can never amount to a "demonstration," a word he uses in a specific sense to mean a proof of which an antithesis cannot, given the rules of logic, be imagined (e.g. that 2 plus 2 = 5). Experience teaches us to reason from cause to effect, because we assume that the unity of nature's laws will persevere; from these two observations we always conclude that "like causes, in like circumstances, will always produce like effects" (*Abstract*, 15). Since we can never know exactly if the future will be conformable to the past, or if events will always "behave" the same way, we must recognize that custom, not reason, guides our lives. All knowledge must then be probable, unless it is tautological; neither custom nor pure reason can lead to acquisition of immutable knowledge. Knowledge which claims for itself immutablility is, at the very least, suspect.

This position with regard to the possibility of human knowledge is likely to produce skepticism, and Hume is concerned to analyze the "sceptical and other systems of philosophy" (*Treatise*, 1:iv, 1; 180). The classical statement on skepticism belongs to the Hellenistic skeptic, Sextus Empiricus, to whom Hume actually refers in the *Enquiry concerning the Principles of Morals*. In addition, he probably derived knowledge of Pyrrhonian skepticism from Pierre Bayle's *Dictionnaire Historique* or from Montaigne's *Apologie pour Raimond Sebond*.[5] Briefly, Hume credits Pyrrhonism with a dogmatic assumption that all questions concerning matters of probability are uncertain, and that certainty is not to be found in the world.

In discussing Pyrrhonian skepticism[6] in the *Treatise*, as well as in later works, Hume maintained that the Pyrrhonian position was logically irrefutable but psychologically untenable; the distractions of human nature subdue extreme skepticism: "I may, nay I must yield to the *current of nature,* in submitting to my senses and understanding; and in this blind submission I shew most perfectly my sceptical disposition and principles . . . If we believe, that fire warms, or water refreshes, 'tis only because it costs us too much pains to think otherwise" (*Treatise,* 1:iv, 7; 269–70 [my italics]).[7] In other words, we cannot resist the impingement of recurring events upon our minds. Reason is not a guide to life, but neither is unmitigated skepticism. The true philosopher must be ironically aware of the logical disproportions between philosophy and living: he creates a moderate, or moderated, skepticism from his reflections upon this disproportion.

Hume had also raised the problem of inductive reasoning in the first volume of the *Treatise*: he would take literally Pope's line in the *Essay on Man,* "What can we reason, but from what we know?" (1:18). Knowledge for Hume depends upon two activities of the mind: the impingement of simple impressions upon the senses, and the causal ordering of ideas corresponding to those impressions. Thus, the mind creates a series of inferences which it accepts as true, but which at any moment could be falsified. In a rather loose sense, Hume is applying the *post hoc ergo propter hoc* principle of logic to the experience of the human being in a series of events. We may indeed see X precede Y on any number of occasions, but we cannot say that reason teaches us that X causes Y. While we can be relatively sure that the sun will rise every morning, as it has in the past, we can express only a probability, not a fact. The ultimate problem lies in constructing for all events a probability calculus that will tell us specifically what our margin of error can be.

Closely associated with the problem of induction and causality is Hume's philosophy of belief, which he equates with opinion and defines as "A LIVELY IDEA RELATED TO OR ASSOCIATED WITH A PRESENT IMPRESSION" (*Treatise,* 1:iii, 7; 96). This definition emphasizes the way a mind "feels" [Hume's word] about an idea to which it has given assent; as a belief, it is recollected with a much stronger force or vivacity than is an idea to which we have not given assent. For example, we believe that the sun will rise in the morning. The vivacity of that idea is much stronger than a feeling that the sun *won't* rise in the morning. The former idea is, therefore, more active and forceful in our minds than the latter; hence, we act as if it were true. In an appendix to this section, Hume admits that it is impossible to explain perfectly the feeling or "manner of conception," but he describes the function of a belief: it is different from a fictitious idea, not in its organization, structure, or essence, but in the *manner* in which it is conceived. To continue with the preceding example, the manner in which we conceive that the sun will rise tomorrow is more intense than the manner in which we might conceive that the sun will not rise tomorrow. When analyzing any event, we must not begin by believing that it has a cause, but should seek to discover what events, if any, are related to it and in what way they induce us to believe in causality.

Hume's efforts to clarify the meaning of such concepts as "causality" may seem trivial to the twentieth century and obvious to anyone. Yet Hume uniquely raised doubts about a priori assumptions in philosophy and in natural science. By showing that the imputation of certainty to a particular event was a product of mental, not physical, operations, Hume either suggested a new method for solving some of the traditional problems of philosophy, or he suggested that the problems could not be formulated in language accurate enough to contain the possibility of their answer. Until mankind achieved a method of discourse suitable for the solution of problems unsolvable in traditional philosophical discourse, it would have to abandon dispute about these problems or risk indulging in pointless subtleties.

Although the method was new, the results were not always so cogent as Hume could have wished. I have hitherto neglected to mention the concept of "self" as it appears in book 1 of the *Treatise,* in part because of widespread disagreement among commentators on the topic, and in part because of some apparent contradictions in Hume's own words about selfhood in Humean philosophy.[8] These difficulties in conceptualizing self occur in the discussion "Of personal identity" in book 1: other selves "are nothing but a bundle or collection of different perceptions, which succeed each other with an inconceivable rapidity, and are in a perpetual flux and movement" (*Treatise,* 1:iv, 6; 252). Earlier, Hume had said that in order to have a concept of self, one would have had to experience an impression which gave rise to the concept of self; and that impression would have to be unchanging and constant. But we have no such impression, only a succession of various passions and sensations from which it is impossible to derive a specific impression of self: "consequently there is no such idea" (*Treatise,* 1:iv, 6; 252). While Hume distinguishes between two sorts of "personal identity," he considers memory the source of personal identity. Since memory is faulty, we cannot extend our concept of self beyond it; and Hume suggests that disputes about self are more verbal than philosophical.[9]

The ambiguity regarding any concept of self does not prevent Hume from analyzing the "Passions" in book 2 of the *Treatise* in terms of their effect upon self. The self is the object of thoughts of pride and humility; the self is not the cause of such passions, by which Hume means bodily appetites, such as pride and humility. Pride and humility, to continue Hume's example, arise in the mind when it is presented with the idea of their cause—beauty, strength, agility, wit, and so forth; for that matter, almost any stimuli could give rise to pride or humility or to any other passion. The association of ideas in the mind leaps to an identification of the alleged cause of the passion with the object. Hume applies the theory of book 1 to this misconception and asserts that the causes of pride and humility are *natural* but not *original*: "'tis utterly impossible they shou'd each of them be adapted to these passions by a particular provision, and primary constitution of nature" (*Treatise,* 2:i, 3; 281). The same argument is applied to the passions of love and hatred.

In general, much of book 2, "Of the Passions," could be seen as a supplement to book 1 of the *Treatise,* but its digressions are more interesting than illuminating. Hume discusses the four passions of pride and humility, love and hatred, to indicate that the laws of association are as important in mental operations as the law of gravity is in physics; in this way, the argument of book 2 is connected with that of book I.[10] In spite of its defects and sometimes its seemingly pointless forays into eighteenth-century psychology, book 2 is a preparation for the moral theory of book 3.[11]

The passions are first divided into *primary* and *secondary*. Primary passions are instinctive, arising without any antecedent perception "from the constitution of the body, from the animal spirits [lust or hunger], or from the application of objects to the external organs" (*Treatise,* 2:i, 1; 275). Secondary passions are the result of prior impressions of pleasure or pain, and these passions are further subdivided into direct and indirect ones. Direct secondary passions include violent passions—"desire, aversion, grief, joy, hope, fear, despair and security" (*Treatise,* 2:i, 1; 277)—and calm passions, which proceed from the contemplation of things external to us.[12] The indirect secondary passions are the result of prior impressions of pleasure or pain while mixed with other qualities—"pride, humility, ambition, vanity, love, hatred, envy, pity, malice, generosity" (*Treatise,* 2:i, 1; 276–77).

Hume admits that these divisions are "vulgar and specious," and he uses them solely for convenience in order to clarify the affectivity of ideas when related by something to oneself. The separate passions, as well as ideas, can have no effect on another unless the mind imposes upon them a relation that creates either pain or pleasure. Hume is both asserting the subjective affectivity of passions upon individual human beings as well as explaining why X leads to pleasure in Mr. Jones and to pain in Mr. Smith. This classification of the passions strengthens his argument for the mind's function in imposing causal relationships upon various events.

Hume fortifies his attack upon the metaphysical bugbears of ethics in part 3 of book 2, "Of the Will and Direct Passions," by applying his same method: the uncertainty of causality. The constant conjunction of two or more events and an *ipse dixit* moral judgment about them is inadmissible in Humean epistemology and in Humean ethics. In discussing the will, Hume argues that reason *by itself* never leads the will to any action, and that reason cannot successfully overcome the passions in an action of the will. The point is neatly stated in a famous piece of Humean rhetoric: "Reason is, and ought only to be the slave of the passions, and can never pretend to any other office than to serve and obey them" (*Treatise,* 2:iii, 3; 415).[13] Reason influences our conduct in only two ways: by directing the attention of a passion to that which is a proper object of the passions, or by discovering connections between events so as to give rise to a passion. Reason is, in other words, not capable of assessing the events and actions that contribute to the distinction between good and evil.

That premise is the starting-point for Hume's analysis "Of Morals" in book 3 of the *Treatise,* although he does feel that contemplation has some role in the moral approval or disapproval an individual may make of certain situations. Moral distinctions for Hume arise only from a "moral sense."[14] Vice and virtue are not discoverable by reason, and Hume makes feelings, rather than judgments, the substance of morality. Good and evil express themselves in terms of particular pleasures and pains, and no absolute rules of right and wrong can be invoked to explain morality.

In this approach, Hume has deviated from many of the traditional notions of morality. One form of ethics has always assumed that man was capable of knowing his duty, of being able to distinguish between right and wrong, and of making the correct moral choice when confronted with events demanding judgment. Knowledge of moral duty was assumed to be on a par with knowledge of fact. Another form of ethics suggested that knowledge could influence behavior in some way, however small. Hume has rejected both of these views by arguing that knowledge cannot be a motive in the execution of moral "duties."[15] Hume, in fact, seemingly rejects the concept of moral duty altogether, emphasizing instead the role of desires and beliefs. Desire, which Hume does not equate with desire for pleasure, is the basis for personal behavior and action; and beliefs have very little effect on these desires, except to indicate a method by which certain desires can be realized.

The source of moral judgments and moral inclinations lies in the peculiar constitution of man. Hume invokes a doctrine based on *sympathy* in order to explain why certain acts give us pleasure, while others give us pain. When we see an act that improves the general welfare of mankind, it evokes a favorable response in us. Sentiments, either of favor or disgust, evolve from the contemplation of events or people and from the way they affect our sympathies. When an act, event, or person calls forth in us a sentiment of moral approval, we call it "virtuous." Consequently, moral rules should not be oppressively absolute, and morality is really, for Hume, a matter of taste—as is beauty or a sense of humor. Hume has also given short shrift to the method of some rationalists who derive the imperative *ought* from a simple infinitive. In other words, Hume cannot see and will not accept the allegedly logical progression from an assertion ("To love one's neighbor is good.") to the moral imperative ("Love thy neighbor!").

Hume's Imagery in the *Treatise*

Until recently, very little attention was paid to the use of images—metaphors, similes, analogies, figurative language—in philosophic discourse, perhaps because philosophers thought of imagery as belonging to "poetic" discourse and not to the "serious" business of philosophy.[16] T. H. Green, who takes only brief notice of Locke's metaphor of impression in his introduction to Hume's *Treatise,* otherwise ignores Hume's imagery (*Works,* 1:9). Writing about the reception of ideas in the understanding, Locke says, "These *simple Ideas,* when offered to the mind, *the Understanding can* no more refuse to have, nor alter, when they are imprinted, nor blot them out, and make new ones in it self, than a mirror can refuse, alter, or obliterate the Images or *Ideas,* which, the Objects set before it, do therein produce."[17] The metaphor of impression in Hume's *Treatise* describes perceptions which enter into our consciousness with the most "force and violence." The term suggests a perception that is indelible and irreducible; it cannot be divided into small components, and it enjoys some of the stability of the printed word.

Yet this metaphor is not always consistent because Hume describes the mind as a "heap or collection of different perceptions" (*Treatise,* 1:iv, 2; 207). Impressions or perceptions do not enter the mind in orderly coherence; the "heap" metaphor implies that even "collection" is too orderly a term to apply to the agglomeration of perceptions impinging simultaneously on the mind. The mind must take this heap of impressions, as an eighteenth–century printer might have taken a bundle of printed but unsorted sheets and organized them coherently; the means by which the mind organizes these impressions is, of course, experience. The metaphor of impression is further qualified when Hume describes impressions as "internal and perishing existences" (*Treatise,* 1:iv, 2; 194). The memory apparently can recall impressions from the "heap" but others are doomed to "perish" without supplying ideas to the mind. Hume attributes to actions the same perishable quality that he finds in impressions: "Actions are by their very nature temporary and perishing" (*Treatise,* 2:iii, 2; 411).

This description of the mind as a "heap or collection of different perceptions" is one of many: Hume does not lack for other metaphors. In a section entitled "Of the Love of Fame," Hume writes of the "fabric of the mind, as with that of the body," comparing the similarities in several minds to the similarities in bodies (*Treatise,* 2:i, 11; 318). Minds, to continue Hume's metaphor, are all woven the same way; and the inquirer into human nature can assume a similarity of structure, thought processes, and responses. The "fabric" metaphor defines in some way the structure of the mind: "In general we may remark, that the minds of men are *mirrors* to one another, not only because they *reflect* each others emotions, but also because those *rays of passions,* sentiments and opinions may be often *reverberated,* and may *decay away* by insensible degrees. Thus the pleasure, which a rich man receives from his possessions, being thrown upon the beholder, causes a pleasure and esteem . . . and being once more *reflected,* become a new *foundation* for pleasure and esteem in the beholder" (*Treatise,* 2:ii, 5; 365 [my italics]). Untangling this mixed metaphor, we discover that Hume regards other minds as capable of generating sympathetic passions. The metaphor also postulates a similarity between the methods by which separate minds adapt themselves to the expressions of other minds. Or the passions may simply cancel each other out and slowly diminish.

A mirror image has been common enough in English literature for conveying ideas about aesthetics, ethics and politics. Hume, like all philosophers faced with the difficulty of conceptualizing "mind" for their readers, tries whatever seems feasible. The following analogy is, however, more subtle than preceding ones: "Now if we consider the human mind, we shall find, that with regard to the passions, 'tis not of the nature of a wind-instrument of music, which in running over all the notes immediately loses the sound after the breath ceases; but rather resembles a string-instrument, where after each stroke the vibrations still retain some sound, which gradually and insensibly decays" (*Treatise,* 2:iii, 9; 440–41). Hume is at least consistent in mixing his metaphors. The passions, being "slow and restive," will not be produced distinctly but will be mixed with other, if fainter, passions. A passion, apparently, cannot be, in Locke's words, a "clear and distinct" perception; nor can it exist without being related to some other passion. This relationship is perhaps appreciated more clearly in a metaphor Hume used earlier, in which he presented the four passions of pride and humility, love and hatred "plac'd, as it were, in a square or regular connexion with, and distance from each other" (*Treatise,* 2:ii, 2; 333):

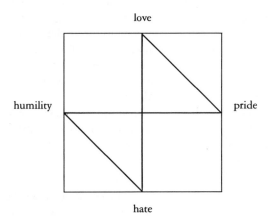

In Hume's moral philosophy and in his discussion of certain basic emotions, his metaphors clearly indicate that no emotion or passion can be experienced or conceived as a distinct entity in the mind. The indistinctness of passions suggests that confusion can easily be the governing principle of a mind incapable of distinguishing anger from hatred or fear from despair.

The preceding metaphors are all used to conceptualize mind as it expresses or experiences passions. In the first book of the *Treatise,* Hume, in describing his theory of knowledge, employs one of his best-known metaphors: "The mind is a kind of theatre, where several perceptions successively make their appearance; pass, re-pass, glide away, and mingle in an infinite variety of postures and situations." Thinking that this metaphor might be misleading, Hume soon adds that "The comparison of the theatre must not mislead us. They are the successive perceptions only, that constitute the mind; nor have we the most distant notion of the place, where these scenes are represented, or of the materials, of which it is compos'd" (*Treatise,* 1:iv, 6; 253). The most striking feature of this image is that of the mind choosing a theatre and the work to which it is spectator, being one of many spectators, and responding to the spectacle on the stage. The ramifications of the image would almost seem to defeat Hume's notion of the mind's capabilities.

These words represent Hume's allegedly atomistic conception of the mind but are certainly at variance with the earlier description of the mind as a "heap" of perceptions. Hume is trying to indicate the manifold ways in which impressions and ideas can make their way into the mind; and, if he uses different metaphors, he is attempting to prevent us from confusing the function of the mind with its structure. Of the latter, it seems, we can have little knowledge but must be content with knowing the way the mind operates. The mind is unable to reject those things in the external world which present themselves to the mind through the senses; it may not acknowledge their force, and they may not convince, but, as long as the senses are active, the mind cannot prevent perceptual activity.

Perhaps the best metaphor, and the most complicated, that Hume uses to define "mind" occurs shortly after the "theatre" metaphor. Using the word "soul" as a synonym for "mind" (a frequent eighteenth-century practice) Hume says:

In this respect, I cannot compare the soul more properly to any thing than to a republic or commonwealth, in which the several members are united by the reciprocal ties of government and subordination, and give rise to other persons, who propagate the same republic in the incessant changes of its parts. And as the same individual republic may not only change its members, but also its laws and constitutions; in like manner the same person may vary his character and disposition, as well as his impressions and ideas, without losing his identity. (*Treatise,* 1:iv, 6; 261).

The intent of this analogy is clear. This conception of "mind" is not atomistic, but sees the mind as a progression of events and things that supplement, shape, and redefine themselves, as well as future events. The mind becomes a process and is not like a book, or Locke's blank slate, or any fixed entity. If I may extend Hume's metaphor, we can think of the mind as undergoing evolution and development, just as the political state does. Unless subjected to violent revolutions, it always contains something of the same structure and function it had when first formed. In other words, the ways in which the mind operates remain, for the most part, the same—as do the operations of the state. The function of each is an indication of its structure; but, unlike physical structures, each is involved in continual process and change.

If the mind is a collection of various perceptions, they must be organized in some way to contribute to our understanding of events and to impart

some sense of certitude in our experience. In order to illustrate the connections between events and facts, Hume relies upon an eighteenth-century
commonplace: the metaphor of the chain.[18] In analyzing the "component
parts of our reasonings concerning cause and effect," Hume speaks of the
"chain of argument or connexion of causes and effects" involved in our acceptance of the fact of Caesar's murder on the Ides of March (*Treatise*, 1:iii,
4; 83). Without the authority of memory or sense-perception, our acceptance of the testimony of historians as fact would be unfounded: "Every link
of the chain wou'd in that case hang upon another, but there wou'd not be
any thing fix'd to one end of it, capable of sustaining the whole" (*Treatise*,
1:iii, 4; 83). A chain of argument used to support any fact must be linked
to something substantial and verifiable.

The same point arises later in Hume's discussion "Of unphilosophical
probability," where he remarks that we can have no assurance about any
event in ancient history without accepting the validity of an immeasurable
"chain of arguments". Hume then points out that an argument has been
raised against Christianity by supposing "each link of the chain in human
testimony" capable only of probability and "liable to a degree of doubt and
uncertainty" (*Treatise*, 1:iii, 13; 145). For strategic reasons—since Hume is
not defending the evidence of Christianity, but historical evidence—Hume
finds fault with this argument. He does, however, explain how the mind
manages to preserve, despite good reasons to do otherwise, some belief in
events long past; the mind retains a "feeling" of probability when, strictly
speaking, probabilities should be reduced to nothing.

The "links are innumerable" in connecting "an original fact with the present impression," but we can give assent to a historical fact because of the fidelity and accuracy with which it has been transmitted to us. Were this
transmission faulty, if all the long chain of causes and effects were composed
of links different from each other and without any relation to the original,
we should never accept the validity of historical fact. The proofs, however, of
historical facts have in all cases resembled one another; and the mind has
thus accepted the facts of history without requiring that they be repeated.
For Hume, even "a long chain of argument" does not diminish the "original
vivacity" as much as it might be diminished were the links in the argument
composed of different and contrary parts. Then the mind would have to ac-
commodate new evidence in judging each historical fact and would be hard
pressed to decide what was fact and what was not. Yet Hume later admits
that a "long chain of objects" can diminish the evidence for an original idea
or historical fact (*Treatise*, 1:iii, 13; 146, 154).

In conjunction with the chain metaphor, Hume often describes the mind in terms of Newtonian and physical concepts. The mind becomes capable of performing certain feats that are analogous to the activity of man: "the mind runs easily along them, jumps from one part to another with facility, and forms but a confus'd and general notion of each link" (*Treatise*, 1:iii, 13; 146). Hume also writes of the mind "passing" or "carrying" certain ideas. This movement in the mind is caused by the principle of associationism; the metaphor would suggest that the principle operates in the mind very much the same way that Newton's laws of motion operate in the external world.

In Section 1 of this chapter, I called attention to Hume's master–slave metaphor describing the relation in Humean psychology between reason and passion: "Reason is, and ought only to be the slave of the passions." That metaphor is a complete reversal of the one Hume used earlier in the section "Of the sceptical and other systems of philosophy." Hume had pointed out that nature and habit soon break the force of skeptical doubts and do not lead man to Pyrrhonistic skepticism. Comparing reason to a monarch and skepticism to its enemy, Hume says that "Reason first appears in possession of the throne, prescribing laws, and imposing maxims, with an absolute sway and authority. Her enemy, therefore, is oblig'd to take shelter under her protection, and by making use of rational arguments to prove the fallaciousness and imbecility of reason, produces, in a manner, a patent under her hand and seal. This patent has at first an authority, proportion'd to the present and immediate authority of reason, from which it is deriv'd."

The metaphor now changes to an expression of a contest between skeptical reasonings, whose authorities are equally diminished in their encounters. Neither reason nor skepticism can or should gain complete ascendance in the human mind. Hume does not facilely suggest that man should synthesize the two, but that he must and always does yield to the "course of nature." The passions are part of the "course of nature," and Hume could easily say of skepticism, as he said of reason, that "skepticism is, and ought only to be the slave of the passions." While reason and skepticism may be enthroned at one time and enslaved at the next, they cannot and should not totally dominate the mind (*Treatise* 1:iv, 2; 186–87, 415).

Numerous other metaphors, some seemingly trivial, appear consistently throughout the *Treatise*; a brief mention of one will perhaps indicate the manner in which Hume conceptualized certain philosophical problems. What might be loosely called a "combat" metaphor describes the struggle between the passions and reason. Hume suggests that the mind might very well be a battlefield in which battles are won according to prejudices, convictions, or impressions. This is the metaphor of the introduction, where Hume, in speaking of the disputes in philosophy, observes that eloquence, not reason, often wins the battles: "The victory is not gained by the men at arms, who manage the pike and the sword; but by the trumpeters, drummers and musicians of the army." The study of human nature is likened to an attack upon a major power center. This metaphor implies that Hume thinks his method capable of putting down or solving traditional philosophical problems. By winning the battle against shibboleths and metaphysical slogans, the philosopher of human nature can build a science of human nature on a new and secure foundation.

Considerably later, in closing his discussion of the passions, Hume varies the metaphor: "I shall observe, that there cannot be two passions more nearly resembling each other, than those of hunting and philosophy, whatever disproportion may at first sight appear betwixt them . . . To make the parallel betwixt hunting and philosophy more compleat, we may observe, that tho' in both cases the end of our action may in itself be despis'd, yet in the heat of the action we acquire such an attention to this end, that we are very uneasy under any disappointments, and are sorry when we either miss our game, or fall into any error in our reasoning" (*Treatise,* 2:iii, 10; 451–52).

Searching for another parallel, Hume finds that the passion of gaming creates pleasure "from the same principles as hunting and philosophy" (*Treatise,* 2:iii, 10; 452). The implication is clear: philosophy involves the truth seeker or the knowledge lover so strongly in its problems or objectives that he or she fails to realize the ultimate effect of, for example, skepticism or dogmatism. Much of the pleasure of philosophy lies in the manner by which one arrives at conclusions about the nature of man or the structure of the universe. The game, not the goal, gives the real pleasure. The conclusions about the nature of man or the structure of the universe may not be pleasant when reached, but the intense pleasure of philosophical study counteracts any attempts to anticipate undesirable consequences.

The richness of the imagery in the *Treatise* repeatedly startles and enlightens a reader, but it can also make the reader feel that Hume's "meaning" can never be stated with certainty and exactitude. Hume's willingness to celebrate the activity of philosophizing, rather than to dogmatize about the conclusions he has reached, is one of the revolutionary aspects of his philosophy. Hume embraces ambivalence and incertitude; he relishes playing the role of a philosopher as much as he delights in the joys of wining and dining. The imagery in the *Treatise* can be constantly mined for new insights about human nature, and if a coherent, unarguable, and totally clear system of philosophy does not emerge from the inquiry, that is to be expected.

While Hume began his *Treatise* with his "combat" metaphor and emphasizes struggles throughout, he chooses quite another metaphor for the conclusion, that of the verb "to anatomize," which Dr. Johnson defined as "to lay any thing open distinctly, and by minute parts." This metaphor was popular during the eighteenth century, and Hume used it upon several occasions, perhaps most notably in the *Dialogues concerning Natural Religion.* Of the function or duty of a philosopher, Hume writes:

The anatomist ought never to emulate the painter: nor in his accurate dissections and portraitures of the smaller parts of the human body, pretend to give his figures any graceful and engaging attitude or expression. There is even something hideous, or at least minute in the view of things, which he presents; and 'tis necessary the objects shou'd be set more at a distance, and be more cover'd up from sight, to make them engaging to the eye and imagination. An anatomist, however, is admirably fitted to give advice to a painter; and 'tis even impracticable to excel in the latter art, without the assistance of the former. (*Treatise*, 3:iii, 6; 620–21)

The anatomist, or philosopher, having a precise and exacting knowledge of the operation of the human mind and its passions, can suggest ways in which all mankind can improve itself. Man must understand the "springs and principles" of human nature in order to create "*practical morality,*" to which the abstract speculations of the philosopher must always be subservient.

Hume was the first to follow his own advice. When the abstract speculations of the *Treatise* failed to achieve the immediate popularity that he desired, he sought to express other ideas in a medium more accessible than a philosophical treatise: the essay.

Chapter Three
The Moral Sciences: Ideas in Search of a Form

Literature: Rhetoric and Emotion

Hume addressed himself to the problem of essay writing in the second volume (1742) of *Essays, Moral and Political*. "Of Essay Writing" appeared only in that edition.[1] In it, Hume commented upon the sparsity of intelligent conversation in the "civilized" world, observing that "Men of Letters" were taking part in daily converse with the rest of mankind and that the "Men of the World" were borrowing their topics of conversation from books. Hume devoted his essays to improving the alliance between the "learned and conversible Worlds": "I know nothing more advantageous than such *Essays* as these with which I endeavour to entertain the Public. In this View, I cannot but consider myself as Kind of Resident or Ambassador from the Dominions of Learning to those of Conversation; and shall think it my constant Duty to promote a good Correspondence betwixt these two States, which have so great a Dependence on each other" (*Works*, 4:368; *Essays*, 535). This particular kind of immodesty was fairly common in eighteenth-century essays; in addition, Hume thoroughly believed not only in the necessity of enlightenment but also in the expansion of the role of the intelligent man in human affairs.[2]

One essay in particular bears the mark of Humean skepticism about the value of emotionalism as a means of improving the conversation among mankind. An essay, "Of the Delicacy of Taste and Passion" (1741), notes a corollary between a "delicacy of passion" and a "delicacy of taste." By the term "delicacy of passion," Hume means what we would today call "excessive sentimentality." People subject to this "delicacy of passion" permit the smallest event to affect both their sense and their sensibilities in a manner disproportionate to the stimuli which called forth the passion.[3] A fictional example of a person exhibiting a "delicacy of passion" can be found in the character of uncle Toby in Laurence Sterne's novel, *Tristram Shandy*.

A "delicacy of taste" is similar to a delicacy of passion, except that its sphere of operation is aesthetics; not manners. A person given to a "delicacy of taste" would be, in modern terms, a hyper-aesthete, one led into raptures at the experience of almost any poem or painting. He or she would be incapable of what has been called "the art of discrimination,"[4] an ability to distinguish the competent from the excellent. Of the aesthete's reaction to a poem or painting, Hume remarks: "nor are the masterly strokes perceived with more exquisite relish and satisfaction, than the negligences or absurdities with disgust and uneasiness" (*Works* 3:92; *Essays,* 4). In the beginning of his essay, Hume had found a "cool and sedate" temper preferable to one afflicted with a "delicacy of passion"; but he finds "delicacy of taste" worthy of being cultivated while a "delicacy of passion" is to be avoided or remedied. To be cured of this excessive sentimentality, one should cultivate a "higher and more refined taste."

Oddly enough, what Hume is proposing is a paradox: by improving one's delicacy of taste, one eventually does not succumb to trivial and frivolous things or events. The improvement of taste eliminates, in effect, grossness and over–sensibility. The mind, by cultivating its resources, learns to differentiate between the kinds of stimuli which had previously evoked a lavish response. By learning to perceive the quality of difference between two events, one is able to understand and to appreciate more fully the "polite arts." The mind becomes accustomed to and relishes a keener, more complex variety of stimuli than it had hitherto been capable of.

Apparently unsatisfied with his first attempt at a definition of taste, Hume returned to the topic in 1757 in the essay "Of the Standard of Taste" in *Four Dissertations.*[5] In common with much of his procedure, Hume emphasizes the different definitions applied to the term "taste" in various contexts, and he makes no attempt to assert or to identify an absolute standard of taste. He considers the ways in which the experience of an individual can substantially alter subsequent perceptions and judgments; he separates perception and judgment, but he seems inclined to make a distinction of degree rather than of kind between them. Such a distinction aims for, and perhaps ends in, an epistemological basis for, or at least an epistemological derivation of, aesthetics. The method of the critic, in suggesting a standard of taste, may be adversely affected by his subjective experience. Hume does not, however, forsake certain predispositions: "where the ideas of morality and decency alter from one age to another, and where vicious manners are described, without being marked with the proper characters of blame and disapprobation; this must be allowed to disfigure the poem, and to be a real deformity" (*Works,* 3:282; *Essays,* 246). As Professor Cohen has suggested,[6] Hume's own method invalidates that judgment; despite one's ability or incompetence to evaluate works of art alien to one's moral and social code, one still makes the judgment.

No absolute standard of taste exists in nature, but standards of taste by which one can judge works of art are the product of experience and contemplation. The duty of the critic is, therefore, to establish standards of taste based upon experience and historical reliability. A standard of taste, according to Hume, will reconcile the various sentiments men may have when regarding an alleged work of art. Into this standard of taste, he both admits and rejects general opinion. Common sense, Hume affirms, leads men to prefer John Milton to John Ogilby and Joseph Addison to John Bunyan; but the same common sense, conditioned by the empirical method of literary inquiry, can provide in a different age contrasting yet valid conclusions about a work of art. Hume's standard of taste is not so much a standard as a method for discovering what the standards of one's age are, of ascertaining the intensity with which one responds to a given work, and of revealing the particular qualities of a work that make it distinguished.

Hume's contributions to theories of taste are not easy to miss in an age that emphasized "rules" criticism and that assumed that standards used to judge a work in one age would be valid for a different work in another age. In opposition to this assumption, Hume posited that the would-be critic should exhibit what he defined in that early essay as a "delicacy of taste": his response to all the components of a work of art should be both intense and general, a sentiment in which Samuel Johnson would concur. Only by the fullest response to the work could an accurate judgment be made. In addition, Hume insists that the method for forming these judgments should be empirical; the more experience a man has with beauties and deformities, the more easily he will recognize them in artistic manifestations. Hume is opposed, therefore, to the view that notions of taste evolve from "on high." To him, the principles of taste are universal and almost equal in all men; only a few men, however, are qualified to judge a work of art because only a few have taken the trouble to exercise and to develop the experience necessary for a proper evaluation of art. As a result of this insistence upon method and experience, Hume will not accept as a work of art anything that requires a standard beyond those supplied by the senses and the imagination.

Some of Hume's contributions to a theory of taste are not new; his argument that a critic must be free of prejudices has been a critical cliché longer than most of us care to imagine. (Indeed, one might argue that some of the most interesting criticism comes from a critic who knowingly exploits his prejudices.) He affirms that *"good sense"* will vitiate the most unproductive prejudices; he recognizes the validity of preferences (one person may prefer sublimity, another raillery); and he asserts that the representations of art that most resemble our age and country please us most. Hume is not free of all the qualities he condemns. He favors literary works that extol bravery, courage, freedom, and other virtues, and he opposes those that exemplify cowardice, license, chicanery, and other vices. His system of morality invades his aesthetic judgments, although he argues that words like "virtue" imply praise, while "vice" implies blame. Paradoxically, Hume's method allows for excrescences in any critical theory when he admits the "right" to be unable to apply all of one's critical strictures because of psychology or physiology.

Usually coupled with "Of the Standard of Taste" is the essay "Of Tragedy," which also first appeared in *Four Dissertations*. A shorter essay than the one on taste, it tries to explain why we are pleased at the representation of sorrow, terror, and anxiety in a tragedy. In the *Treatise,* in a section entitled "Of Compassion," Hume had explained the pleasure of tragedy by appeal to a sympathy theory, arguing that the spectator's identification with the processes in a drama created a favorable, pleasant response (*Treatise,* 2:ii, 7; 369). "Of Tragedy" is a considerable alteration and revision of that sympathy theory.[7]

Hume takes into account the Abbé Dubos's representation of a sympathy theory of tragedy and considers some other explanation for the pleasure derived from it. In answer to this theory, Hume posits that "This extraordinary effect proceeds from that very eloquence, with which the melancholy scene is represented" (*Works,* 3:261; *Essays,* 292). Describing why the sympathy theory is insufficient, Hume relies on a number of informative verbs: "excite," "overpower," "convert," "join," "alter," and "convey." Such elements as the forceful expression of passions and the "beauty of oratorial numbers" in a tragedy create, because they are applied to an interesting subject, an intense feeling of pleasure that is not allied to any identification one makes with the characters of a drama. Hume admits that tragedy is an imitation, but he argues that imitations are always agreeable. We do realize that the tragedy is a fiction, and this realization "softens" the passions engaged by a tragedy and converts them into a "new feeling"—one neither sympathetic nor realistic but adventitious. The emotions we, as spectators, feel are not exactly extrinsic to the situation that calls them forth. They are emotions transformed by the context in which we experience tragedy. In one sense, Hume is saying that our idea of tragedy and the pleasure it gives us are derived from a recombination and conversion of original impression in our minds. The imitation of tragedy on the stage, combined with appropriate histrionics, produces pleasure in us because the experience is different not only in kind but in degree from that of ordinary life.

The literary criticism in these two essays is rhetorical, not philological, perhaps because rhetoric was one of Hume's early (and lifelong) concerns, and the importance of rhetoric to Hume and to his works should not be minimized. In other essays, Hume addressed himself to other rhetorical features of art. For example, one of the elements involved in the transformation of passions was eloquence. In the second volume of *Essays, Moral and Political,* Hume titled one essay "Of Eloquence" (1742). He observes that the modern period is superior to the ancient in philosophy but much inferior in eloquence; that England can honor its poets and philosophers, but that it has no orators to speak of. What it calls "eloquence" is simply "good sense, delivered in proper expression" (*Works,* 3:169; *Essays,* 104). The speakers in England are temperate and calm and dare not employ the bold figures of speech used by Demosthenes and Cicero. But Hume is not convinced that ancient eloquence is unsuitable to the modern temper.

Although Hume does not define eloquence denotatively, he does give an intensive, or connotative, definition. Dr. Johnson, in his *Dictionary,* had defined eloquence as the "power of speaking with fluency and elegance; oratory." Hume's definition involves more of a value judgment than Johnson's. Eloquence appeals chiefly to the passions and can override reason because its language is not the calm and decorous appeal of "sweet reason." Hume disputes the assumption that the "superior good sense" of the eighteenth century makes eloquence archaic or impractical: "our orators [could be] more cautious and reserved than the ancient, in attempting to inflame the passions, or elevate the imagination of their audience. But, I see no reason, why it should make them despair absolutely of succeeding in that attempt. It should make them redouble their art, not abandon it entirely" (*Works,* 3:169; *Essays,* 104).

Spoken eloquence involves the use of elaborate figures of speech, elevated rhetoric, a voice of energy and modulation. Its appeal is visceral, not intellectual; therefore, eloquence is judged both qualitatively and quantitatively. When the principles, or passions, or sentiments in man are properly stimulated, he responds with satisfaction and is able to distinguish works of genius from works of capricious wit. This judgment is even more true of eloquence than the liberal arts: the more an eloquent speaker can move the public or a great mass of people, the greater he is.

While Hume is saying that an eloquent appeal is more forceful and more pleasing than a calmly reasoned speech, he does not suggest that eloquence should be the means by which the emotions of men are falsely swayed. Even

the most impassioned speech is not exempt from order and coherence, but
the method of presentation ought to make the most of an effective rhetorical
structure. And, of course, Hume confines eloquence to those subjects for
which it is fitted: the principle of decorum is almost an accepted fact.

In this essay and others, Hume is interested in differentiating among various subjective responses to an event, particularly the response of a large
group of people when contrasted to a small group or an individual. What is
appropriate in one circumstance is not in another, for reactions to any appraisal of events become more subtle when they are individualized. This
point is reiterated near the beginning of one of his longer essays, "Of the
Rise and Progress of the Arts and Sciences" (1742), in which Hume observes that "those principles or causes, which are fitted to operate on a mul-
titude, are always of a grosser and more stubborn nature, less subject to
accidents, and less influenced by whim and private fancy, than those which
operate on a few only" (*Works,* 3:175; *Essays,* 112).

Hume's aesthetic framework provides for two different degrees of events
to engage our sentiments, our taste, our passions. Some events are large-
scaled, perhaps even coarse; their appeal is to large multitudes, and they
must be evaluated in terms of the efficaciousness of that appeal. These
large-scaled aesthetic events, designed for the masses, would be inappropriate in the parlor or in a man's closet. Perhaps an event of this kind could be
scaled down, as one might take the sentiments found in a piece of rhetorical
eloquence and fit the sentiments into the rhetoric of a short poem. The intensity of the aesthetic event and its appeal are not so much reduced as
transformed into a medium more appropriate for small audiences. An aesthetic event of this kind allows for, even requires, a subtilized response from
an individual or a small group of people.

More important than the differentiation of aesthetic responses is Hume's
insistence upon the emotional value of the work of art. In fact, Hume has all
but excluded truth as a value from an aesthetic construct; a work of art is
judged not so much on its fidelity to "truth to life" or "reality," or on some
other hard-worked cliché, but on the quality and extent of emotional response it elicits from the spectators. Critical judgments about works of art or
aesthetic events derive their cogency from their accuracy. The orthodox theory of "imitation" or "mimesis," so essential to most critics of the seventeenth and eighteenth centuries, has been discredited in favor of one that
emphasizes creativity, uniqueness, and suggestivity. Where possible, art was
to be measured by empirical standards. The emotions pertinent to or elic-
ited by the work of art under consideration were the guides. Admittedly,
Hume hazarded some false psychological assumptions; but he insisted that

a work of art was not something sifted from the "rules" but an independent emotional experience involving the spectator temporarily in emotions or passions different from those of everyday experience.

Morals: Diversity and Humanity

The essays discussed in the previous section represent Hume's inquiry into literary theory. While we need not bother excessively about what kind of essays they are (literary, political, or moral), we can note that almost any of Hume's essays could be classified as "moral" in the eighteenth-century sense of that term. Alexander Pope's *Epistles to Several Persons* were also titled *Moral Essays* and comprehended a wide variety of subjects. The third definition Dr. Johnson gave in his *Dictionary* for moral was "popular; customary; such as is known or admitted in the general business of life." Yet, in reading Hume's "moral essays," we need not give such a wide meaning to the term. Hume's "moral essays" could include "Of the Liberty of the Press," but the contents would seem to define it more as a political essay. Hume never specified which of his essays was "moral," but it is worthwhile to note that any number of topics could be considered under that term.

One of the topics to which eighteenth-century writers addressed themselves, and one which perhaps no age ever ignores, was that of man's "dignity" or "meanness." Hume took up the topic in "Of the Dignity or Meanness of Human Nature" (1741). He had initially planned to call it "Of the Dignity of Human Nature," which gives us a clue to Hume's sentiments. Asserting that sentiments favorable to mankind are more likely to promote virtue than misanthropy, while sentiments denigrating mankind promote meanness, Hume persuades himself that the dispute concerning the dignity or meanness of human nature is more often verbal than real. He agrees that no one would deny the actual difference between vice and virtue, wisdom and folly, or other polarized qualities. In spite of these determinable differences, we affix blame or merit not by appeal to a "fixed unalterable standard in the nature of things" but by comparison. When we compare ourselves to animals, we are naturally overwhelmed with our superiority. Animals comparing themselves to human beings might not be so overwhelmed with our superiority. We may even exaggerate notions of human excellence beyond what we experience in ourselves, a vice to which Pope called attention in the *Essay on Man*. Comparisons, however, induce contempt for man because we find only a few whom we consider wise, virtuous, or beautiful. Without appealing to an absolutist standard of excellence, Hume points out that the appellations of "wise" or "beautiful" are the products of comparison. If the lowest of mankind were as wise as Cicero or Bacon, we could still find few "wise" men on earth. Differences are of degree, not of kind.

Hume is apparently trying to tread that unreliable ground between absolutism and relativism. His success is perhaps tenuous, but he had been preparing the reader for the only proper kind of comparison, those principles, or guidelines, by which humans are moved to decisions or judgments. To Hume, much of the dispute in the controversy is linguistic. He cannot understand, for example, the reasoning of those who maintain that self-love, in any form, is the spur and spring of all human action. Should a misanthrope persist in calling kindness to others self-love, the error is linguistic, and he would have to admit that this kindness, nevertheless, has an immense influence upon human actions. The fallacy lies, Hume maintains, in assuming that all acts of virtue or friendship must have a selfish motive.

Applying the same logic here that he did to theories of causality, Hume argues that a virtuous sentiment precedes and produces pleasure; a virtuous sentiment does not derive from the pleasure. On another level, it is argued that virtuous men are not unreceptive to praise and have therefore been pronounced vain. But who would ascribe an act of any kind entirely to one motive? Vanity and virtue, Hume alleges, are interconnected; and the love of fame, stemming from one's praiseworthy actions, is similar to and intermixed with the love of praiseworthy actions for their own sake. Hume concludes that the love of glory for virtuous deeds certainly indicates an actual love of virtue. The implication is clear: how could one not love virtue if one loved the acclaim one received from being virtuous?

In suggesting that words which describe deeds cannot go beyond the available evidence, which he was to do again in the *Enquiry concerning the Principles of Morals,* Hume seems to be simplifying any discussion of ethics. He was doing that and more: he was raising questions about the nature of language and its autotelic qualities. Language could not have some elusive meanings available only to those gifted with a kind of linguistic "second sight." Words would have to mean what they seemed to mean, not someone's idea of what a word "really" meant. Interlaced with this skepticism about a hidden meaning or motive behind the words that one uses to describe moral acts is an awareness of the logical danger of confusing the meaning of a word with what it suggests. Language, Hume says, should not suggest more meanings than the evidence warrants.

Hume develops this point of view, with an excellent example, in the essay "Of National Characters" (1748). By this term, Hume meant those qualities we assign to an individual because of his geographical or cultural origin.

Quashing the assumption that these physical causes could have some effect upon the formation of national character, Hume asserts that even the most superficial observer would realize that a nation's character was the result of moral causes. When we attribute national character to physical causes, we do so from an inclination to invest a general term with more authority than it could reasonably command. We allow the contiguity of certain physical phenomena to a people to impose upon their culture certain presumptions about their moral qualities (people living in hot countries are more warm-blooded than those living in cold countries, etc.). For Hume, language can convey precise information only when used with an awareness that precludes its invitation to transform contiguity into causality.

One of the ways in which Hume tries to make his analysis precise is by relying upon historical example and not upon a priori precepts. In "Of National Characters," for example, all of the presumptions made in the name of national character are subjected to a historical methodology. Generalizations which do not fit the lessons of history are thus discarded. While this methodology, rather obvious to us, works well when Hume's skepticism restrains his personal inclinations, it is not so successful when he is tested by his sense of national pride. The essay "Of Polygamy and Divorces" (1742) incorporates Hume's attention to linguistic improprieties and to a historical methodology, but it also concludes that "The exclusion of polygamy and divorces sufficiently recommends our present EUROPEAN practice with regard to marriage" (*Works,* 3:239; *Essays,* 190). Hume arrives at this conclusion by his reluctance to admit "barbarism" into the workings of human nature and from his aversion to tyranny in any form.

To approach the subject of polygamy and divorce in a casual essay as if it required subtle philosophical discriminations would perhaps be inappropriate in the eighteenth century. Hume does, however, allow himself a generalization in this essay that lapses from his customary perspicuity: "To render polygamy more odious, I need not recount the frightful effects of jealousy, and the constraint in which it holds the fair-sex all over the east." Relying on the scanty information available to him about the East, Hume generalizes beyond his evidence. The available literature from and of the East indicated that sexual jealousy was an emotion more peculiar to the Western, or European, world. In some editions of this essay, Hume quoted a piece of Turkish wisdom, without realizing that it could imply an absence of sexual jealousy in Eastern nations. A Turkish ambassador in France, Hume reports, found the Turks simpletons in comparison to the Christians: "*We are at the expense and trouble of keeping a seraglio, each in his own house: But you can ease yourselves of this burden, and have your seraglio in your friends' houses*" (*Works,*

3:234n; *Essays,* 628). Hume defends European womanhood against this ungallant observation, but he is still blind to the apparent absence of jealousy, or at least the Western kind of jealousy, in Eastern nations. In this instance, his nationalistic pride overwhelms philosophic detachment.

Hume's observations about divorce are cogent, if his premises are accepted. He makes the common objection to divorce because of its effects on children, but his second argument premises that males, in spite of their delight in liberty, will adjust to necessity, and, eventually, the proximity of their spouses will create harmony and friendship. (This assertion of Hume's was purely conjectural: he never married.) Marriage chiefly subsists, not by love, but by friendship. To this rather constrained sense of marriage, he adds the proviso that only those people whose interests are closely allied should marry. Hume's purpose in these essays was to vindicate Western preference in regard to marriage and to justify monogamy. He succeeded only by discarding some of his skeptical inclinations and by short-changing the reader on historical examples. He used literary and historical examples as equally forceful, a mixture of evidence he seldom committed.

Hume's interest in historical problems may have provided the impetus for a set of four essays, all written in the first person, discussing the positions of certain classical philosophies: "The Epicurean," "The Stoic," "The Platonist," and "The Sceptic" (1742). The intention of these essays, Hume noted, "is not so much to explain accurately the sentiments of the ancient sects of philosophy, as to deliver the sentiments of sects, that naturally form themselves in the world, and entertain different ideas of human life and of happiness" (*Works,* 3:197n; *Essays,* 138n.). In them, Hume adopts both the rhetoric and the logic of the various sects; and he often satirizes the ideas he is representing.

The image Hume presents of Epicureanism is typical of his century.[8] Man is envious of nature because it produced him and must always be the source of creative inspiration and energy; however, man cannot possibly equal nature's achievements. To the Epicurean, nothing is so ridiculous as philosophers' attempts to produce artificial happiness out of reason and reflection. The human mind and its bodily confinements are not self-sufficient in the pursuit of pleasure, which, when it comes to the Epicurean, all too quickly departs. Cheerful discourse, not reason, leads to wisdom; and men are often led astray from the correct pursuit of pleasure by the love of glory. Life's ephemerality should impel them to the most intense gratification possible for their senses.

Epicureanism suffers no great injustices in this summary of the ideas Hume presents as those of that sect. The rhetoric for this literary occasion, however, calls attention to what Hume must have considered absurdities in Epicurean ideology. The excesses, ironically emphasized by exclamation points, imply that Epicureanism is more of a pose than a position; that it sacrifices logic and good sense to its own image.[9] Confusing aesthetics with ethics, the Epicurean throws his life away in vain pursuit of pleasure, foiled by a term he never defines. Although Epicurus considered *ataraxia* ("tranquility") the highest goal of pleasure, Hume never mentions this contemplative side of Epicurean thought; he prefers to caricature Epicureanism with the exotic flowers of an over-fertile rhetoric: "But see, propitious to my wishes, the divine, the amiable PLEASURE, the supreme love of GODS and men, advances towards me. At her approach, my heart beats with genial heat, and every sense and every faculty is dissolved in joy; while she pours around me . . . all the treasures of the autumn. . . . O! for ever let me spread my limbs on this bed of roses, and thus, thus feel the delicious moments with soft and downy steps, glide along" (*Works,* 3:199–200; *Essays,* 141). After rhetoric of this sort, almost sexual in its imagery, few readers would be surprised to discover in the *Dialogues concerning Natural Religion,* the comment that "the old *Epicurean* Hypothesis . . . is commonly, and I believe, justly, esteem'd the most absurd System, that has yet been proposed" (*Dialogues,* 209). Although the speaker in this instance, Philo, representing Hume's views, alludes to the Epicurean cosmogony, Hume would no doubt include the Epicurean ethic.

Compared to the Epicurean, the Stoic fares much better in Hume's representation. The Stoic argues that man's essential difference from the brutes—his "affinity with superior beings"—urges him into art and industry; and nature supplies him with unfinished materials to refine for his own use and convenience. Man should acknowledge nature's beneficence, not be content merely to accept it, and should seek both physical and mental self-improvement. Human skills, when developed, lead to happiness, the purpose of all human industry. But the pleasures of the Stoic are not those of the Epicurean: only those pleasures and enjoyments acquired by labor and industry are permanent; all else is transitory. The man who seeks pleasure on a bed of roses soon discovers that this "pleasure" also creates indolence, disgust, and anxiety. Happiness must result from security, and the achievement of wisdom requires compassion. The reward of virtue is celestial and earthly glory.

The presentation of Stoic doctrine is relatively favorable, and the rhetoric is not fixed upon any ironic framework. Still, Stoicism is not free of excesses, some of which are similar to those of Epicureanism. Like that philosophical sect, Stoics make too much of the harmony of minds and of the effect that personal virtue may have on other individuals. Devoting themselves to the pursuit of virtue, they become more interested and more involved in the intricacies, rather than in the object, of that pursuit. Hume's strongest criticism seems, however, to be devoted to the implied denigration of human nature in Stoicism. Although exalting man for struggle and triumph, for vindicating the intelligence with which nature equipped him, Stoicism makes man too much a slave to nature. Thus, the consolations it offers must militate against precepts which are sometimes self-vitiating. Nor should the consolations of philosophy have a strictly utilitarian value, with all activity subordinated to the principle of self-improvement. In spite of its high goals and higher pretensions, Stoicism, as Hume paints it, can exert a pressure on man that turns his desire to improve himself into a necessity for self-glorification.

Hume mentions Plato only infrequently in his correspondence and literary works, and it comes as no surprise to find the Platonist decisively dismissed in his essay. The shortest of the four essays (barely a thousand words), "The Platonist" expresses no surprise that the vicissitudes of human nature should be so extreme. To him, the activities of human life are but a tiny portion of the divine; and the furious pursuit of popularity and sensual indulgence hardly equips the mind for its most solemn duty: the contemplation of the Supreme Being. The Epicurean's pursuit of pleasure leads finally and inevitably to a sense of guilt that is exacerbated by a worn-out body. The Stoic is little better: he, can hardly wait for the popular recognition of his own, highly-touted and self-regarding virtue. Because Stoics devote themselves to the products of men's minds, they forget the adoration due the Divinity. The most perfect products are those of the mind, and what is a more natural course for man, in the quest for true virtue and true wisdom, than to confine himself to the contemplation of the perfect? Of all examples of virtue pretended to by man, the most worthy is the Deity.

Each of these three essays—"The Epicurean," "The Stoic," and "The Platonist"—ends with some remark about the purpose of the Deity in human affairs. The Epicurean envisions a god, "if any governing mind preside," who would be satisfied to see his creatures achieving their purpose on earth—the pursuit and attainment of pleasure. For this end, and no other, the Epicurean holds, was man created; the knowledge that our pleasure would give our creator pleasure sustains us and frees us. In opposition to this view, the Stoic, who is more certain of the being of God, finds satisfaction in virtue on earth. The man of morals, having done his best on earth, is appropriately unconcerned with the promises extended in the concept of a life beyond death. He acknowledges the benevolence of the creator and is content with the one opportunity he has to add luster to the name of virtue. These mild endorsements of a Supreme Being are quickly overshadowed by the brief homily of the Platonist, whose discourse always informs his predecessors of the omnipotence and omniscience of God. Man's chief virtue is the contemplation of the perfection of God; and in a state beyond this life, he shall enlarge the dimensions of that contemplation. Man must not be misled by his own stupidity into thinking that pleasure lies elsewhere and that his task on earth, a task he can never complete, will become the occupation of an eternity.

The increasing insistence upon the role of a Supreme Being in each of these philosophical sects, as Hume represents them, does not culminate with a rationalistic apotheosis in the last of the four essays, "The Sceptic." The first three essays make important revelations about Hume's position on certain ethical problems, and Hume heightens their importance in the criticism that "The Sceptic" makes of these other doctrines. This essay is about as long as the other three combined and is certainly livelier than they are.

The Skeptic argues that philosophers pay too much attention to principles and too little to the variety of operations in nature; they are, therefore, most suspect when reasoning about the methods of attaining happiness. The Skeptic doubts that human nature and its urge towards happiness can be explained by any one set of general principles. More importantly, he raises questions about the functions and duties, if any, of a philosopher. One principle which philosophy teaches is that allegedly innate properties have no bearing on the value-terms assigned to things. The aesthetic or ethical implications in language lie not in the object but in the "sentiment of the mind which blames or praises." A diversity of sentiments among mankind precludes universal agreement on the constituents of beauty and worthiness; this diversity of sentiment should make us aware of nature's autonomy.

No analogies can be drawn between, for example, the "truths" of celestial mechanics and the approbation one gives a work of art. The Skeptic does not think that taste, colors, and the sensible qualities are necessarily found within one's body; rather they are part of the cultural inclination of the particular human being. The Skeptic does agree, however, that the "happiest disposition of the mind is the *virtuous*," which is defined as that "which leads to action and employment, renders us sensible to the social passions, steels the heart against the assaults of fortune, reduces the affections to a just moderation, makes our own thoughts an entertainment to us, and inclines us rather to the pleasures of society and conversation than to those of the senses" (*Works*, 3:221; *Essays*, 168). Men's actions are guided by constitution and temperament, not abstract generalizations. The Skeptic concludes

that virtue is always the best choice for man, but human life is so frag-
mented that no one should expect uninterrupted happiness, or misery.

If we can assume that the viewpoint of the Skeptic in some measure represents Hume's, then we have another of those careful attempts on his part
to tread a thin line between an "objectivist" view of ethics and of aesthetics
and a "subjectivist" view. He is emphatically anti-objectivist, but this opposition does not automatically consign him to the subjectivist camp. Instead,
Hume pushes the aesthetician and the ethicist strongly down the road to a
contextual consideration of an individual's response to an act or event.

The worth of an object derives not from any qualities it may be presumed
to contain within itself, but from the passion (roughly, desire) with which
we pursue it. This passion, when pronouncing judgment, does not render its
verdict simply from a consideration of the object itself but from all of the
circumstances and accidents which attend it. A passion is not a unique response creating a standard by which an object is judged; it is, instead, a con-
catenation of natural proclivities and custom. Thus, the philosophy of the
Skeptic offers no remedy for those who are born with, or into, the kind of
disposition that scorns and abominates mankind. Yet who would say that
any other philosophy can rehabilitate those who are ill-disposed towards the
rest of humankind? The mind can perhaps be reformed by habit, but the
conviction that the virtuous life is best is likely to impress only the man already virtuous.

Of this essay, John Laird, one of the better commentators on Hume, has
said that it "proceeded to be rather more sceptical than Hume generally permitted himself to be on ethical subjects," while more recently Robert J.
Fogelin has claimed that the essay "represents Hume's position in everything but tone and minor detail."[10] Hume probably was more skeptical in
this essay about everything than in any of his other writings. The opening
words of the concluding paragraph are sometimes cited as an instance of
philosophical despair: "In a word, human life is more governed by fortune
than by reason; is to be regarded more as a dull pastime than as a serious occupation; and is more influenced by particular humour, than by general
principles" (Works, 3:231; Essays, 180). We ask two questions of life and
find neither answer satisfactory. If we involve ourselves in it with passion
and anxiety, we find that we give it too much concern; if we resign ourselves
to indifference, we miss the pleasure of the game. We waste our lives reasoning about life only to discover that life is gone and that death treats the
philosopher and the fool alike. Yet the role of the philosopher, Hume concludes, offers us one of the most diverting and amusing occupations which
life offers, and Hume's metaphor of the "game" was not idly chosen.

The somberness of this essay is not always found in the other "moral" essays. Some exhibit a light touch and reflect the amusement that the philosopher finds in whatever diversion life offers. Hume was attempting in these essays to be both Addison and Bishop Butler, to entertain and to instruct his readers, preferably at the same time. In essays like "The Sceptic," he suggested totally different ways in which one could regard the explanations offered for the aesthetic or ethical value in some object. In some, he artlessly defended practices common to the European frame of mind. In others, he simply demolished assumptions about history or human nature that were part of the accepted opinion of his day.

Politics: Whig Principles and Tory Prejudices

Hume's political thought can be something of a trial for the average reader since his ideas cannot be conveniently fitted into any prescribed or proscribed political ideology. In addition, the reader has to contend with an eighteenth-century vocabulary that does not always convey a concept amenable to modern standards of classification.[11] Much of Hume's political practicality derives from his moral persuasions, and he is prone to refer to social virtues as "artificial" and as distinct from "natural" virtues—the uniquely personal ones. The *Enquiry concerning the Principles of Morals* devotes some sections to considerations of moral acts involved in the social and political spheres, and almost all of the 1741–42 essays with political titles are permeated with moral judgments.

While an essay like "The Sceptic" gives the impression of a person unwilling to make judgments about the habits and peculiarities of others, we find that Hume elsewhere has no qualms about depicting the French government of Henry III as one filled with "oppression, levity, artifice on the part of the rulers; faction, sedition, treachery, rebellion, disloyalty on the part of the subjects" (*Works,* 3:98; *Essays* 15). In the same essay, "That Politics may be Reduced to a Science" (1741), Hume asserts that a republican and free government whose checks and controls had little effect, and which also "made it not the interest, *even of bad men,* to act for the public good," would be absurd (*Works,* 3:99; *Essays,* 16 [my italics]). Apparently, man must worry about the public good and upgrade it before he can turn his attention to the improvement of individual morality.

To neglect the principles of decency and morality is a common failing, as Hume observes in "Of the First Principles of Government" (1741): "When men act in a faction, they are apt, without shame or remorse, to neglect all the ties of honour and morality, in order to serve their party" (*Works,* 3:110;

Essays, 33). These same men, however, should they form their faction on a principle of right or morality, could be unswervingly stubborn in their devotion to justice or equity. Still, the reader cannot evade Hume's implication that justice and equity derive, not from noble motives, but from a convenient rallying-point. The state will thus have a function in the formation of public morality. Virtue and a strong sense of morality, the foremost requirements for happiness, are formed neither by the hard-shelled admonitions of religion nor by the most subtle and refined principles of philosophy; virtue and general morality in a state "must proceed entirely from the virtuous education of youth, the effect of wise laws and institutions" (*Works*, 3:127; *Essays*, 55). Peace and security in life derive from good government, not from an abundance of material possessions and comforts. The benefits of good government and the morality of man are interdependent.

If this insistence upon a moral basis for governments seems to suggest that Hume accepted the idea of a "social contract," which he called the "original contract," then I must point out that Hume tentatively embraced the idea in the *Treatise* and quickly abandoned it. In the *Treatise*, he asserts that "government, *upon its first establishment*, wou'd naturally be suppos'd to derive its obligations from those laws of nature, and, in particular, from that concerning the performances of promises." Yet he accepts only a part of the social contract theory by maintaining "that tho' the duty of allegiance be at first grafted on the obligation of promises, and be for some time supported by that obligation" (*Treatise*, 3:ii, 8; 593), it later becomes independent of all contracts. A government formed upon this basis derives from the intrusion of change, such as the acquisition of wealth or power, among a body of people, requiring that some sort of human promises be made to supplement natural law.

Hume's concept of the usefulness and value of the "original contract" had itself changed when the essay "Of the Original Contract" (1748) appeared in *Three Essays, Moral and Political*, then in the third edition of *Essays, Moral and Political*. In this latter edition Hume roughly describes a theory attributing the origin of government to an original contract. He affirms that one cannot deny that government was formed by an original contract if this meant that men, living in the woods or deserts, voluntarily gave up their native liberty to accept certain conventions whose obviousness precluded any necessity of placing them in a formal document. Any original contract proceeded from the native equality, or something close to it, of men; or they would not have otherwise willingly abandoned their will to the authority of an established government.[12]

In a paragraph which Hume added to the posthumous edition of these essays, he argues that even this sketchy consent was imperfect and could not have been effective in establishing a regular administration. The exercises of authority required by such primitive forms of government, in which a tribe might be ruled by a chief of some kind, were unique; they had no established or preordained rules but were guided by the exigencies of each emergency. And, of course, the more this chief exercised his authority, the more accustomed people became to submitting to it. Thus, he acquired some control over them and established the custom of submission to authority.

Hume apparently had more trouble with this political concept—the origin of government—than with any other.[13] He quickly disposed of the idea that government arose from the will of a Deity by pointing out the pettiness into which the concept of rule by divine right extended. The formation of government had to be accounted for somehow since it was a human and not a divine institution. Hume could never free himself from the idea that some kind of agreement or inclination among people created the rudiments of government. As a political theorist, however, he seems to have concluded that conceptualization of the "origin of government" was not possible.

The only essay added to the posthumous 1777 edition was titled "Of the Origin of Government" and dealt with the same problem. In it, Hume alleges that the origin of a government was slow and erratic; it did not spring into being by the immediate, spontaneous agreement of men, even if they may have articulated some sort of temporary original agreement. For one thing (and Hume's moral sense injects itself into the argument here), "such is the frailty or perverseness of our nature! [*sic*] it is impossible to keep men, faithfully and unerringly, in the paths of justice" (*Works,* 3:114; *Essays,* 38). The incurable weakness of human nature leads man into antisocial action. Even if the original cause of government had been some kind of contract, it would never have long subsisted because one person, or many, would be tempted to break the agreement for some private advantage. To circumvent large-scale antisocial action, man must establish the concept of obedience in order to support justice.

Accounting for the origin of government, Hume discovers that it must arise from the interplay of political forces, from the consolidation of habit, and from the human inclination to order and power. Men ruled by the love of power can be instrumental in shaping a government. The force of their personalities and devotion to "their" state impose a kind of order upon other men by subordinating the wills of others to that of one leader. This interplay of political forces involves authority and liberty in perpetual opposition, although neither one can prevail for long, if a government is to be established and to survive.

Indeed, neither liberty nor authority can or should gain dominance. Liberty represents the perfection of a civil society, but paradoxically, authority is necessary for it to exist, to insure that the partitions of power are justly administered. Justice itself, among other desiderata associated with liberty, may be suspended should some alien force threaten the welfare of a government which has emerged from various political forces that shaped it into something stable and reliable.

When discussing the various ways in which liberty takes shape in the world, Hume points out (in this same essay) that a sultan, while the master of life and fortune of any of his subjects, could not increase their taxes, any more than the French monarch, who can impose new taxes at will, could regulate and decide the lives of the sultan's subjects. The various ways in which liberty was regarded throughout the world was a topic of perennial interest to Hume, and one of the essays of 1741 bore the title "Of the Liberty of the Press." In it, Hume remarks that nothing would more astonish the foreign visitor to England than the liberty of the press and the journalistic censure attendant upon every decision made by the crown or by Parliament. To Hume's mind, the mixed form of government, one neither totally monarchical nor entirely republican, accounts for this liberty more than any fact.[14] So long as the republican part of England's government can prevent it from being overwhelmed by the monarchical part, the liberty of the press will be allowed to continue, for liberty of the press is one of the strongest props of republicanism.

Hume's attitude toward what he called a "mixed form of government" was one of his most enlightened but one also misunderstood by those in his century who wanted him classified as either Tory or Whig, so that they could pelt him with ready–made refutations. Hume found the mixed government of Britain to be predominantly republican although held in check by a strong monarchical tradition.[15] Although he altered his opinion in later life, in 1741 he saw the power of the crown increasing after a long period when popular government was ideologically and politically powerful. The wealth of the monarchy, however, militated against the continued preeminence of republicanism.

In answering the question of his essay "Whether the British Government inclines more to Absolute Monarchy, or to a Republic," Hume prefers, in abstract, a monarchy to a republic in Great Britain. If the present form of mixed government is to come to an end—and Hume hopes that it will continue, even while recognizing that all governments have some terminus—he also hoped it would come in the form of absolute monarchy, "the true *Euthanasia* of the BRITISH constitution" (*Works*, 3:126; *Essays*, 53). Why?

The dangers of popular government are far more terrible. The kind of republic Britons might get upon the dissolution of the present form is not the "fine imaginary republic, of which a man may form a plan in his closet," and indeed which Hume outlined in "Idea of a Perfect Commonwealth" (1752), but one unlikely to have any respect for justice and liberty. Hume suggests that it is better to let a new government form itself by whatever forces shape it under an absolute monarch than to permit a totally republican form to degenerate into anarchy. For this reason, Hume is frequently lined up with the Tories, who, if truth be said, would at the very least have suspected the motives of a man who denied their divine–right theory as an account of the formation of monarchical government.

Toward the end of his life, however, in 1775, Hume had come to think that republicanism was sometimes the best form of government. In a letter to his nephew, also named David Hume, he judged that modern practices had corrected all the traditional, historical abuses associated with monarchies. He confessed his preference: "[Republicanism] is only fitted for a small State: And any Attempt towards it can in our [Country], produce only Anarchy, which is the immediate Forerunner of Despotism" (*HL,* 2:306 [words in brackets are conjectures by Greig]). Another immediate forerunner of despotism is revolution since it overthrows established governments and seeks to start anew. Hume is almost always on the side of an established government, assuming it is not tyrannical, and he prefers to keep it rather than substitute one uncertainty for a greater one. Hume also admired the revolution in the American colonies, thought it justified, and confessed, also in 1775, to Baron Mure of Caldwell, that "I am an American in my Principles" (*HL,* 2:303).

What is the reader to make of these seeming inconsistencies and others like them which compose Hume's political essays? The suggestion I can offer is only speculative, but such a solution seems preferable to an accusation of inconsistency and political illiteracy against Hume. Basically, Hume was a political theorist and not a politician. Custom and his frame of mind led Hume into a skeptical analysis of conventional political wisdom; instead of continuing the principles beyond the a priori precepts of certain political ideologies, Hume tried to substitute an empirical methodology in both politics and economics. The essay "Of the Populousness of Antient Nations" is an excellent example of an attempt to fuse historical inquiry, skeptical doubts, and empirical conclusions.

As a philosopher, Hume found himself more at home with the theoretical constructs of political science than with the popular sentiments that oversimplified the complications of a continually emerging government.

The "Idea of a Perfect Commonwealth" leaves no doubt that Hume was basically libertarian and that his personal preference was for a government that insured a high degree of individual liberty. Yet personal preferences, regardless of their propinquity, were expendable if the exigencies of government demanded it. Hume's function was to raise doubts, to propose alternatives, and to say the unpopular when necessary. The tasks of mollifying the populace and administering the nation's polity belong to others.

Economics: Historical Perspective and the Passions

The extent and the effectiveness of Hume's economic thought are not necessarily indicated by the quantity of his writings on economics. He wrote only nine essays that, strictly speaking, could be called economic essays: "Of Commerce," "Of Luxury," "Of Money," "Of Interest," "Of the Balance of Trade," "Of the Balance of Power," "Of Taxes," "Of Public Credit," and "Of the Jealousy of Trade." All were published in 1752 in his *Political Discourses,* except the last, which was published in 1758. Hume's discussion of economics is neither systematic nor thorough; nevertheless, his ideas on economics have been thought to be among the most valuable written in the eighteenth (or any) century and superior to anything before Adam Smith.[16]

Since Hume was a contemporary of and adviser to Adam Smith, almost any discussion of Hume's economic thought is immediately compared to Smith's. Basically, Hume and Smith are in sympathy so far as the methodology of economic inquiry is concerned, although Smith's inquiries are much more developed. Smith is less concerned than Hume with the psychology of human beings involved in economic transactions, and Smith often assumes the "universal psychology" attributed to every man, regardless of race, creed, or color. In contrast, Hume considers variations in men's behavior, and his economic ideas belong most properly in the pattern of his other thoughts.

Hume is a transitional figure in the movement from mercantilist economic theory to classical economic theory, and he cannot be said to belong to either school. He was one of the first writers to demonstrate the interrelations of economic theory and economic practice and their further relation with social and political events. For Hume, economics is the science of explaining the way in which money, trade, taxes, public credit and commerce are produced by the changes in human wants, which are, in turn, affected by environment.[17]

"Of Commerce," generally regarded as Hume's most important economic essay, contains the outlines of his economic psychology, or the relationship between the state and the individual. He asserts what is commonly allowed, that "The greatness of a state, and the happiness of its subjects, how independent soever they may be supposed in some respects, are commonly allowed to be inseparable with regard to commerce; and as private men receive greater security, in the possession of their trade and riches, from the power of the public, so the public becomes powerful in proportion to the opulence and extensive commerce of private men" (*Works*, 3:288–89; *Essays*, 255).

Hume admits that some exceptions may be admitted to this rule because of the variations in behavior patterns. Historically speaking, Hume continues, the state is greatest when its "superfluities" are used to increase public welfare; but, I hasten to add, Hume does not have in mind a "welfare state." Instead, he is following the psychological ideas suggested in his other works, that economic matters develop less from arbitrary laws of cause and effect, but develop instead from attitudes, customs, experiences, and habits. In keeping with his view in the *Treatise* that the passions are more often the "springs" of behavior than reason, Hume makes the passions the starting point of his economic theory. This procedure removed the economics from the politics of mercantilism and centered it in the "science of human nature."

For Hume, labor is the ultimate source of wealth, and passions are the ultimate source of labor. Passions, therefore, are the ultimate source for the wealth and production of the world. Passions, however, do not necessarily govern the way in which wealth is used. For example, poverty can occur when the means for attaining economic advantages are so simple and expedient that men are led into indolence, as they are in the Mediterranean countries. When economic advantages are not easily attained, men must have some potential profit before embarking on the dangers concomitant with production: "Men must have profits proportionable to their experience and hazard" (*Works*, 3:298; *Essays*, 267). Throughout his essays, of course, Hume puts the psychology of economics in historical and geographical perspective; transactions involving capital or labor are obviously affected by the culture in which they occur.

Commerce, which arises from the pleasure of profits and the luxury they can bring, is not estimable exclusively in monetary terms: "Money is not, properly speaking, one of the subjects of commerce" (*Works*, 3:309; *Essays*, 282). While Hume's monetary theory is in places ambiguous,[18] it is, as the preceding sentence would suggest, dominantly classical. Hume is also the originator of the quantity theory of money.[19] That is, Hume argues that the supply of money is unimportant since the prices of goods will always be proportionable to the actual quantity of money. Money, like a priori ideas, has no intrinsic value. The public may receive advantage from a greater supply of money, but it does so only during wars and in trade with other countries. Money itself does not increase trade. Those countries accumulating the greatest wealth usually have the greatest expense.

Their accumulation of money or wealth, therefore, gives them no special advantage in commerce because the greater expenses of producing that wealth make it possible for other countries to undersell them. The domestic happiness of the state is not increased by the quantity of its money. If the policy of the state works to increase the quantity of money, the result is desirable: it "keeps alive a spirit of industry in the nation, and encreases the stock of labour, in which consists all real power and riches" (*Works*, 3:315; *Essays*, 288). As he had done in his earlier writings, Hume insists on the subtle distinctions necessary in economics between causes and effects: money is not a cause of plenty and happiness, but it can be an effect of labor and industry.

"Of Public Credit" is likely to be of more interest to the casual reader than most of Hume's other economic essays because Hume is specifically interested in the problems arising from and associated with the public, or national, debt. Hume's ironic opposition to the accumulation of public debt to be paid off by other generations would give aid and comfort to modern conservatives opposed to "deficit financing": "it seems pretty apparent, that the ancient maxims [saving great sums against any public exigency] are, in this respect, more prudent than the modern; even though the latter had been confined within some reasonable bounds, and had ever, in any instance, been attended with such frugality, in time of peace, as to discharge the debts incurred by an expensive war" (*Works*, 3:361; *Essays*, 350–1).

Hume, like many of his latter–day counterparts, thinks that ministers of state and politicians are unlikely to exercise restraint in borrowing, a position pretty well borne out by historical evidence. Incorporating sociological analysis and historical perspective, he suggests that the increase of the public debt will, as a matter of course, lead to bankruptcy and to political deterioration. Hume ascribes the inclination towards a mounting public debt to the "natural progress of things"; from a knowledge of the natures of men and politicians, Hume suggests two possible consequences of an increasing debt. One would produce what he calls the "*natural death*" of public credit, as a result of governmental overextension; another consequence would be the "*violent death*" of public credit as a result of an inability or reluctance to accept voluntary bankruptcy and the subsequent submission of the state to a conqueror.

The relations of a state to its neighbors form the subject of two essays containing some of Hume's most original thought. "Of the Balance of

Trade" is an exposition of the inadequacy of mercantilist attempts to increase the internal quantity of money or commodities by imposing artificial limits on international trade.[20] Hume argues that the amount of currency or cash in a country tends towards an equilibrium as a result of a balance between its exports and imports. Free trade prevents the escalation of prices out of proportion to the prices asked in other countries. In a series of rhetorical questions, Hume doubts the ability of a country to maintain a disproportion between its supply of money and its labor and commodities. He specifically questions the ability of a state to lose its labor and industry and yet retain its gold and silver; it need never fear losing its currency so long as its industry and labor are maintained.

Six years later, in "Of the Jealousy of Trade," Hume was to reject the protectionist theory of international trade agreements, although he had conceded the necessity of tariffs in the earlier essay. No nation was likely to have its domestic industry damaged by the prosperity of neighbors, but Hume said he wished to go farther and to observe "that where an open communication is preserved among nations, it is impossible but the domestic industry of every one must receive an increase from the improvement of the others" (*Works*, 3:345; *Essays*, 328). Although the reader finds some evidence for Hume's doubts about the effectiveness of this principle, he can never doubt the moral outlook of Hume's economics, which found unlikely the proposition that a nation's wealth, commodities, and industry would be increased by its conquest of neighboring states.

Hume's economic views are not easy to summarize, but their relevance to the economic problems facing many countries today is often breathtaking. Perhaps his most important contribution to economic thought was his insistence that man ought to reason as subtly and as abstrusely on economics as he did on other branches of "moral science." That was the contention of the opening paragraphs in "Of Commerce," and Hume followed his own suggestion conscientiously. He never ignored the role of custom and habit in shaping economic changes; in fact, custom and habit were the source of all economic change. History and psychology were the means by which Hume attempted economic analyses, and he focused attention upon both the myths of economics, as well as upon the general principles to be derived from the study of domestic and international transactions. His inquiry into economics relied upon the same tools he used to inquire into human understanding and into the principles of morals.

Chapter Four

Courage and Perseverance: The Two *Enquiries*

Human Understanding: The New and The Old

In chapter 1, we noticed the advertisement in which Hume repudiated the philosophy of the *Treatise* and desired his readers to regard only his later writings as representative of his thought. Today, of course, few people pay any attention to Hume's request and regard the *Treatise* as his major philosophical work, although nineteenth–century commentators tended to take Hume at his word and, with some notable exceptions, ignored the *Treatise*. The nineteenth–century editor of the standard Oxford editions of the two *Enquiries* and the *Treatise*, L.A. Selby–Bigge, is in many ways responsible for focusing attention on both works.[1] An earlier nineteenth–century edition (1874–75) of Hume's philosophical works, by T.H. Green and T.H. Grose, devotes two volumes to the *Treatise* and two volumes to the bulk of Hume's other works (excluding the *History of England*). Almost one–third of the two volumes of this edition of the *Treatise* is devoted to the elaborate commentary by Professor Green, and we could hardly assert that the *Treatise* has been neglected at Hume's request.

Many commentators, however, persist in accepting the *Enquiry concerning Human Understanding* as a revision of the *Treatise,* an activity which Selby–Bigge's comparative tables have encouraged. No one will deny that corollaries between the two exist, nor would anyone assert that a consideration of Hume's first *Enquiry* distinct from the *Treatise* amounts to a new discovery. Yet it is important to regard the work not so much as a recasting of the ideas of the *Treatise,* complete with appendices and reformulations, but as an independent contribution to the history of thought. Hume intended it to be considered that way and intended the same for the second *Enquiry.* A comparison of the *Treatise* with the two *Enquiries* will obviously yield interesting results, but respecting Hume's wishes and considering the *Enquiries* as independent works has much to recommend it.[2]

In the opening section of the first *Enquiry,* Hume proposes that the science of human nature may be approached in two ways. The first way is to regard man as a creature of action, not contemplation; philosophers who consider man as an active creature responding to active stimuli try, therefore, to represent the concept of virtue with all the eloquence and persuasiveness they can command. The other approach regards man as a reasonable rather than an active creature. The philosopher utilizing this approach wishes to set the limits by which man's nature can be scrutinized and regulated. Seeking to excite his curiosity about the fundamental principles of nature, he avoids the pose of certainty and avoids imposing standards of manners upon men. Of these two forms, the first is more likely to be popular with mankind because it makes few demands upon interaction with the problems and paradoxes of human life. And indeed, this "easy philosophy" enjoys a greater fame than "abstract philosophy." In spite of the facile dichotomy and the many thinkers who repair to it, nature has enjoined man to a mixed life, one of contemplation and action; to go too far to one extreme is to invite dissolution or melancholia: "Be a philosopher, but, amidst all your philosophy, be still a man" (*Works,* 4:6; *ECHU,* 13).[3]

Hume is raising not only a legitimate question for his inquiry, but a necessary question: the way in which the discipline of philosophy and metaphysics can instill accuracy in the ordinary business of human life. Metaphysics encourages objections and invites contempt from the generality of mankind, as indeed bad metaphysics should. The function of the philosopher is not to encourage the isolation of his discipline, but, as Addison suggested in *Spectator* 10 (12 March 1711), to bring "Philosophy out of Closets and Libraries, Schools and Colleges, to dwell in Clubs and Assemblies, at Tea-Tables and in Coffee-Houses."[4] The mind must learn to reject certain philosophies as inherently misleading and to cultivate a skepticism proper to the vicissitudes of daily life, while avoiding that skepticism that totally subverts reflection or action. A proper skepticism is not fooled by the rhetoric of certainty any more than it is debilitated by the specter of total chaos. In opposition to the penchant of traditional philosophers, or even some modern philosophers, who hope, like Newton, to find some general principles of human nature by which all actions can be predicted or explained, Hume suggests that such an undertaking does not lie within the province of human understanding. Events in the mind are more linked to one another than to some general emanation from nature or the universe. The philosopher can apply his energies most properly to the elucidation of whatever phenomena best contribute to the human understanding of human nature.

The second section, "Of the Origin of Ideas," restates with some alterations the propositions of the opening pages of the *Treatise*. We need not repeat the distinctions Hume makes except where the *Treatise* is amplified, slighted, or corrected. He had, for example, insisted in the *Treatise* on the term "image" to define ideas; the same word is implied in the first *Enquiry*. As Professor Flew has pointed out, this inclination to think of ideas as images oversimplifies the idea-forming activity of the mind. To justify his division between impressions and ideas, Hume makes experience his arbiter: if we trace an idea back to its origins, we always find that it derives from some initial, livelier impression. If a man is deprived from birth of one of his senses, such as the sense of sight, he can have no idea of what color means.[5]

The main purpose of this short chapter comes in the last paragraph, where Hume uses this admittedly imperfect distinction between ideas and impressions as ammunition for an attack upon the splenetic metaphysics of what the eighteenth century called "schoolmen." If we are confronted with a philosophical term which seems to have no meaning, a far too frequent occurrence for Hume, we should simply inquire from what impression that idea arose. Although Hume does not openly exhibit Locke's interest in the proper use of words (book 3 of Locke's *Essay* is entitled "Of Words"), his intentions are similar: to fix the philosophical function of language within certain definable rhetorical and logical limits.

Perhaps the most noticeable difference between the *Enquiry concerning Human Understanding* and the *Treatise* lies in the diminished form of the observations made about the association of ideas. The third section, "Of the Association of Ideas," consisted of three paragraphs in the 1777 edition of the *Essays* and *Treatise,* although it was about six times as long in editions Hume published during his lifetime. Hume notes that no philosopher has attempted to define the various classes of association, and he suggests three: resemblance, contiguity in time or place, and cause or effect. Instead of expanding upon these possible classifications, Hume prefers to speculate about the effects the connection of ideas would have on our passions or our imaginations. That speculation constitutes the omitted portion of the 1777 edition. What reason he may have had for omitting this speculation from his final edition can only be conjectured. In writing the *Abstract,* he thought the way in which the "author" of the *Treatise of Human Nature* made his most impressive contribution was in his use of the principle of the association of ideas. In the first *Enquiry,* this suggestion was considerably modified, and Hume finally decided that the simple fact that the principle existed was as much as he cared to mention. Many modern editions of the first *Enquiry* omit these paragraphs, which contain some of Hume's more interesting applications of the principle of the association of ideas to literary theory and works of art.

Hume asserts that the association of ideas here cannot be the loose or casual ones of ordinary experience, but must command some kind of unity. The most unusual connecting principle is that of cause and effect, particularly when a historian tries to draw conclusions about the behavior of peoples and societies. Comparing the writing of history to the writing of poetry illuminates our understanding of the way in which cause and effect, as organizing principles of the poet, can call forth strong emotions in us. The mind, presented with a reorganized unity, is powerfully affected by the actual imputation the poem makes of cause and effect. The responses created by these perceptions and reflections increase our enjoyment of the work of art by heightening our sensitivity to the rhetorical exigencies of art confronted with life. Hume leaves the fruitful topic reluctantly, and the reader of the first *Enquiry* certainly wishes for some additional exploration of this promising approach to literary criticism.

The first three sections, however insidiously provocative they may be, are nothing but a prologue for the heart of the book, sections 4 through 7.[6] In these four sections we find Hume's skepticism asserting itself both rhetorically and formally. Experience, which is Hume's methodological criterion, leads an inquirer into two modes of understanding which Hume represents as *"Relations of Ideas"* and *"Matters of Fact."* The first group consists of propositions which are intuitively or analytically certain; they are rhetorically tautological. The second group consists of propositions which are not certain, only possible; they are formally verifiable. Into this second class of propositions enter the skeptical doubts about the operations of the understanding. Any proposition, Hume affirms, the contrary of which is intelligible or subject to verification, can never achieve certainty, only a high rate of expectability.

The division of propositions is one of Hume's more important contributions to philosophy as well as to the development of theories of literature based upon subjective reevaluation of experiences. This dichotomy, sometimes called *Hume's Fork,*[7] is a step or two, perhaps several, away from the unsatisfactory psychology of the first three sections and of the psychological explanations of the understanding found in the *Treatise.* What Hume calls *Relations of Ideas* are propositions whose truth–value can be ascertained a priori; their validity cannot be denied without involving self-contradiction. For example, one could not assert that $2+2=5$ without contradicting the a priori axioms of arithmetic. Hume's statement about the first class of propositions is itself an a priori assertion; no experience can prove to us beyond all possibility of uncertainty that relations of ideas are self–verifying. We accept these propositions as intuitively true or as analytically certain because they are not matters of fact but of logic and rhetorical convention. To define "network" as Dr. Johnson did—"Any thing reticulated or decussated at equal distances, with interstices between the intersections"—is to articulate a tautology. In some instances the tautology can be illuminating if it contains words whose implications we comprehend.

The problems involved in analytic propositions (what Hume calls *Relations of Ideas*) are considerably beyond the scope of this discussion, but it should be clear that Hume's major interest was not in analytic but in synthetic propositions, ones which make an empirical assertion. The truth–value of synthetic propositions can be ascertained only a posteriori; that is, synthetic propositions must be subjected to a kind of verification they do not inherently contain. To add to the complexity of "Hume's Fork," modern philosophers have pointed out that Hume's assertions about his second class of propositions are themselves a priori propositions. When Hume states "The contrary of every matter of fact is still possible; because it can never imply a contradiction, and is conceived by the mind with the same facility and distinctness, as if ever so comfortable to reality" (*Works*, 4:23; *ECHU*, 25), he argues a priori. That proposition itself cannot be verified by an appeal to the class of propositions it defines. From this position, Hume goes on to argue that man experiences the events of everyday life not as a manifold unity but as distinct entities. This contention is the source of one of the easy objections made to Hume's philosophy; namely, that it is atomistic and must inevitably involve itself in one of Zeno's paradoxes.

Hume has prepared the reader, however, for one of his important insights, the proper and improper use of the evidence of experience in determining matters of fact. He asks "*What is the foundation of all conclusions from experience?*" (*Works*, 4:28; *ECHU*, 32). The immediate answer is that our experience of causes and effects and our conclusions drawn from experience do not emanate from reason or from any activity of the understanding. When we experience a certain contiguity of events, we assume, extralogically, that at any given time those events will exhibit a similar "causal" relationship. We experience the rising of the sun every day, and from the series of experiences we have of the rising of the sun, we act on the assumption that the sun will rise in the following days. Custom instills in us certain expectations about the natural process of events, and those expectations are usually justified.

These expectations are not deductively justifiable, only inductively. Regardless of the extensiveness of our experience, we cannot project an infinite series of cause and effect; we can appeal to no authority except custom to "prove" that the sun will rise tomorrow. We have experience of event X in a thousand circumstances; we "know" that X will always occur in those circumstances. This inference is the product of experience, but it defies all the processes of syllogistic logic. Any conceivable and hitherto unexperienced event can inject itself into familiar circumstances and cast to the four winds all our assurance and certainty. We can never, therefore, assert the logical irreversibility of any two connected events. Certainty is unobtainable in postulating that event X, which has occurred precisely at noon every day since recorded history, will occur tomorrow or the day after. Any number of unlikely, but possible, events can reverse that expectation.

The appeal to custom is the argument of section 5, "Sceptical Solution of these Doubts." Our experience, Hume states, would never be of any use to us, as it plainly is, if we did not function according to custom and expectancy, avoiding the harsher dictates of logic and reason. The constant conjunction of two events imposes its own autonomy upon our psyche, and we convert matters of fact, of past experience, into some workable calculus of probability. In daily life, Hume hardly doubted that his customary expectations would not be vindicated in the separate experiences of forthcoming days. Like other ordinary human beings, he formed certain patterns of belief, fashioned from the expectations of experience. Sufficient to contain the process of routine events, the evidence of experience was a reliable guide in discussing past matters of fact. But experience, Hume thinks, should also teach us that the unexpected is never far from our daily lives and that custom can actually prevent us from inquiring into matters taken for granted. The evidence of past experience is projected, on faith, into the future, but it should never be trusted to comprehend the unexpected, the unexpectable: man is a creature of limited and finite experience.

Human Understanding: Causes and Chaos

Before Hume turns to his discussion of the idea of necessary connection, he devotes the three short pages of section 6 to "Of Probability." The discussion of probability constituted three sections in the *Treatise,* and the new presentation is mute recognition of the difficulty of mixing psychology with philosophy. Chance, Hume maintains, does not exist in the world since every future event has some probability. We cannot reconstruct the various causes of different events, but we do form certain beliefs about natural processes. Some causes always produce similar effects, at least upon human beings: fire always burns and water always suffocates any human being. But the relative certainty that may arise from this similarity of causes and effects may not appear in other examples. When two similar causes produce different results, we are forced to reconsider our imposition of past certainty upon future likelihood. Again Hume emphasizes the subjective quality of these experiences and implicitly suggests that man has little effect upon the force of events. His language also associates the mental process with other natural phenomena: "This concurrence of several views in one particular event begets immediately, by an inexplicable contrivance of nature, the sentiment of belief" (*Works*, 4:48; *ECHU*, 57); Hume uses the metaphor "begets" three other times in this section to explain the operation of probability, and the likening of probability theory to procreation, perhaps, betrays Hume's impulses towards naturalism. He explicitly challenges others to account sufficiently for the impact of mental uncertainty upon any system of philosophy when they attempt to deny the validity of his assertions. Received theories of man, or of human experiences, are all defective in treating such difficult subjects. Hume was unwilling to relinquish totally his insight, whatever its defects, about the subjectivity of any theories of probability.

In discussing the idea of necessary connection (section 7), Hume elaborates upon an argument made in the first part of section 4; and in the last section of the *Enquiry*, he summarizes this argument: "If we reason *a priori*, any thing may appear able to produce any thing. . . . It is only experience, which teaches us the nature and bounds of cause and effect, and enables us to infer the existence of one object from that of another" (*Works*, 4:134–35; *ECHU*, 164).[8] Hume is concerned with both the logical and the psychological problems involved in reasoning from a set of propositions to a conclusion; and he sees the inexactitude of language as the chief obstacle to any inquiry about the limits of knowing. Nothing in "moral" communication enjoys the precision that one finds in mathematics, mainly because mathematics represents one kind of knowing and morality another kind.

The first part of section 7 considers the influence, if any, that volition has on the various components or organs of the body; but the immediate cause of that effect is not easily known. Few principles in nature are more mysterious than this alleged influence of some "spiritual substance" on the "material substance" of our bodies. Applying the epistemology of public impressions and private ideas to this anomaly, Hume questions our ability to know precisely the activity of the will upon the body. This conjecture leads to his second argument about the degrees of authority our will has over the various organs of our body.

Why, for example, should the fingers be immediately responsive to the will, but not the liver or heart? The extensiveness or power of our will can be known from experience only; no a priori assumption explains the workings of all the organs of the body, yet even the effect of our will upon such obviously responsive organs as the fingers is not so simple as it seems. For the volition does not act immediately upon the organ concerned, but upon muscles and nerves. A series of unknown events finally produces the intended result, and we do not know the means by which it was achieved. These difficulties with the idea of volition, Hume discovers, by no means lead us to an awareness of a power within ourselves to comprehend what we call acts of will. Hume raises the same objections against the assertion that ideas in the mind are subject to the same power or influence of the will, and also against the idea of attributing to the Deity the effects stemming from an act of the will.

Having argued that a priori knowledge of one event's causing,, or not causing, another event is impossible, Hume now trains his attention on the instances of "necessary connection." His approach, in summary, is that events seem to occur uniquely, that one event follows another, but that we can never observe or experience any link between them: "They seem *conjoined,* but never *connected*" (*Works,* 4:61; *ECHU,* 74). It would seem, then, that, since we have no experience of this "necessary connection," we are impelled to the conclusion that we can have no idea of necessary connection and that such words are without philosophical or even commonplace meaning.

That is not, however, Hume's position, for he thinks that there is one approach which will avoid this seemingly inescapable conclusion. The idea of "necessary connection" arises from the continued similarity and constant conjunction of certain events. This constant repetition enforces on us an expectation of recurrence and a belief that X, having always preceded and produced Y, will do so again: "This connexion, therefore, which we *feel* in the mind, this customary transition of the imagination from one object to its usual attendant, is the sentiment or impression, from which we form the idea of power or necessary connexion" (*Works,* 4:62, *ECHU,* 75). Nothing in the original events themselves can contain the concept of "necessary connection." It must arise from the subjective reconsideration by a human mind, acting within ascertainable limits, of events whose connection is suggested, but not necessitated by contiguity.

In discussing the idea of "necessary connection," Hume has again, I think, tried to walk along that line between "objectivity" and "subjectivity," to accept for a minute the vague implications of those words. In fact, he has tried to avoid making such a distinction since such bifurcation of one's experience is both simple and simpleminded. Explicitly, Hume has now questioned the utility of such concepts; implicitly, he has illustrated the confusion in which they involve even the most careful thinker. The activity of the mind in perceiving phenomenal events is itself not an isolatable event. Who can imagine a mind that did not perceive events with which it was existentially confronted? The mind cannot refuse to perceive these events; at the least, it must receive them. Hume attempted to construct a methodology that would consider the mind both as process and participant in phenomenal events. In the act of perceiving, the mind is aware that it is perceiving and is inextricably involved with the events it observes. The process of events in the "external world" and of events in the "mind" are, Hume implies, incapable of being totally separated; and one must take into account this condition when reasoning about human nature.

The two sections following Hume's analysis of the idea of necessary connection are entitled "Of Liberty and Necessity" (section 8) and "Of the Reason of Animals" (section 9). Controversy over the freedom of the will was for long a perennial staple of philosophy, and an examination of the problem of reason in animals usually emphasizes the limitations of any analogy drawn between animals and men.[9] Hume's argument in section 8—that disputes over liberty and necessity are more verbal than real—is cogent; however the real interest of the section lies in his tacit preparation for the dissection of miracles. Hume regards any attempt to refute a given hypothesis on the ground that it endangers religion and morality as not only uninformed, but unintelligent. When a man inquires into the role that the Deity may play in human moral decisions, he is inviting confusion. Of the difficulties attached to this or to any inquiry about liberty and necessity, Hume ironically asserts,

These are mysteries, which mere natural and unassisted reason is very unfit to handle; and whatever system she embraces, she must find herself involved in inextricable difficulties, and even contradictions, at every step which she takes with regard to such subjects. To reconcile the indifference and contingency of human actions with prescience; or to defend absolute decrees, and yet free the Deity from being the author of sin, has been found hitherto to exceed all the power of philosophy. Happy, if she be thence sensible of her temerity, when she pries into these sublime mysteries; and leaving a scene so full of obscurities and perplexities, return, with suitable modesty, to her true and proper province, the examination of common life; where she will find difficulties enow to employ her enquiries, without launching into so boundless an ocean of doubt, uncertainty, and contradiction! (*Works,* 4:84: *ECHU,* 103).

Hume's analysis of miracles exemplifies the above contention. As the reader will recall from chapter 1, "Of Miracles" is unequivocally the most controversial work Hume ever wrote. In addition, it contains some of his most subtle reasoning and to the devout, some of the most frightening logic ever assembled in one short essay. A miracle Hume defines as a "violation of the laws of nature" and asserts that the testimony offered in support of miracles is never totally reliable. The general assumptions of the first part of this section involve a priori maxims which nonetheless lead ineluctably to a posteriori conclusions. No testimony offered in the defense of a miracle can be sufficient to validate it, unless that testimony is itself so powerful that its falsity would be more miraculous than that very miracle which it supports.

Hume then subjects the evidence offered in support of miracles to the test of customary experience and to the frequent variation and unreliability of the sources cited in support of the miracle. Pointing out that reports which favor the passions or, particularly, the religious inclinations of the reporter cannot, by definition, be impartial or disinterested, Hume asks if we can actually obtain reliable evidence for miracles. Most evidence will be distorted because it is partisan; scrupulous, impartial inquiry is unlikely. In a paragraph of great cogency, he observes, "Upon the whole, then, it appears that no testimony for any kind of miracle has ever amounted to a probability, much less to a proof; and that, even supposing it amounted to a proof, it would be opposed by another proof; derived from the very nature of the fact, which it would endeavour to establish" (*Works,* 4:105; *ECHU,* 127).[10]

Experience alone can invest human testimony with authority, the same experience which has regularized nature. How can we react when the experience of the laws of nature is violated by what is alleged to be a miracle? We must decide which is more extraordinary: the miracle or the testimony offered in support of it. The result is invariably inconclusive: "and therefore we may establish it as a maxim, that no human testimony can have such force as to prove a miracle, and make it a just foundation for any such system of religion" (*Works,* 4:105; *ECHU,* 127).

Both Hume's language and his methodology are uncompromising. He has denied the validity of the usual evidence advanced in support of a miracle, since that evidence satisfies none of the criteria he established for miracles. Knowing only too well the eccentricities of human beings, he has suggested that human credulousness created more miracles than any other single cause. The evidence that Hume finds acceptable in supporting miracles is more quantitative than qualitative. Near the end of the essay, he allows that a sufficient uniformity of agreement about a violation of the laws of nature would validate a claim to miraculousness. The kind of events men offer as miracles however, are so narrow and chaotic that empirical credibility cannot be extended them. The most persuasive argument that Hume uses, however, is one Bertrand Russell was to use two hundred years later:[11] that miracles invoked in support of one system of religion almost always conflict with or contradict the miracles of another—and conflicting assertions cannot both be true. So many witnesses dispute the various miracles of opposing sects that the testimony destroys itself. How is one to decide among the evidence offered for countless miracles? In the land of the blind, the one–eyed man is king; in the land of miracles, we are all blind.

Hume's concluding remarks are judiciously ironic. He quotes with approval Bacon, on the suspiciousness of "relations" which depend upon religion, observing that Bacon's reasoning "may serve to confound those dangerous friends or disguised enemies to the *Christian Religion,* who have undertaken to defend it by the principles of human reason" (*Works,* 4:107; *ECHU,* 129–30). Religion, Hume asserts, is founded on faith; its only defense, if it need one, is faith. Considering the Pentateuch, Hume finds that we are presented with a book written in a barbarous age by ignorant people. It records events long past even testimonial verification and is full of any number of miracles, prodigies, and incomprehensibilities. "I desire any one," Hume says, "to lay his hand upon his heart, and after a serious consideration declare, whether he thinks that the falsehood of such a book, supported by such a testimony, would be more extraordinary and miraculous than all the miracles it relates" (*Works,* 4:108; *ECHU,* 130). Our own experience will not permit us to assert a series of empirical propositions we have, in fact, never experienced. The acceptance of the contrary more easily coincides with our natural inclination and experience than the miraculous events recorded in the Pentateuch, or any other work for that matter.

Remembering one of Hume's prior observations that began "upon the whole," the eighteenth-century reader, as well as the modern reader, might have found one of the last sentences a real shocker. "So that, upon the whole, we may conclude, that the *Christian Religion* not only was at first attended with miracles, but even at this day cannot be believed by any reasonable person without one" (*Works,* 4:108; *ECHU,* 131). If the testimony for a miracle has never amounted to a probability, still less to a proof, and if no one can believe the Christian religion without accepting the validity of at least one miracle, the conclusion of the syllogism is inescapable: the Christian must believe what can never be proved and must assent to a "continued miracle in his own person." He must believe the contrary of what experience and even common sense tell him. Small wonder that Hume was regarded, and still is in some quarters, as a dangerous infidel, although much of the preceding argument would probably not shock those who followed the Calvinistic evaluation of reason. Small wonder, too that some twentieth-century commentators fail to take Hume seriously.[12] Yet Hume's position, when thought through, actually strengthens the validity of the self involved in the personal experience of religion. Religion must be strong in a man's mind and heart, not by laws, customs, platitudes, or logic, but by a conscious faith. Religion without faith is a fraud; and faith, according to Hume, without miracles is impossible.

Throughout this section of the first *Enquiry,* the reader sees Hume's skepticism at work on a topic too often clouded by sentimentality or taboos. He treats miracles as what they have pretended to be—a particular branch of knowledge; acceptance of them is alleged to be wisdom of the most exalted kind. But they cannot be dealt with by any of the rules which conventionally govern inquiries into human phenomena. If miracles are amenable to the logic and reason which guide inquiries into history, for example, then they are incapable of probability or proof. Miracles and other events that involve faith do not belong to ordinary methods of discourse but must achieve whatever validity they can by the rules of faith. They do not have the force of knowledge and should not be accepted as knowledge.

Any sections following "Of Miracles" would almost have to be anticlimatic. They very well may be, but they shouldn't. Section 11, "Of a Particular Providence and of a Future State," is mistitled since providence and futurity are hardly mentioned. The original title, which appeared in only the first edition, was "Of the Practical Consequences of Natural Religion," a designation which clarifies its relation to "Of Miracles." In it, Hume, writing in dialogue form for the first time in his literary career, poses as the recipient of the skeptical observations of a friend, whose principles, however curious and relevant, he cannot accept. This pose is strategic since Hume would have been ill-advised to spend one section demolishing empirical arguments for miracles, only to follow it with a demonstration of the difficulties inherent in the analogical method of reasoning upon natural religion. This is what the "friend" does; and Hume, instead of disagreeing, supplements the arguments against natural religion that his friend makes. The chief mistake in analogical reasoning lies in the human penchant to attribute to the Deity the same conduct and intelligence we have. The result is unbounded conjecture, and inquiry from effect to cause based upon this analogy. The argument here is one expanded by Philo in the *Dialogues concerning Natural Religion,* and it can be more thoroughly considered there.

Hume does, however, take this opportunity to vindicate the practical harmlessness of philosophical inquiry: "I think that the state ought to toler-

ate every principle of philosophy; nor is there an instance, that any government has suffered in its political interests by such indulgence. There is no
enthusiasm among philosophers; their doctrines are not very alluring to the
people" (*Works,* 4:121; *ECHU,* 147). The only exception Hume makes for
his generalization is the prevalence of doctrines or reasonings manifestly inimical to the best interest of scientific inquiry or of political uniformity.[13]

Hume's strategy is similar in section 12, the last, "Of the Academical or
Sceptical Philosophy," where he alleges that "The *Sceptic* is another enemy
of religion," while leaving the reader to infer that he, Hume, is not such a
person. The essay contains, however, Hume's best statement of the proper
role of the skeptic. Cartesian skepticism withers quickly before Hume's
blast at the a priori assumptions it involves, while the skepticism that leads
to solipsism or nihilism is simply labeled "trite." The first two parts of the
section, by demolishing various forms of "improper" and useless skepticism,
lay the groundwork for the usefulness and durability of a mitigated skepticism as outlined in the third part of the essay. When we consider the narrow
limitations of any inquiry, Hume suggests, we cannot hope for too much
since we do not have the means to achieve those hopes; nor should we expect
too little since the world is not chaotic.

The kind of skepticism that Hume advocates is often Pyrrhonistic, but it
fixes boundaries upon human inquiries. It is, as numerous commentators
have observed, a species of naturalism.[14] Through questioning the evidence
offered in support of a theory demonstrating the uniformity of nature,
Hume nevertheless found himself, in practical terms, accepting the uniformity of nature. He cannot accept as fact what his experience does not
teach him. Newton observed that the inductive method of reasoning could
never produce certainty, but that as methodology, it was the best we had.[15]
Hume's skepticism accepts the truth of his proposition, "Whatever *is* may
not be"; and it attempts to cope with the divergent experiences of human
nature with a full awareness of that handicap.

Although perhaps not representative, the last paragraph of the first
Enquiry is deservedly the most famous. In historical context, it is not so
dashing as it seems; for the "school metaphysics" that Hume berates had
long ago passed on to its reward.[16] Yet its rhetorical energy gives us a clue to
Hume's attitude towards a priori theorizing and empty speculation. It can
easily bear requoting:

When we run over libraries, persuaded of these principles, what havoc must we
make? If we take in our hand any volume; of divinity or school metaphysics, for instance; let us ask, *Does it contain any abstract reasoning concerning quantity or num-*

ber. No. *Does it contain any experimental reasoning concerning matter of fact and existence?* No. Commit it then to the flames: For it can contain nothing but sophistry and illusion" (*Works,* 4:135; *ECHU,* 165).

The Principles of Morals: Semantics and Secularism

Hume's design in the *Enquiry concerning the Principles of Morals* is indeed hopeful: to attempt the same reformation in ethics as Newton had done in "natural philosophy," and to reject any system of ethics not established by facts or observation. The results are certainly different from those of previous ethical systems. Hume's ethic is completely secular, more so than those of Spinoza, Bayle, Montaigne, Hobbes, or even Francis Hutcheson. Hume's secularism is thus not unique, but it is different from the secularism of Hutcheson's ethic, to take one of Hume's contemporaries as an example. Hutcheson's secular ethic operates within human limits and limitations, but it relates moral activity to the Deity and speculates about the role of the Deity in moral decisions, something Hume conspicuously avoided.

Hume's methodology is deceptively simple. By close observation of noteworthy human transactions, he plans to identify and to isolate those mental qualities accounting for personal merit. He attends to the terminology applied in moral judgments in order to discover what similarities in criteria exist. Our language makes rhetoric an inescapable part of any system of ethics since many words are inextricably associated with specific sets of ideas about morality and behavior. To gain proper perspective, Hume adds a historical dimension to his approach. Activities or qualities of the mind which excite general approbation are called "virtuous"; activities or qualities of the mind which are blamed or censured are in general termed "vicious."[17] Hume plans to follow the generally reliable method of experimental reasoning and to infer general maxims from sequences of particular instances. The best method for establishing a system of ethics is first to discover what human interchanges have been accounted ethical. Hume's procedure involves an attack on one of the features of human behavior most often used in the eighteenth century as a basis for moral theories—self-love.[18]

In all editions of the second *Enquiry* which appeared during Hume's lifetime, the second section, "Of Benevolence," was first devoted to a discussion of self-love. In the first posthumous edition of 1777, however, the section on self-love was relegated to an appendix, where it has gone unnoticed by almost all of Hume's commentators. Since the various ideas suggested by the concept "self-love" provided seventeenth- and eighteenth-century moral theorists with fruitful means of unifying and formulating ethical systems, Hume's discussion of self-love is of more than cursory interest. Moreover, much of what Hume says about self-love in the relocated part of section 2 prepares the reader for his inquiry into the origin of moral principles. Hume's ethical postulates and assertions cannot be fully understood without understanding his attitude toward and his concept of self-love. For these reasons, a useful starting-point for an exegesis of Hume's moral philosophy can be found in his views on self-love.

The relocated section does not constitute the totality of Hume's views on self-love, for he either mentions or discusses the concept in the *Treatise*, in his essays, in the *History of England*, and in the *Dialogues concerning Natural Religion*. The second *Enquiry* presented his most sustained consideration of the topic. Hume begins by noticing the existence of a principle asserting that benevolence, friendship, public spirit, and other like virtues are not what they seem. Refusing to take this assertion at face value, Hume makes several ad hominem observations about the kind of "heart" to be found in the enunciator of such views. Another view holds that no passions are disinterested, that friendship is an extension or outlet for self-love: regardless of our putative motives in any moral transaction, the ultimate motive must be self-love.

In spite of this insistence upon self-love as the source of seeming benevolence, the philosophers who advocated some kind of self-love as the ultimate ethical doctrine were themselves friendly and generous (for example, Epicurus, Atticus, and Horace; Hobbes and Locke). An Epicurean or Hobbesean admitted the existence of friendship in the world, and Hume cannot, as a matter of rhetoric and logic, accept the attempt to call it another form of self-love. Hume admires results: he esteems the man whose self-love leads him into acts of charity or benevolence, regardless of the motives other people ascribe to his acts. Distinguishing between two kinds of benevolence (general and particular), Hume argues that both kinds must exist in human nature. Any resolution of them into some "nice consideration of self-love" is more curious than important. Hume remarks, ironically, that all attempts to prove benevolence, for example, to be something other than it is, have been fruitless; such attempts proceed from the "love of *simplicity*, which has been the source of much false reasoning in philosophy" (*Works*, 4:269; *ECPM*, 298).

An ethical system based on self-love is attractive, Hume continues, because it accounts for the origin of benevolence in selfishness. As we inquire about the origin of our passions, we do not suppose that they came from the least obvious and least familiar causes. The more intricate and refined a system is, the more we are apt to suspect it. Eliminating elaborate and inessential theories dependent upon self-love to explain human motives, Hume argues that we ought always to assume that the simplest and most obvious cause for the operation of the passions is the correct one. He points out that animals show kindness to other animals and to humans; yet we do not impute their motives to self-love. Surely we can be as charitable toward human beings as we are toward animals. Parental devotion also cannot be attributed to self-love. Perhaps the most resonant objection that Hume makes is metalinguistic. Hume asks why we have a word such as "gratitude" if it is to have no meaning or reality, if we are to have no methodology for knowing what the word means. If we are to consider gratitude as only disguised self-love, then we ought indeed to reduce all human acts to species of self-love. Not even the advocates of an ethical system based entirely on self-love have adopted this procedure, as Hume points out, and they have certainly not practiced it.

Returning to his observations about the great dangers of oversimplification in philosophical reasoning, Hume observes that the hypothesis allowing the existence of disinterested benevolence is simpler than one asserting self-love. To make self-love the source of all charity is to confound and needlessly complicate inquiries into the principles of morals. In addition, certain passions, like the love of fame, must precede self-love; if we seek fame, we must first obtain it before our self-love can allow us to enjoy it. To distinguish between self-enjoyment and self-love is necessary if we are to comprehend moral acts. Self-love cannot explain all of our actions and reactions: "If I have no vanity, I take no delight in praise: If I be void of ambition, power gives me no enjoyment: If I be not angry, the punishment of an adversary is totally indifferent to me" (*Works*, 4:271; *ECPM*, 301). Without experience to teach us the difference between pain and pleasure, self-love could exert no influence on us. Some inclinations or appetites must exist prior to whatever self-love may arise in an individual, otherwise nothing would call it forth.

Hume finally appeals to the "original frame of our temper" to establish the possibility of "real" benevolence and friendship. Reason and experience accord more with the attribution of benevolence and friendship to a natural propensity on the part of an individual than they do with self-love. Self-enjoyment may result from the pleasure we have in benevolence, but self-enjoyment and self-love are not identical. Indeed, Hume says, the passion of anger may carry us into undesirable pursuits; and self-love could do little to restrain our vindictiveness. Philosophy can at least permit humanity and friendship the same privileges ascribed to enmity and resentment. Human nature is not capable of being explained by an appeal to some abstract universal principle. At the risk of an anachronism, I should say that Hume finds masochistic the practice of attributing only evil passions and malign motives to human beings. And a projection of individualized consciousness is not sufficient for inquiry into the reasons for the principles of morals.

Why Hume relegated this part of section 2 to an appendix can only be conjectured. Generally speaking, he viewed self-love as one of the least admirable of human passions, although he did not find it so opprobrious as other vices; yet the concept is essential in and to his ethical system. The difficulty with self-love as an ethical concept is that it usually involves a "ruling passion" theory of ethics—one Hume specifically abjured as the basis of ethics. On several occasions he said that human behavior could not be explained by appeal to some passion or principle to account for the totality of ethical conduct. None of the ideas or concepts—such as "benevolence," "justice," or "utility," which Hume discusses in the *Enquiry concerning the Principles of Morals*—is sufficient in itself to form or to animate a theory of ethics; nor does he intend that one of them should be sufficient.

For convenience, I have been referring to Hume's "system of ethics" and its formation; but to credit Hume with a system of ethics is perhaps misleading. As the title indicates, Hume is inquiring into the principles of morals, an activity that is different from erecting a system of morals. Hume's general conclusions, which will seem simple-minded to those unfamiliar with the history of ethical speculation, are not likely to shock or even to enlighten a modern mind. His ethic is primarily descriptive, not prescriptive; and thus it has neither the rhetoric nor the sweeping autonomy of systems of ethics. Instead of the imperative sentences that we might expect from a discussion of morality, Hume's are chiefly declarative. I hasten to add that he commits himself by implication to a traditional ethical position. Hume's language clearly implies those qualities he finds virtuous and those vicious.

The key to Hume's moral outlook is probably best found in section 5, "Why Utility Pleases."[19] The sections after it discuss qualities useful and agreeable to ourselves and to others, indicating the extent to which Hume emphasizes the importance of utility in moral acts. "Why Utility Pleases" is a more important section than the three following ones because Hume seeks in it to explain rather than to enumerate the data-bases of ethics. Interestingly enough, Hume is concerned in this section to demonstrate the inadequacy of self-love as a concept sufficient to explain all action. This undertaking reinforced Bishop Butler's answer to theories of ethics that denied the possibility of disinterested moral action.[20]

To give utility the same praise that we would give any social virtue would seem "natural" in ethical inquiry; but, Hume notes, philosophers have not often done so because of the difficulty of accounting for the origin of usefulness as an ethical criterion. Suggesting that confusion of the two notions of utility has been one of the reasons for this difficulty, Hume distinguishes between utility which lends virtue to its owner and utility in an inanimate object. Social virtues naturally recommend themselves to the mind, long before admonitions or education do. The public utility of these virtues causes them to be considered meritorious, and the ends these virtues promote please either from selfish interests (self-love) or from generosity and humanity. Hume again asserts that moral systems cannot be derived from or based on concepts of self-love; to allege that benevolence and humanity are only forms of modified self-love is to forsake linguistic accuracy for a generalization supporting the tradition of man's innate sinfulness. Theories of self-love cannot sufficiently account for the agreeableness and pleasure of usefulness. The approbation accorded usefulness is universal and not particular; it cannot be reconciled with a denial of the possibility of disinterested moral action.

Hume does admit, however, that self-love is a forceful and extensive principle in human nature and that philosophers who sought to account for all activity in its terms can perhaps be excused for their shortsightedness. Because the interests of the individual seem coextensive with those of his society, other philosophers enforced a unity upon moral activity that did not, in fact, exist. To support his argument on strictly empirical grounds, Hume marshals category after category of examples which cannot be sufficiently justified by a self-love theory of ethics. Considering the subject on both a priori and a posteriori grounds, Hume argues against the oversimplification of ethics into theories of self-interest and self-love. What else, he asks, but a general goodwill towards one's fellow creatures could account for utilitarian value that disinterested spectators assign to social virtue? In qualities that are useful to ourselves, such as efficiency in the dispatch of our business, self-love does not and cannot account for the pleasure which that quality in us would give to other people; but anyone is pleased to observe a man who does his job well. Even those qualities that are solely pleasing to us cannot always be resolved into self-love. Agility of mind is both useful and pleasant to ourselves, but it was not created by our self-love. In short, the usefulness of these pleasing qualities enlarges our capacity for understanding ourselves and others better than we otherwise would.

The purpose of ethics is to inquire into the criteria for determining good and bad actions in order to ascertain whatever personal merit any individual has. Neither reason nor sentiment is sufficient in and of itself to arrive at correct moral equations. For Hume, personal merit "consists altogether in the possession of mental qualities, *useful,* or *agreeable* to the *person himself* or to *others*" (*Works,* 4:245; *ECPM,* 268). While philosophers may have disputed this activist definition of personal merit (or virtue), common life, where most moral transactions take place, implicitly accepts and acts upon those principles. Certain qualities, like the "monkish virtues" of "celibacy, fasting, penance, mortification, self-denial, humility, silence, solitude" are always rejected by "sensible" men because they have no function. They are not valuable to society, and they usually render their owner unfit for human intercourse. With this observation, Hume explicitly rejects both the ascetic and the Puritan tradition in ethics; in fact, he labels these ascetic qualities "vices."

In coming to a conclusion about the proper subject matter of morals, Hume excludes such passions as avarice, ambition, and vanity from an account of the origin of morals. Those passions are incorrectly thought to be forms of self-love, but Hume does not think they can account for the formation of moral sentiments. Morality must be dependent upon a universal propensity in mankind to agree about an object or person deserving approval. Since the sentiment of humanity is more widespread than that of self-love, self-love cannot be the foundation of morality. The concern of morality lies in the establishment of general principles; morality does not assert or propound a ruling passion that governs all men regardless of what they think.

In the "Conclusion," Hume articulates the essential differences between the language of self-love and that of ordinary moral transactions. By qualifying nouns with a possessive adjective (e.g., *his rival*), a person relates the events of his experience specifically to himself and not to the generality of humanity. To describe a man as "odious" or "depraved," however, is to expect the concurrence of one's listeners, or, anyway, not to be astonished at any disagreement. The language of ethics, Hume implies, is amenable to the kind of experience and verification that one applies in "natural philosophy" or history. Its judgments are understood because they are universal, and men throughout history experience much the same sentiment or passion upon hearing lies or viewing cruelty.[21] Because human emotions and affections share a number of similarities in all human beings, the same linguistic criteria for determining a useful chair could apply to determining a courageous decision.

Hume insists upon a dichotomy between what we may call "private moral experiences" and "public moral activities." The general sentiments of human beings, not their private passions, constitute the origin of morals. The difference is great: "Whatever conduct gains my approbation, by touching my humanity, procures also the applause of all mankind, by affecting the same principle in them: But what serves my avarice or ambition pleases these passions in me alone, and affects not the avarice and ambition of the rest of mankind" (*Works*, 4:249; *ECPM*, 274). Moral language is formed on the vast distinction between these two species of sentiment. Specific manifestations of self-love are controlled and modified by the universal principles that have been incorporated into the sum and substance of our language. What Hume calls "benevolent concern for others" is not, of course, equally diffused in all men. And the objects of that concern may well vary, since education or reason will direct concern toward specific people. Yet every quality of the mind, useful or agreeable to its owner or to others, also renders pleasure to the generality of mankind and is usually thought meritorious.

Hume's views as outlined here may seem facile, even naive, to a modern reader. So far as I can tell, they did not to the eighteenth-century reader; for none of the eighteenth-century reviews or discussions of the *Enquiry concerning the Principles of Morals* which I have examined has charged Hume with such. The reason may be attributable to the latent skepticism, which becomes straightforward in the last part of Hume's conclusion, of the second *Enquiry*. Confessing that he cannot at present imagine any forcible objections to his contention that personal merit is made up of the utility or agreeableness of personal qualities, Hume realizes the probability of error. The confusion and errors resulting from what was thought precision in measuring the bulk of the earth and the order of the universe are sufficient examples to deter anyone from being dogmatically certain about any reasoning based upon perception and experience. His hypothesis, while seeming so obvious, must, to the skeptical mind, invite dispute and correction; otherwise it would have been unanimously accepted long ago. Hume, therefore, ironically suggests that men's certitudes are likely to fool no one but themselves.

This skepticism leads Hume into a consideration of one's obligation or duty to promote virtue and to discourage vice. And the skeptic asks what hope can we have of convincing mankind to accept the rigorous and austere ethic that grows out of the sentiments of all mankind. The advantage of the principles Hume has articulated lies in their usefulness to the individual. Fame and honor, even ingenuity and politeness, are qualities no one would willingly forgo if one is educated. The opposition of selfish and social sentiments is no more accurate than the opposition of selfishness and vanity, or the opposition of selfishness and ambition. Before self-love can direct our energies and passions, we must have already engaged our affections, our natural propensities. If we wish the approbation of our fellow men, we can do no less than exemplify the virtues that language has traditionally defined. Giving all possible credit to vice, we would not find it more rewarding than the practice of virtue with whatever view to self-interest we may have. And we will discover that the principles of morals are general guides, not autonomous rules. The wise individual knows the exceptions to the general rules and uses them judiciously.

Reason impels man to accept the moral principles described by our language. If he does not, if he cannot find reason for seeking and promoting personal merit, then, Hume skeptically concludes, he is unlikely to be convinced by any argument. A man who does not understand the general sentiments of mankind or the language in which morality is phrased is beyond the reach of human communication. This is not to suggest that Hume's moral theory is "naturalistic." Reading the *Enquiry concerning the Principles of Morals,* we must keep in mind Hume's observation in the *Treatise,* "that nothing can be more unphilosophical than those systems, which assert, that virtue is the same with what is natural, and vice with what is unnatural" (*Treatise,* 3:i, 2; p. 475).

In this discussion I hoped to enforce two ideas about Hume's method and purpose in the *Enquiry concerning the Principles of Morals.* First, I think it is clear that Hume wished to lay to rest forever the notion that all acts were the product of self-love, or that the narcissistic element in man was too strong to include the possibility of disinterested moral action. Second, Hume found in the forms of language a possible structure for ethics, and he tried to show the inescapable interconnections between discourses about ethics and the language used to make those discourses. To reformulate ethics along these lines precluded any attempt to separate the business of ethics from that of everyday life. In addition, these guidelines provided an ethic whose authority was secular, not sacred, and was consequently more universal than any ethic derived from religious precepts. No one will argue that Hume's inquiry is perfect as an attempt to establish the principles of morals, but we can say of it, as Dr. Johnson said of his *Dictionary,* "In this work, when it shall be found that much is omitted, let it not be forgotten that much likewise is performed."

Chapter Five
Hume as Historian

The History of England:
Background and Methodology

As early as 1745, Hume considered writing a history of England. For the next decade, he collected facts, information, and ideas for this history. Although the first volume of his *History of England* was not published until 1754 (the second volume in 1757), Hume was nevertheless planning, in the 1740s, what kind of history he would write.[1] In the surviving manuscript notes for his history, we can see that Hume made careful outlines of certain parts of English history, apparently trying to familiarize himself with the material to be assimilated and the sources necessary for that assimilation.[2]

To write a history of England was no easy task, although several people, as I pointed out in chapter one, had attempted either a comprehensive or a selective history of England. While Hume's history is not exactly comprehensive, it attempted to do more than any of his predecessors had done. Hume's most important predecessor was Rapin-Thoyras, and the defects of his history of England were not always outweighed by its achievements. Hume set for himself one of the most important goals of any writer in the eighteenth century: to write a readable and intelligent history of England, free of fractious partisanship, impartial where possible, judicious even when unnecessary.

To attempt to be fair and impartial is, of course, the intention, if not the claim, of most authors. Yet some of the difficulties attendant upon writing a complete history of England were not unknown to Hume's contemporaries. James Ralph's exhausting *History of England,* covering the years 1688 to 1702, had noted some of the imponderables of writing history in its introductory review of the Restoration.[3] Ralph points out the vagaries of writing about events when they are not yet history, and the importance, once they are past, of achieving a proper perspective for viewing them. Unfortunately, Ralph observes, all Englishmen are members of some party or faction; because they share common creeds, to judge the past virtues or sins of their party or faction may be very painful or even impossible. "Thus," Ralph

says, "should an *Historian* arise, who had Application to collect the best
Materials, Capacity to comprehend, and Skill to digest them, Genius to animate his Work, and Integrity and Resolution so to decide upon every Character and every Fact, as Equity should prompt, as Truth should authorise,
instead of making Converts, by the honest Exercise of his Talents, he would
possibly make Enemies; and all the *Sore* among the *Living* would clamour
in Behalf of the *guilty Dead*."[4]

In Ralph's estimation, the perils of writing history lie more with the putative historian than with the frequent irreconcilability of facts and events.
He is nonetheless hopeful: "But should so valuable a Man ever arise among
us, I hope he would venture upon the Task, however difficult and discour-
aging, of reducing our shapeless Annals into Form and Comeliness, with
Spirit superior to any such ungrateful Consequence."[5] Although neither
man may have known the other, James Ralph outlined in 1744 the kind of
historian Hume hoped to be. Ralph's history covered periods that Hume
did not cover, but which, in 1763, he thought of covering; and he sought to
obtain Ralph's materials for that purpose. To his publisher, Andrew Millar,
Hume wrote, "I am told, that Mr. Ralph is dead, who had certainly made a
large Collection of Books and Pamphlets for his Work. I should be glad to
know into whose hands they are fallen, and would purchase them, if they
could be got at a reasonable Price" (*HL,* 1:382). If nothing else, Hume admired the scholarship that went into Ralph's work. I do not know if Hume
was aware of Ralph's work when he began the actual writing of his own history of England; that he may not have been seems unlikely in view of the
wide reading and lengthy preparation for his *History of England.* He may
have decided to omit a history of the periods after the "Glorious Revolution" since Ralph had already covered them and since Hume was not inclined to write a history of his own times. His printer, William Strahan,
encouraged him to continue the history, but by the end of the 1760s, Hume
did not feel up to the task and allegedly told Strahan, "I must decline not
only this offer, but all others of a literary nature for four reasons: Because
I'm too old, too fat, too lazy, and too rich" (*Life,* 556).

Hume did agree with Ralph's general sentiments about the problems of
writing history and of being a historian. Before undertaking the task, he
thought carefully about the problems with which he would be faced. Since
no one before him had attempted to write the kind of history that Hume
wished to write, he had no model to follow; however, he did have some general ideas about the form and function of a history.

As we have seen in chapter 1, in a letter of Hume's to John Clephane, he confided that he was engaged upon a project which would keep him busy for several years, his *History of England*:

My friends flatter me (by this I mean that they don't flatter me), that I have succeeded. You know that there is no post of honour in the English Parnassus more vacant than that of History. Style, judgement, impartiality, care—everything is wanting to our historians; and even Rapin, during this latter period, is extremely deficient. I make my work very concise, after the manner of the Ancients. It divides into three very moderate volumes; one to end with the death of Charles the First; the second at the Revolution; the third at the Accession [Hanover], for I dare come no nearer to the present times. The work will neither please the Duke of Bedford nor James Fraser; but I hope it will please you and posterity. Κτῆμα εἰς ἀεί (*HL*, 1:170–71)

Hume did not attempt the projected third volume. He completed his history up to 1689. The conclusion of the forgoing letter indicates to what extent Hume thought he was being impartial, since John, fourth Duke of Bedford, exemplified everything that Whigs stood for, while James Fraser was an enthusiastic Jacobite.[6] Thus, before the *History of England* was published, Hume had hoped that it would please the judicious and would be "a possession for all time," as he quoted Thucydides.

Even after protests were raised about Hume's alleged political bias, he still thought himself moderate. John Clephane received another letter from Hume after the first volume of the *History* was published, where Hume articulated, in a famous passage, part of his methodology: "My views of *things* are more conformable to Whig principles; my representations of *persons* to Tory prejudices" (*HL*, 1:237). Finding himself numbered among the Tories more often than among the Whigs was ample proof, Hume added, of men's higher regard for persons rather than things. Yet Hume thought this regard was as it should be, for he had no wish to write a history consisting only of fact, fact, fact.

To avoid the dullness and sterility of history as fact, fact, fact is not, however, to write a history that is fantasy, fantasy, fantasy. Writing a history of anything requires that one have, obviously, some conception of history, some plan of organizing materials, and some discretion in the choice of representative events. We may never be absolutely certain what Hume's concept of history was, nor can we isolate all his intentions in writing a history of England. We can, however, recreate, from various scattered comments, some idea of the form and function of history as Hume conceived it. The presentation of historical facts and events necessarily involves discrimination among one's sources. The discriminations and judgments made about the sources and presentation create the perspective from which a history is written.

In outlining Hume's concept of history, we could first turn to an essay that appeared in 1741, "Of the Study of History." This essay appeared in every edition of Hume's essays through 1760, but it was removed from the edition of the *Essays and Treatises on Several Subjects* published in 1764 because it was one of the essays Hume thought "too frivolous." Although not as weighty as some of his other essays, it does contain some helpful observations. In the essay, Hume jokingly asserts that the study of history recommends itself to the female sex as suited for their education and instruction more than the usual books of amusement or instruction. History will convey to them two important truths: (1) that the male sex is not so perfect as they imagine, and (2) that love is not the sole governing passion of men and is often overcome by other passions. Hume continues in this vein for two paragraphs and then admits his ironic raillery. Yet his suggestions, he alleges, are not without merit; for history is indeed an agreeable entertainment because it transports the mind to other cultures and other societies. A knowledge of history is necessary for the well-educated man or woman. Ignorance of history is unpardonable in a person pretending to be educated. To these advantages, Hume adds history's capacity for introducing one to new realms of inquiry; moreover, it can promote virtue without leading to the difficulties poetry might entail.

While Hume began his essay frivolously, he suggests in its last paragraph two important functions of history. Because a historian is, according to Hume, unlike a poet, and must represent passions in all their glory or iniquity, he inculcates a sense of virtue. He must be judicious, but he is not always impartial; he may err in his judgment of particular persons, but he must not do so in representing vice and virtue in their proper perspective. Hume's observations about the philosopher's contemplation of history are even more instructive. Taking an abstract view of men, manners, and things, the philosopher is often unmoved by the general sentiments of human nature. Because he does not enter into that which he contemplates, the philosopher often does not feel the difference between vice and virtue. That which is temporally distant loses much of its humanity when viewed from a philosophic standpoint. The study of history, Hume continues, prevents this distortion by mediating between the extremes of indifference to virtue or vice and the extremes of atrophy of natural sentiments. Writers of history, as well as readers, respond to instances of vice or virtue since they must pay attention to characters and events. The temporal distance from the characters or events described usually precludes any interest on the part of the narrator or reader, but it encourages correct moral or political judgments. History, for Hume, is about men, their moral actions and transactions, not about laws, edicts, and decrees.

We saw in chapter 2 some of the epistemological problems which confront the reader or the chronicler of history. The greatest epistemological problem that confronted any historian, Hume no less than his predecessors, was that of the reliability of the data from which a history was to be constructed. As years pass and as men become more and more removed from the important events of history, the evidence for their occurrence becomes harder to verify. Hume's solution to the difficulty, first raised in the *Treatise,* was neither original nor imaginative. He relied upon the metaphor of the "chain of argument" to suggest the continuity that is somehow preserved in any narrative, spoken or written, of historical events. He invokes the doctrine of "common sense" to suggest that few will doubt that a man such as Julius Caesar existed. As a matter of expedience, Hume is right: few will ever doubt that Julius Caesar existed. Important events and men are testified to in many documents as well as by tradition. But, Hume points out, events and men of lesser importance do not share in this extensiveness. Given a similarity in the reports of one historical occurrence, the historian can safely include it as "fact" in his composition. What is the historian to do, however, when the reports conflict or seem otherwise unreliable?

Hume's method for dealing with such instances is simple. The limits of experience prevent absolute assertions about the truth-value of any proposition. Moreover, the propositions of history are not the same as those of scientific facts, which are capable of re-verification. To determine the truth-value of historical propositions, the historian must confine the evidence to the context in which they appear. Historical propositions are subject to means of verification different from the procedure for other propositions. In the *Treatise,* Hume mentioned two admittedly unoriginal guides to determining the truth-value of historical propositions. In writing the *History of England,* he employed a methodology consistent with his assertions about the principles of human nature. (This is not to say that Hume's *History* is "philosophical," although one might easily read it with that preconception.) The methodology exhibits Hume's willingness to judge the validity or reliability of the reports from which he composed his history.

An example of this methodology can be found in the *History,* in chapter 2, in which Hume covers the period from 827 to 978. In discussing Anglo-Saxon King Edgar, he relies upon a number of documents which spell out the administrative details of his reign. He notes some disagreement among

Scottish historians about the allegiance of the Scottish king, Kenneth III, to Edgar. Hume ignores these problems and points to the primary way in which Edgar maintained authority: by cultivating the monks and others who, by pretending superior sanctity and purity, had more influence with the people than any other group. When the union of crown and church proved to be successful, Edgar exploited it by condemning the secular clergy. The monks were enjoined to rid the monasteries of reprobates and backsliders, which they did. Yet Hume is appropriately skeptical about the evidence offered to support the allegations against the secular clergy:

We may remark, that the declamations against the secular clergy are, both here and in all the historians, conveyed in general terms; and as that order of men are commonly restrained by the decency of their character, [not to mention superior motive,] it is difficult to believe that the complaints against their dissolute manners could be so universally just as is pretended. It is more probable, that the monks paid court to the populace by an affected austerity of life, and representing the most innocent liberties, taken by the other clergy, as great and unpardonable enormities, thereby prepared the way for the encrease of their own power and influence. (*History*, 1:99 [passage in brackets omitted from Hume's last revised edition].)

The "innocent liberties" to which Hume refers include gaming, hunting, singing, dancing, and living with one's wife—"liberties" denied the regular clergy.

The passage omitted from the last revised edition of the *History* contains, I think, a clue to Hume's methodology in narrating history where the facts are scarce or contradictory. He is suspicious of any generalization contrary to ordinary experience and custom. Having no firsthand, reliable accounts of various events, Hume imposes upon the popular, yet questionable, generalizations, some of his ideas about the mechanics of human nature. The limits of historical truth and reliability are fixed by the implications of Hume's moral and epistemological presumptions. Within this framework, Hume can and does make certain assertions about evidence he thinks untrustworthy. (I think we can agree that any assertion about people's motives must, as a matter of logic and psychology, influence the historian's conclusions.)

Hume remarks, for example, that the members of the secular clergy were of decent character and entered into their work with motives superior to those of the regular clergy (or so Hume seemed to imply). Thus, one part of Hume's methodology in writing his history involves his ideas about men's motives in choosing X rather than Y. The limitless implications of this methodology are restrained by Hume's reluctance to substitute one questionable generalization for another and by his inclination to distrust the professionally pious. While an eighteenth-century reader may have been incensed at the implications of Hume's remarks about the monks' affectations, he might, with better reason, have questioned Hume's mixture of evidence. What Hume says about the reasons for the monks' aversions to the secular clergy is acceptable, but we might very well wonder about the way in which the conclusion was reached.

In short, Hume distrusts generalized accounts of specific events. Lacking historical evidence, he tries to explain what *might* have happened in terms of the principles of human nature. This explanation we might expect of Hume, whose first interest was philosophy. One twentieth-century commentator remarked of the philosophy in the *History* that "It is only when the *History of England* is read with a critical eye that the immense amount of thought involved in it becomes apparent, and the reader realizes that what seemed to be a simple, straightforward narrative of fact is really a highly polished and skilfully articulated philosophy of history. Moreover, the philosophy is so subtly insinuated into the texture of the work, so artistically blended with it, that the task if effecting a separation is by no means easy."[7] While I do not think we can find isomorphic correlations between the ideas in the *History of England* and Hume's ethical and metaphysical positions, we can safely assume that his philosophical inclinations predisposed him to treat the uncertain in history the same way in which he treated it in philosophy. He specifically admits to this procedure in discussing Queen Elizabeth's reign: "whoever enlarges his view, and reflects on the situations, will remark the necessary progress of human affairs, and the operations of those principles, which are inherent in human nature" (*History*, 4:19).

When the facts are too few or too general, the historian fills in what he can with observations based upon his particular insight into human nature. What is he to do when the facts are many? Hume addressed himself to this problem in opening his discussion of Henry III, with the following observation: "Most sciences, in proportion as they encrease and improve, invent methods by which they facilitate their reasonings; and, employing general theorems, are enabled to comprehend, in a few propositions a great number of inferences and conclusions. History also, being a collection of facts which are multiplying without end, is obliged to adopt such arts of abridgment, to retain the more material events, and to drop all the minute circumstances, which are only interesting during the time, or to the persons engaged in the transaction" (*History*, 2:3–4). Hume then remarks that this truth is nowhere more evident than in the reign of Henry III: no mortal would be patient enough to read all the trivia and frivolities by which the weaknesses of "so mean a prince as Henry" were distinguished.

We might object to this procedure, as Professor J. B. Black did[8], by seeing in it a subjective interpretation of history, which would discourage historical research by assuming that all facts are not potentially valuable. Yet we must remember that Hume was writing what was really the first successful history of England, and he foresaw these difficulties. The histories of others had often failed simply because they crammed too much minutiae into their narratives, and James Ralph's history was a good example of this practice. Hume's history was indeed different in its selectivity, and part of his methodology involved a wish to have his *History of England* be a popular and commercial success. The view articulated above represents Hume's attempts to cope both with the vastness of English history and its relative importance. Events of interest only to the professional student of history could be safely omitted if no injustice were done to the events that actually shaped men's lives. For convenience, I have suggested that Hume's *History* was comprehensive; perhaps it would be more exact to say that Hume wanted his *History* to be both comprehensible and comprehending. He wanted it to appeal to the average intelligent reader of this time; he wanted to exhibit both a grasp of the important affairs of state and an ability to see them in the proper perspective; and he wanted this perspective to inculcate certain moral attitudes.

This desire to limit the scope of a historical discussion, as well as the physical size of the volumes, is expressed in Hume's letter to the historian William Robertson. Robertson's *History of Scotland* appeared 29 January 1759; Hume read it and made several comments about the style and the methodology. Having finished one history, Robertson was looking for the subject of another and apparently wrote to Hume for some suggestions. Hume pointed out the difficulties, and the advantages, of ancient Greek history and then mentioned Thomas Leland's *History of the Life and Reign of Philip, King of Macedon* (1758): "There is one Dr Leland, who has lately wrote the Life of Philip of Macedon, which is one of the best Periods: The Book, they tell me, is perfectly well wrote; yet it has had such small Sale, & has so little excited the Attention of the Public, that the Author has Reason to think his Labour thrown away. I have not read the Book; but by the Size, I should judge it to be too particular. It is a pretty large Quarto; I think a Book of that Size sufficient for the whole History of Greece till the Death of Philip" (*NHL*, 48). While neither the modern historian nor the modern reader may approve of this arbitrary limit, Hume's reasons seem justifiable in his own terms. He did not "use" his *History* to preach to his readers, but he did impose arbitrary limits on his narrative exposition in order to appeal to as many readers as possible.

The preceding statements suggest that Hume was interested only in those periods of British history which had some profound effect on the course of British civilization. And, indeed, those periods received the most attention, as Hume himself realized. He remarked in the first chapter (actually, one of the last parts of the *History* to be written) that

Ingenious men, possessed of leisure, are apt to push their researches beyond the period, in which literary monuments are framed or preserved; without reflecting, that the history of past events is immediately lost or disfigured, when intrusted to memory and oral tradition, and that the adventures of barbarous nations, even if they were recorded, could afford little or no entertainment to men born in a more cultivated age. The convulsions of a civilized state usually compose the most instructive and most interesting part of its history; but the sudden, violent, and unprepared revolutions, incident to Barbarians, are so much guided by caprice, and terminate so often in cruelty that they disgust us by the uniformity of their appearance; and it is rather fortunate for letters that they are buried in silence and oblivion. (*History*, 1:3–4)

Hume's history is, he says, devoted to the ways in which civilization is advanced and not to the fables and traditions associated with a body of people. Hume's chief interest in writing history lies in the representation of the various forces—moral, political, and economic—which shaped the progress of British civilization and which improved political stability. The result was, he hoped, a "more full narration for those times, when the truth is both so well ascertained and so complete as to promise entertainment and instruction to the reader" (*History*, 1:4).[9]

Hume thus accepted, of his many guidelines, two cherished criteria of Renaissance and eighteenth-century critics: the entertainment and instruction of readers. History's value could be both hedonistic and utilitarian. Hume wanted to bring into proper focus all the events which contributed to the formation of civilized manners in Great Britain, to ascertain and examine the human motives and passions that lay behind the formal paraphernalia of government. He was admittedly selective when incorporating facts into his history, but he avoided what he would have called the "vulgar error" of ignoring facts that contravened the instructiveness of his examples. This methodology, faulty in some ways to the modern historian, led Hume into various judgments about the events or characters in his narration. Because of his selectivity and because of the wish to instruct and to entertain—among

other reasons—Hume permitted his *History of England* to display some of
his philosophical positions, political attitudes, and moral judgments.

The History of England: A Scottish Perspective

"I believe this is the historical Age and this the historical Nation: I know
no less than eight Histories upon the Stocks in this Country; all which have
different Degrees of Merit, from the Life of Christ, the most sublime of the
whole, as I presume from the Subject, to Dr Robertson's American History,
which lies in the other Extremity" (*HL,* 2:230). Hume made this observation in August 1770 in a letter to his printer, William Strahan. "This Country" is specifically Scotland. Robertson was indeed one of the greatest
historians of the day, of any day, but Hume seems to have felt that the Scots,
by virtue of their history prior to the union with England in 1707 (and to a
certain extent after that), had an especially valuable perspective from which
to view the events in "these islands," as well as a contribution to make to the
study of history in general. Hume's comment to Strahan is consonant with
an earlier one made in a letter to Hugh Blair, on 28 March 1769: "History,
I think, is the Favourite Reading, and our other Friend [i.e., Robertson], the
favourite Historian" (*HL,* 2:196–97).

Hume had entitled the first volume of his history *The History of Great
Britain,* turning to the less accurate but more cosmopolitan *History of England* for the remaining volumes. In the late twentieth century, with nationalistic movements, sentiments, and prejudices seemingly gaining in
strength day by day, it is perhaps difficult to remind ourselves that "enlightened" Scots in the middle of the eighteenth century regarded the Act of
Union of 1707, uniting Scotland with England, as a mitigated blessing, but
a blessing nevertheless. Like many other Scots, Hume was interested in de-
veloping a culture and a civil polity that would, by means of commerce and
learning, enhance the constitutional interdependence of the two countries.
When Hume arrives at a discussion of the history of Scotland in chapter 13
of his *History,* he notes, without any apology, "We now come to give an account of the state of affairs in Scotland, which gave rise to the most interesting transactions of this reign [i.e., Edward I], and of some of the
subsequent; though the intercourse of that kingdom with England, either in
peace or war, had hitherto produced so few events of moment, that, to avoid
tediousness, we have omitted many of them, and have been very concise in
relating the rest." He then speaks of the government of Scotland having
been "continually exposed to those factions and convulsions, which are incident to all barbarous, and to many civilized nations" (*History,* 2:83).

Examining the moment when Edward I succeeded in his attempts to subordinate Scotland to the interests of England, Hume approaches the inevitable rebellion of the Scots, under the guidance of one of Scotland's greatest patriots and military heroes, William Wallace, with judicious detachment, even insouciance: "This man, whose valorous exploits are the object of just admiration, but have been much exaggerated by the traditions of his countrymen." A few sentences later, however, Hume invokes the rhetoric of narrative romance to describe Wallace: "He was endowed with gigantic force of body, with heroic courage of mind, with disinterested magnanimity, with incredible patience, and ability to bear hunger, fatigue, and all the severities of the seasons; and he soon acquired, among those desperate fugitives, that authority, to which his virtues so justly intitled him" (*History*, 2:125–26). Hume's language here is as extravagant as it ever gets, and while it is possible that he is mocking the exaggeration to which he had earlier alluded, Hume's narration continues to present Wallace in these superhuman terms.

Wallace was in his mid-thirties when Edward ordered his execution at Tower Hill. Asserting that Edward's "natural bravery and magnanimity" should have led him to respect similar qualities in Wallace, Hume regards Wallace's execution as the "unworthy fate of a *hero,* who, through a course of many years, had, with signal conduct, intrepidity, and perseverance, defended, against a public and oppressive enemy, the liberties of his native country" (*History*, 2:135; my italics). What the "liberties" of Scotland were at that time Hume fails to say, but one is obliged to wonder if they flourished in spite of the "factions and convulsions, which are incident to all barbarous nations." However, the designation of Wallace as a "hero" is unusual, and Hume does not often resort to this kind of vocabulary in describing mortal men.

Hume's almost hagiographic memorialization of Wallace would probably not have sounded extravagant or excessive to many of his countrymen, and the "barbarous" treatment of "that gallant chief" inspired another leader, Robert Bruce. In his account of Bruce, Hume deliberately relies on Scottish historians: "not that their authority is in general any-wise comparable to that of the English; but because they may be supposed sometimes better informed concerning facts, which so nearly interested their own nation" (*History*, 2:137). Hume's choice of words betrays his historian's unease at the empirical validity of his sources, but the careful juxtaposition of "supposed" and "sometimes" excuses their lack of authority when compared to English historians. It is not, however, their authority that Hume is invoking, but their knowledge. Hume seems to have forgotten what he had said

about testimony in the first *Enquiry*: "The wise lend a very academic faith
to every report which favours the passion of the reporter; whether it magni-
fies his country, his family or himself, or in any other way strikes in with his
natural inclinations and propensities" (*Works*, 4:104; *ECHU*, 125).

Once again, Hume deploys the vocabulary of narrative romance: Bruce,
we are told, "had long harboured in his breast the design of freeing his enslaved country"; Bruce sought allies "to live or die . . . to redeem the Scottish name"; he laid before his fellow Scots the "joyful prospect of recovering
from the fraudulent usurper" their old independence; he appealed to them
to follow their "rightful prince, who knew no medium between death and
victory," and appealed also to their "valour," their "generous ancestors," and
urged them "to perish, like brave men, with swords in their hands." Of
course, Bruce's plea, "assisted by the graces of his youth and manly deport-
ment," has the proper effect, and most of the men accept his leadership; one
man does not, and Bruce has to dispatch this doubter, John Cummin, by
stabbing him, after which one of Bruce's supporters, Sir Thomas
Kirkpatric, makes assurance double sure by stabbing poor Cummin again.
After two paragraphs in which the bravery, courage, and virtue of Bruce
have been extolled in no uncertain way, and in language that one would not
immediately associate with a skeptical philosopher, Hume seems to remember that historical judgment requires less involvement in his own narrative:
"This deed [i.e., the murder of Cummin] of Bruce and his associates, which
contains circumstances justly condemned by our present manners, was regarded in that age, as an effort of manly vigour and just policy" (*History*,
2:138–39). Hume's reader is likely to feel that Hume's belletristic representation of Bruce's activities is more of an endorsement than a condemna-
tion. In resorting to the passive voice, Hume evades the problem of
providing verification or evidence for his assertion.

What heroes can England produce that could possibly compare to these
larger than life figures, whose heroic deeds and unshakeable courage are offered as paradigms? No reader of English literature or English history is
likely to be unaware of Shakespeare's magnificent Henry V: here was a hero
for his own age and for all time. Perhaps a Scottish historian might have different ideas. Hume pays the appropriate attention to Prince Hal's dubious
youthful activities and brings us to the famous battle with the Percy family.
Here, Prince Henry is Henry IV's "gallant son, whose military achievements
were afterwards so renowned," but it is the Scotsman, Douglas, Henry IV's
opponent who "performed feats of valour, which are almost incredible," not,
one presumes, unlike those of Wallace and Bruce. Hume notes with satisfaction that some of the King's enemies were punished or beheaded, but

Wallace "was treated with the courtesy due to his rank and merit." (*History,* 2:341). Even in this familiar episode of English history, Hume lingers on the attractive features of a Scottish demeanor.

The misgivings that Henry's youthful activities had aroused in the English proved to be well-founded but irrelevant: Henry became a model monarch, and his character appeared even brighter when it was contrasted with his former behavior. In Hume's account, he proves to be courteous and magnanimous, as well as a good administrator. But Shakespeare made him, at the battle of Agincourt, the greatest of English heroes, a theme of honour and renown. Hume's account is, however, of the battle itself, and not Henry's role in it, although Hume does say of Henry that "perceiving his advantage, [he] ordered the English archers, who were light and unincumbered, to advance upon the enemy, and seize the moment of victory." Ten thousand French were killed in the battle, Henry "was master of 14,000 prisoners," and the English losses "exceeded not forty; though some writers, with greater probability, make the number more considerable" (*History,* 2:365–66). So much for the victory that

> . . . gentlemen in England now a-bed
> Shall think themselves accurs'd they were not here,
> And hold their manhoods cheap whiles any speak
> That fought with us upon Saint Crispin's day.
> (*Henry V,* 4:iii, 64–67)

Perhaps it is unreasonable to expect Hume to lavish the powerful colors on his rhetorical palette upon a King who had already dwarfed any of the canvases depicting him, and Hume was certainly not going to compete with Shakespeare for the honor of describing Henry V's heroism.

Warriors and fighters have been traditional heroes, their virtues sung and their exploits imitated. Hume is not impervious to military achievements, but his particular interest in the *History of England* was in those periods when civilization began to displace barbarism, when polite culture and learning flourished in the kingdom, when the human sciences as well as the physical sciences advanced. Hume's admiration for at least one Englishman is unqualified: "In Newton this island may boast of having produced the greatest and rarest genius that ever arose for the ornament and instruction of the species. . . . He was . . . long unknown to the world; but his reputation at last broke out with a lustre, which scarcely any writer, during his own lifetime, had ever before attained" (*History,* 6:542). Is it accidental that Hume describes Sir Isaac Newton not as an Englishman, but as a "genius" of "this island"? Just before this description of Newton, he had noted "there arose in England some men of superior genius," a group including Robert Boyle and Newton, so Newton's Englishness could not have been overlooked. Among the other men of genius are John Wilkins, Christopher Wren, John Wallis, Thomas Sydenham, and Robert Hooke—all Englishmen.

Hume had, however, managed to find a Scottish genius as well, although he makes no appearance with Newton and others. Indeed, Hume has to bring him into his narrative almost by irrelevant force. In discussing events during 1645, shortly after Cromwell's procession to power, he brings up the loyalty of the Earl of Montrose to the king, who had among his supporters, "lord Napier of Merchiston, son of the famous inventor of the logarithms, the person to whom the title of a GREAT MAN is more justly due, than to any other, whom his country [i.e., Scotland] ever produced" (*History*, 5:462). Earlier, Hume had alluded to "the famous Napier" (*History*, 5:155). The discovery, or invention, by John Napier (1550–1617) of logarithms un-doubtedly transformed mathematics, but Hume seems to require his pres-ence in his *History* to endorse the political activities of his son. Nevertheless, he was, for Hume, an authentic Scottish "great man," if not quite a "hero." As it happens, Hume conveniently overlooks the role of Henry Briggs (1561–1630), the English mathematician who made the trip to Edinburgh to meet Napier and whose work in collaboration with Napier refined and defined the system of logarithms.

Because Hume was, in so many respects, a cosmopolitan and worldly fig-ure, at ease in the salons of Paris as well as on military expeditions, his Scot-tish background and prepossessions can be overlooked. Duncan Forbes, in his study of Hume's "philosophical politics," notes that Hume's "concern for literature and his dislike of the English . . . comes through loud and clear in the letters; the latter, rising to a pitch of *Schadenfreude* at time, is, among other things and especially, an inflammation of a life-long complaint against the 'great men' of England and his fierce desire to be independent of them, his dislike of English snobbery and the hauteur of the English ruling class. . . . When Hume talked about the English 'barbarians,' it was often the great men, not the mob, that he had in mind."[10] This view may be slightly exaggerated—Hume did, after all, have a number of English friends and was not so parochial as many Scotsmen of his day were—but Hume's nationalism was more creative than resentful. In his *History of En-gland,* his vocabulary and his narrative strategy nevertheless disclose an ea-gerness to validate and to venerate achievements by men who were Scots first and from "this island" next.

The History of England: Principles in Retrospect

To observe that we can find in a historical work the presuppositions and principles of the author is hardly astonishing. No one doubts that the beliefs and opinions of an author influence or affect his writing in one way or another. He can be bitterly polemical, as Bishop William Warburton was, without realizing just how far from the mainstream of ideas he is. To someone like Warburton, the most extravagant statements may seem too obvious for clarification; certain principles become so much a part of the writer's personality, as well as the rhetoric with which one expresses oneself, that they seem indistinguishable from the objects of perception. In contrast, another author may be keenly aware that his opinions, prejudices, and ideas are uncommon and often, unacceptable. Attempting to avoid fractious partisanship, this author over-compensates for his ideas and may completely obliterate them. He goes out of his way to be fair to the opposition, with the result that he sometimes appears to be numbered among those whom he opposes. To tread the thin line between these two extremes is a cliché every writer invokes, and Hume, as we have seen, invoked it, at least in a modified form. As Hume himself tells us in his autobiography, his *History* had the misfortune of both extremes. Because he bent over backwards to be fair to policies and people not meeting his approval, Hume was accused of being one of them; because of his reputation as a dangerous freethinker, he was accused of injecting atheism into his work, though there is also plenty of evidence in the *History* to confirm Hume's deep and thoughtful hostility to religious bigotry and cabals.

To find Hume's opinions and judgments about events and people in the *History of England* requires little effort. What distinguishes them at once from his philosophical speculations and reasoning is the rhetoric. Hume is nowhere *less* skeptical about the efficacy of moral judgments, for example, than in the *History of England*. These judgments are not fixed by either the rhetoric or the logic that we discover in his abstract contemplations about the principles of morals, politics, or economics. It is always the prerogative of any writer to make moral judgments, regardless of the work under consideration. In Hume's case, one could ask what is otherwise the purpose of "moral science" if not to make assessments or judgments. No reader of Samuel Johnson's writings can be unaware of the tenacity with which moral attitudes and prescriptions affix themselves to almost all of his literary principles. In fact, Dr. Johnson would probably have approved of most of Hume's moral and political judgments in the *History of England,* if he had read it.[11] While Hume is not so openly moralistic as Dr. Johnson—and he had of course displeased Johnson with his skeptical inquiries into the principles of religion and morality—his moral judgments could easily coincide with Johnson's, except when Hume's judgments were made as a result of what Hume considered an abuse of religious power.

Writing of the early Anglo-Saxon kings, Hume discovered innumerable abuses of religious power, most of which resulted from the imposition of clerical authority in secular matters. The misfortunes of King Edwy illustrate the abuses. Hume narrates Edwy's passion for Princess Elgiva, whose "softer pleasures" led to their being discovered, apparently, *in flagrante delicto*. Dunstan, the Abbott of Glastenbury, and Odo, the Archbishop of Canterbury, hoped to improve their political position by exploiting their awareness of this dalliance. Edwy managed, however, to defeat them and succeeded in banishing Dunstan. During Dunstan's absence, however, his cabal was active; it first tortured and then banished Elgiva. When she attempted to return, Odo had her murdered; with the return of Dunstan, Odo instituted a revolt against King Edwy, who was excommunicated. The death of Edwy passed the crown to his brother Edgar. In discussing the peaceful reign of Edgar, Hume, whose displeasure at the treatment of Edwy and Elgiva is clear, remarks, "Such is the ascendant which may be attained, by hypocrisy and cabal, over mankind" (*History,* 1:2, 100). Hume's judgment is a combination of moral indignation and religious disaffection. In this instance, Hume is pointing up the disproportion between the values of a religious temperament and their secular application.

Like many of Hume's moral judgments, the preceding one harshly evaluated the sacrosanct veil that barbarous activity in the name of religion wrapped around itself. Transactions between church and state were invested with an authority that few would challenge and even fewer question. In this respect, the *History of England* is one of the best introductions to Hume's profound and principled detestation of the tyrannies to which religious convictions give rise. Religious authority, powerful by itself because of fear and superstition, when joined with secular power could achieve an effective and often brutal "ascendant" over the populace. Because of the preeminence of religious customs and dogmas, any measures taken on behalf of religion were beyond criticism or correction. In some respects, eighteenth-century England shared this same attitude that anything done in the name of religion or done to promote piety was sacred and inviolable. That such an attitude could create much hypocrisy is obvious.

Hume emphasized the barbarity and wickedness of this kind of religious hypocrisy in order to show the disruptive influence of religious authoritarianism when injected into civil and secular concerns.[12] Despite Locke's eloquent plea in his *Letter concerning Toleration* (1689), religious power in the eighteenth century still interposed itself between the citizen and the state, sometimes with disastrous results, of which the abortive attempt in 1753 to legalize the naturalization of Jews is one example. Whatever its causes and whatever its effects, Hume deplored the interferences of churchly authority in civil or secular matters. The *History of England* often relates the chaos produced by this interference.

Hume is often severe about the foibles and aggrandizements of the church or of any institution which attempts tyranny. In contrast to this severity, the reader finds Hume frequently sympathetic to misfortunes resulting from the frailty of human nature—if tyranny is absent. An example appears in Hume's account of King Edgar's quest for suitable bedmates. On one occasion, in Andover, Edgar requested the compliance of his host's daughter, whose charms had overwhelmed him, for the night. The mother, determined not to dishonor her family while nonetheless appearing to acquiesce to the King's impetuosity, agreed; but she substituted an attractive waiting-maid, Elfleda, for her daughter. The King, pleased with Elfleda's charms, was not displeased with the deception and took Elfleda as his favorite mistress. Shortly after doing so, he heard of the still greater beauty of a country woman, Elfrida. Wishing to know more, he sent his favorite, Earl Athelwold, to find out if reports of Elfrida's beauty and charms were true. They were, but Athelwold was determined to have her for his own and reported to the King that her wealth and position had blinded potential suitors to the plainness of her face.

Satisfied with this account, and hearing from Athelwold that he would like to take Elfrida as his wife in order to improve his own fortune and position, King Edgar relinquished his claim. But clever deceptions must, unfortunately, come to an end. The King learned of Athelwold's trickery, and demanded to visit him and his new wife. Athelwold cautioned her against revealing the truth for fear of his life, but Elfrida, jealous that she had been deprived of a potential queenship, appeared in all her splendor. Hume concludes his narration in this manner: "she excited at once in his [Edgar's] bosom the highest love towards herself, and the most furious desire of revenge against her husband. He knew, however, to dissemble these passions; and seducing Athelwold into a wood, on pretence of hunting, he stabbed him with his own hand, and soon after publickly espoused Elfrida" (*History,* 1:2, 102). Then Hume simply begins another paragraph by saying "Before we conclude our account," leaving his readers to decorate their imaginations as best they can with the rhetorical ornaments he provides.

To the modern reader, a standard of morality which condemns religious hypocrisy and usurpation of civil power and which seems tacitly to condone the *crime passionel* is at least curious. Yet we should not shorten Hume's view to fit our own standards. First, he catalogues many more instances of religious chicanery—and judges them harshly—than instances of murder for the sake of sensual gratification. Elsewhere in the *History* he condemns murders and executions which were thought justifiable to a large number of his countrymen. His treatment of Charles I is a case in point. We have to remember that he had a most unfavorable opinion of the Dark Ages and Middle Ages, as may be seen in Appendices 1 and 2 of the first volume of the *History*. The murder of one person in order to gain his wife would have seemed, in those times, a common instrument of revenge to Hume. The Anglo-Saxon and Anglo-Norman kings and peoples were barbarians, and he did not expect civilized behavior from them.[13] Finally, we can acknowledge that historians or philosophers have to have more courage to condemn religion than to condemn murder. To disapprove of murder hardly testifies to moral courage, but to disapprove of certain religious activities, in a time when they might be widely admired, condoned, or practiced, does testify to moral courage. Even so, Hume is almost always harsher upon institutional tyranny than he is on personal, or individual, tyranny.

Tyranny takes many forms, of course, and Hume is particularly sensitive to political tyranny carried out in the homiletics of Christian piety. Although Hume was not an apologist for any form of religion, be it Christian, Jewish, or Buddhist, he was inclined to defend minority religions against the impositions of majority ones. In the reign of Henry II, mentioned in section 1 of this chapter, Hume discusses persecutions of the Jews, and in this section, we see an example of the way in which the speculative part of his methodology leads to some of his moral judgments. Disapproving of the high interest rates in this period (*ca.* 1272), Hume conjectures about the fortunes, literal and figurative, of the Jews: "It is easy to imagine how precarious their state must have been under an indigent prince, somewhat restrained in his tyranny over his native subjects, but who possessed an unlimited authority over the Jews, the sole proprietors of money in the kingdom, and hated, on account of their riches, their religion, and their usury: Yet will our ideas scarcely come up to the extortions which in fact we find to have been practised upon them" (*History*, 2:12, 68). This conjecture is then supported by a series of instances demonstrating the ways in which the Jews were tyrannized.

In order to express his distaste for this tyranny, Hume inquires into the motives of tyrants. They offered as a "better pretence for extortions, the improbable and absurd accusation, which has been at different times advanced against that nation . . . that they had crucified a child in derision of the sufferings of Christ . . . It is in no wise credible, that even the antipathy born them by the Christians, and the oppressions under which they laboured, would ever have pushed them to be guilty of that dangerous enormity" (*History*, 2:69). Hume's rhetorical disapproval also disputes the evidence produced against the Jews; as ever, he opposed tyranny that hid under the name of piety. In addition, he suggests that any ensuing violence would have been the result of the Jews' unstable position. Their usury, Hume argues, was understandable when recognized as an attempt to make some compensation for the indignities and the continual peril that were the whole of their existence.

Hume attributes acts of violence against the Jews in Henry III's reign partially to bigotry but primarily to "avidity and rapine." The desire to convert Jews to Christianity by no means corresponded to the biblical injunctions to proselytize. For a Jew to become a Christian and perhaps escape lifelong persecution was a financial hazard: in France, any Jew embracing Christianity forfeited his real and personal property to the king or any of his followers. Of this practice, Hume makes the following ironic remark: "These plunderers were careful, lest the profits, accruing from their dominion over that unhappy race should be diminished by their conversion" (*History*, 2:67). This sentence, incidentally and two others preceding it (which I summarized at the first of this paragraph) did not appear in the first edition, nor in any of the editions published in Hume's lifetime. While I should not argue that this inclusion, made as one of Hume's last revisions, necessarily proves anything, it does indicate Hume's inclination to make moral judgments about popular or unpopular subjects.

The treatment of the Jews also gives Hume many opportunities for packing together facts, irony, judgment, and humor. He describes the reign of Edward I, successor to Henry III. During Edward's reign a statute was enacted to banish all Jews from England. This banishment Hume attributes to the King's rapacity and zeal and to the poverty of the crown: "Among the various disorders, to which the kingdom was subject, no one was more universally complained of than the adulteration of the coin; and as this crime required more art than the English of that age, who chiefly employed force and violence in their iniquities, the imputation fell upon the Jews." Note the ambiguities that arise from describing the same feature with three different nouns: "disorders," "crime," "iniquities"; note also, the inability of the English to manage sufficient "art" to counterfeit coins and to be obliged to disrupt life by force and violence; note, finally, the deliberate inexactitude of "fell," so that the Jews are implicitly absolved of the crimes alleged against them. Little wonder, then, that Hume can describe the King's behavior in hanging two hundred and eighty Jews and banishing fifteen thousand from the kingdom, as "egregious tyranny" (*History,* 2:13, 76, 78).

About the time this volume of the *History of England* was being written, the Pelhams were attempting to legalize the naturalization of the Jews. Of the Naturalisation Bill, W. E. H. Lecky remarks that "There is no page in the history of the eighteenth century that shows more decisively how low was the intellectual and political conditions of English public opinion. According to its opponents, the Jewish Naturalisation Bill sold the birthright of Englishmen for nothing: it was a distinct abandonment of Christianity, it would draw upon England all the curses which Providence had attached to the Jews."[14] Opposition to the bill and prejudice against the Jews was widespread and tenacious during the 1750s. For Hume openly to accuse English kings of "egregious tyranny" against the Jews, when many of his countrymen probably thought Edward had done the right thing, was not so courageous as his unpopular questioning of religion's postulates. It was, however, a moral judgment that many men, from an excess of prudence, would not have made. Hume sought no special consideration for the Jews just because they were Jews, but he objected strongly to their persecution and even more strongly to the trumped-up reasons offered in justification of that persecution.[15]

I have focused only briefly on Hume's representation of the treatment of the Jews, but it does offer a method, albeit somewhat artificial, for displaying Hume's penchant for a certain kind of moral judgment in his *History,* a moral judgment which, as we have seen, is often mixed with politics. Indeed, while Hume's *History* is unmistakeably a political history, politics and morality are often so closely intertwined as to be indistinguishable. The logic and rhetoric of Hume's various inquiries into the principles of morals in no way fixed the language of his own moral judgments; he would have been the first to admit this seeming disparity. His naturalistic ethic left plenty of room for individual moral judgments, and he had no hesitation in making them. For example, the chicaneries of the Earl of Somerset during the reign of James I earn this reproof: "The favourite had hitherto escaped the enquiry of justice; but he had not escaped that still voice, which can make itself be heard amidst all the hurry and flattery of a court, and astonishes the criminal with a just representation of his most secret enormities" (*History,* 5:60–61).

Somerset had been charged, along with other accomplices and his wife, the countess, with the murder of Sir Thomas Overbury. The accomplices were eventually punished, but Somerset and his wife were pardoned. Of this action, Hume asserts "It must be confessed that James's fortitude had been highly laudable, had he persisted in his first intention of consigning over to severe justice all the criminals: But let us still beware of blaming him too harshly, if, on the approach of the fatal hour, he scrupled to deliver into the hands of the executioner, persons whom he had once favoured with his most tender affections" (*History,* 5:63). A few sentences later, Hume specifically attributes the King's mercy to the "great remains of tenderness, which James still felt for Somerset."

Hume clearly believes that the persistent voice of conscience reminded Somerset of the enormity of his crimes. While we may find no exact corollary in his philosophical writings for this sentiment, we can derive it from Hume's conception of the moral sense. In the *Treatise,* he argued that moral decisions were derived from a moral sense, that morality was something we "felt" rather than judged (*Treatise,* 3:i, 2). Hume obviously could not have known whether Somerset had escaped that "still voice," but he assumed a uniformity of sentiment among mankind. Thus, the voice of conscience would be felt as easily in Somerset's time as in Hume's. Although Hume has little sympathy for Somerset, he sympathizes with James's difficulties in punishing a fallen friend. Hume recognized loyalty as one of the most important virtues, and he frequently admires it in the *History of England,* even when its results are deplorable.

Deplorable results in human transactions were usually mitigated by Hume's sympathetic understanding of human frailty. He made no such concessions to acts born of religious sentiments, but he applauded religious innovations which promoted certain moral principles. The rise of the Independents during the reign of Charles I is a case in point. Here Hume permits an epistemological distinction between two religious sects, the Independents and the Presbyterians, to lead to a qualified approval of the Independents' activities. The "enthusiastic spirit"—or religious fanaticism—of the time encouraged fervent piety: "In proportion to its degree of fanaticism, each sect became dangerous and destructive; and as the independents went a note higher than the presbyterians, they could less be restrained within any bounds of temper and moderation. From this distinction, as from a first principle, were derived, by a necessary consequence, all the other differences of these two sects" (*History,* 5:442).

The Independents opposed the intrusion of clerical authority into secular life, as well as that of the magistrate into religious matters. Believing in none of the hierarchical distinctions of rank set up by other churches, the Independents promulgated the idea that an individual could have instantaneous communication with God for the purpose of consecration and thus validation of what few sacraments they accepted. To Hume, all this is more-or-less good, and he contrasts their freedom to Catholic dogmatism and to the Presbyterians' elaborate and doctrinaire tenets. As for the Independents, they, "from the extremity of the same zeal, were led into the milder principles of toleration . . . Of all christian sects, this was the first, which, during its prosperity as well as its adversity, always adopted the principle of toleration; and, it is remarkable that so reasonable a doctrine owed its origin, not to reasoning, but to the height of extravagance and fanaticism" (*History*, 5:443). Even with the cautious qualification, "milder principles of toleration," Hume has found a good word to say about a religious sect, even if he seems nonplussed at the outcome of their fanaticism.

The skepticism in Hume's moral principles, I think we have seen, had less influence on his value judgments in the *History of England* than his inclinations and preferences. Frequently he does avoid making a moral or political commitment, either by implication or by direct statement. When the occasion demands that some judgment or evaluation be made, Hume does not shrink from the task. In writing a history of England, he had accepted, as part of his duty, the necessity of pointing out flaws and errors in men and institutions. Although he did not use the *History of England* to dramatize his ideas, his philosophical presumptions guided him in the representation of history's events.[16]

I do not wish to suggest that Hume's *History* is totally philosophical. It is "philosophical" only in so far as it reflects his attitudes towards some of the traditional concerns of philosophy; yet almost any history will reflect some of its author's preconceptions about human beings or institutions. Hume's primary occupation in the *History of England* is to dramatize the progress, change, and evolution of constitutional government. While he emphasizes the society and culture of each epoch, his principal interest lies in the improvement of governmental stability, of civil and individual liberty, and of political unity.[17] In his treatment of the data of history, he often reveals the way in which knowledge of the past should illuminate and clarify an age's present problems. In this sense, then, the importance of his *History of England* lies both in its emphasis on constitutional order and its representation of a specific set of moral and political values.

These assertions may not always be applicable to particular events that Hume treats. Any attempt to analyze the *History of England* in terms of a specific concept, prejudice, or faction is automatically doomed to failure. It could be read without reference to any of Hume's other works, but an intensive reading of the *History of England* enlarges our understanding of those other works, and vice versa. Although it has been superseded in accu-

could have any force because it would be expressed in a manner whose accuracy we could never possibly verify—emotionally, physically, or intellectually. To know God, or even God's attributes, we must have a means of knowing; and Demea's principles are self-vitiating.

Philo does not reply directly to Cleanthes; he simply reinforces his earlier criticisms of the design argument. He points out that the assignment of one particular cause to one event does not explain the cause of that cause. By extrapolating from our experience certain human events that "prove" design in the world and hence an "Author of Nature," we lead ourselves into a series of infinitely regressing causes. Whatever procedure or methodology we may use to prove design in nature, we can never escape human curiosity; when we go one step beyond our experience in the search for causes, we cannot help inviting an infinite regression. Philo even suggests a method which Cleanthes could pursue but wisely does not: "By supposing [the present material World] to contain the Principle of its Order within itself, we really assert it to be God; and the sooner we arrive at that divine Being so much the better" (*Dialogues*, 185; *Works*, 2:408).

Cleanthes replies to this criticism by saying that once he has found his Deity, he is content to go no farther. In part 5, after Philo has reasserted the unique quality of the creation of the world, a quality of which we have no experience, Cleanthes affirms that the hypothesis of design recurs in all Philo's arguments. He regards this concession as a "sufficient Foundation for Religion." This discussion advances iconoclastically enough through part 6, and in part 7 some of the drama begins to unfold when Philo points out that the universe bears a greater resemblance to animal bodies and vegetables than to the productions of human art. If Cleanthes agrees with his previous contention that like causes produce like results, then he must agree that the origin of the world should be attributed to generation or vegetation rather than to reason or design. A comet's tail, Philo says, can contain the "seed" of a new world. The metaphor of vegetation would seem to be more informing and accurate than the hypothesis of design. Oddly enough, it is Demea who makes a strongly Humean criticism of this reasoning: "What *Data* have you for such extraordinary Conclusions? And is the slight, imaginary Resemblance of the World to a Vegetable or an Animal sufficient to establish the same Inference with regard to both?" (*Dialogues*, 203; *Works*, 2:422).

Philo agrees with Demea. He was simply demonstrating a way in which Cleanthes' logic, pushed to its inescapable implications, defeats his own arguments. After some second thoughts, Demea opines that the vegetative quality of the world, if true, would still be another instance of the validity of the argument from design. From what other faculty but design could such

racy by more "scientific" histories of England (or Britain), it is still one of the most readable histories of England. Few would deny that Hume presented the events, institutions, and characters of English history with clarity, energy, and insight. Its sheer readability makes it as rewarding to read as Gibbon's *Decline and Fall,* and it now has the great advantage of being readily available in an excellent, inexpensive text. We may read it with a constant sense of Hume's lively and enlivening irony: writing for example, about the supporters of Charles I, Hume comments, "Being commonly men of birth and fortune, to whom excesses are less pernicious than to the vulgar, they were too apt to indulge themselves in all pleasures, particularly those of the table" (*History,* 6:141). We ignore the question-begging in order to relish the humor. Small wonder, then, that, in the 1960s, a newspaper columnist and cracker-barrel philosopher, Harry Golden, mentioned it as one of the seminal works of literature which the student, interested in reading for the sake of reading, ought to read.[18]

Chapter Six

Hume and Religious Skepticism

Religion and Philosophy: "The Natural History of Religion"

The Reverend William Warburton wrote about Hume's "natural History of Religion," when it was to be published by Millar:[1] "The design of the first essay is the very same with all Lord Bolingbroke's to establish *naturalism*, a species of atheism, instead of religion: and he employs one of Bolingbroke's arguments for it . . . He is establishing atheism; and in one single line of a long essay professes to believe Christianity."[2] Warburton then attributes to Hume a mischief that even the most fanatical Antichrist could not have accomplished. He was right in perceiving that Hume's piety was outweighed by his skepticism; but, like many otherwise capable minds of the eighteenth century, Warburton was totally incapable of distinguishing between the mildest skepticism and atheism. The only alternatives to Christianity or to theism for many eighteenth–century divines were atheism or paganism. Even the Deists, who were aware of greater subtleties in religious inquiries, were often incapable of seeing how different Hume's skepticism was from any brand of atheism.

People like Warburton were doubtlessly irritated not so much by Hume's observations about particular religious problems as they were by his method. "The Natural History of Religion" embodies a historical–anthropological method to account for the "origin of religion in human nature" (*NHR*, 25; *Works*, 309). The statement that religion's origin could be found in human nature and not necessarily in divinity—that it had an origin no more "noble" than any of our passions—surely irritated Warburton and his fellow religionists. Hume has, in other words, not accepted their premises; indeed he has implicitly argued that the premises for religious argument are faulty. By not accepting the a priori assumptions of traditional theology, Hume confounded his readers and critics; by ignoring the alleged logic and rightness of their approach, he undoubtedly shocked them.

Hume's first argument in "The Natural History of Religion" takes the form of an inquiry into human nature's belief in a Deity. He finds that early forms of religion must have been polytheistic. Gradually, as people became more sophisticated, these forms became monotheistic: "The mind rises gradually, from inferior to superior: By abstracting from what is imperfect, it forms an idea of perfection" (*NHR,* 27; *Works,* 4:311). The ideas of perfection thus formed are transferred to some abstract idea of a deity. In early man, Hume argues that the regularity and order of the universe excited no curiosity; and early man assumed that at least one god existed for each phenomenon he did not understand.

In order to emphasize the mystical and quasi-mystical elements in religion, Hume directs attention to our general ignorance about causes, saying that unknown causes create ideas of omnipotence. Fear of what we do not know enslaves us. We assign human qualities to phenomena whose causes are unknown to us: we see human faces in the moon or armies in the clouds. From this propensity, Hume argues, arises a willingness to create a deity for every unexplainable phenomenon. Generally speaking, men tend to allegorize the unknown by means of the known: "And thus, however strong men's propensity to believe invisible, intelligent power in nature, their propensity is equally strong to rest their attention on sensible, visible objects; and in order to reconcile these opposite inclinations, they are led to unite the invisible power with some visible object" (*NHR,* 46; *Works,* 4:325). Hume allows that men are not capable of comprehending an unseen, non-sensible intelligence. He questions the reasons adduced for assigning, as manifestations of that quality, certain items or events in the world they do experience.

Two important and interrelated themes emerge from "The Natural History of Religion": (1) Hume regards religious sentiment as one of the passions of mankind; and (2) he finds no logical correlation between the a priori principles of religion and their origin in human nature. Religion thus has no more authority over the human mind, than any other passion would have, in so far as it is just another passion. Because religion deals with supernatural and seemingly unexplainable phenomena, it draws to itself an authority, a certitude missing in other passions. Because it offers man exaltation by means of something he cannot comprehend, he assumes that its origin can be only divine.

The logic of the first theme, broken down, leads irrevocably to the second. Religious sentiments that have prevailed in the world, or part of it, turn out to be nothing but "sick men's dreams." The principles that men attribute to the pervasiveness of a deity in the world are no more to be regarded than the "playsome whimsies of monkies in human shape, than the serious, positive, dogmatical asseverations of a being, who dignifies himself with the name of rational" (*NHR,* 94; *Works,* 4:362).

Hume is contending that the high–minded, exalting principles that are the theoretics of a religion bear little resemblance to the ways in which they appear in the ordinary world. Men emphatically and passionately attest to the alleged importance of religion in their lives: they act as if they had no confidence in the principles they have embraced. The most intelligent men in all ages have accepted the most absurd and ridiculous theologies as unquestionable: the most libertine men have advocated some of the most exalted or demanding ideas. The moralities promulgated by many religions have been the most stringent and the most noble in the world: they have produced chicanery and misery beyond measure. Finally, Hume continues, death—the surest prospect of mankind—has been assuaged by the promise of the soul's immortality; but, not even this security is sufficient to vanquish the terrors of the devout at death's approach.

The questions that Hume has raised in this deceptively short essay are not amenable to easy exegesis; they are monumentally important to those who find religion either emotionally or intellectually valuable. For a person exhibiting what Hume calls a "delicacy of taste" and who might call it "poignant" or even "poetic," the conclusion is startling: "The whole is a riddle, an aenigma, an inexplicable mystery. Doubt, uncertainty, suspence of judgment appear the only result of our most accurate scrutiny, concerning this subject. But such is the frailty of human reason, and such the irresistible contagion of opinion, that even this deliberate doubt could scarcely be upheld; did we not enlarge our view, and opposing one species of superstition to another, set them a quarrelling; while we ourselves, during their fury and contention, happily make our escape into the calm, tho' obscure regions of philosophy" (*NHR*, 95; *Works*, 4:363). Those whom William James called the "tough-minded," however, might find the conclusion inescapable.

Religion and Philosophy:
Dialogues concerning Natural Religion

Hume's final work, *Dialogues concerning Natural Region*, is in many ways his best. In the last quarter century it has attracted almost as much commentary as it had in the past. Certainly the best-written of his works, it does not suffer from the expansiveness of the *Treatise;* yet the *Dialogues concerning Natural Religion* manages to display almost all the important philosophical discoveries enunciated in it. Lacking the range but not the accessibility of the *Enquiries,* it is probably the best work for the student just beginning to read Hume, although it is not the one upon which Hume's reputation as a philosopher would be built. I think, however, that *Dialogues concerning Natural Religion* is Hume's best work because it uses the topics of religious belief and skepticism as starting points for a subtle induction into the problems of philosophy. It is also the most cogent presentation of religious views in eighteenth-century English literature, or, for that matter, literature of any century.

The work consists of a series of intellectual and religious exchanges among three interlocutors: Philo, the skeptic; Cleanthes, the empirical theologian; and Demea, the defender of revealed religion. Their roles are not quantitatively equal because Philo has the greatest number of words. Their proportions are: Philo, 67 percent, Cleanthes, 21 percent, and Demea, 12 percent.[3] This quantitative disparity carries over into the substance of the arguments. Although Pamphilus, the narrator, whose religious education was charged to Cleanthes, pronounces Cleanthes the victor at the end, this concession is an example of Humean irony.[4] Cleanthes is not merely a straw man, nor is Demea. They both express certain philosophies of religion affirmed by tradition. If Philo is permitted to speak twice as much as the other disputants combined, the imbalance is surely not unjust; for centuries after the birth and death of Christ, the skeptical voice went unheard, if indeed it existed. Even the emphasis upon *natural religion,* as distinct from supernatural religion, might have made John Knox lament the gross impiety of the age. It is a shocked Demea who protests that both Cleanthes and Philo pay no attention to the a priori arguments, not only for God's existence but for his benevolence, omnipotence, and omniscience.

The names of Hume's protagonists perhaps reveal something of his design in the *Dialogues.* Borrowing from Cicero, Hume calls his skeptic Philo.[5] In antiquity, Philo (160–80 B.C.) was the founder of the so-called fourth Academy, and academic philosophy had become synonymous with skeptical philosophy. Cicero studied under Philo, and in his discourse *De Natura Deorum,* the character Cotta represents the Academic or skeptical point of view. Some of the arguments of Hume's Philo are modeled on Cicero's Cotta. In addition, Cicero's character Balbus studied under Cleanthes (331–232 B.C.) who succeeded Zeno as head of the Stoic school of philosophy. Hume's Cleanthes, like Philo, takes some of his arguments and examples from Cotta in *De Natura Deorum.* Hume had also used the name "Cleanthes" in the *Enquiry concerning the Principles of Morals* (section 9).

Other parallels between Cicero and Hume can be found, particularly in the endings of their separate dialogues. Cicero, at the end of *De Natura Deorum,* gives the victory to the orthodox stoic, Balbus: "The Conversation ended here and we parted. *Velleius* judged that the Arguments of *Cotta* were truest; but Those of *Balbus* seem'd to me to have the greater probability."[6] Pamphilus, the narrator in Hume's *Dialogues,* concludes: "*Cleanthes* and *Philo* pursu'd not this Conversation much farther; and as nothing ever made greater Impression on me, than all the Reasonings of that day; so, I confess, that, upon a serious Review of the Whole, I cannot but think, that *Philo*'s Principles are more probably than *Demea*'s; but that those of *Cleanthes* approach still nearer to the Truth" (*Dialogues,* 261; *Works,* 2:468). The way in which the conclusion of the *Dialogues* is not modeled on Cicero seems at least as interesting and important as (if not more than) the parallels between the two conclusions.

Authors other than Cicero contribute to the intellectual genealogy of Philo, Cleanthes, and Demea. One of the more likely sources for some of Cleanthes' arguments is Bishop Joseph Butler, author of *The Analogy of Religion* (1736). Butler's *Analogy* and his *Sermons* both employ methods of reasoning similar to the expositions of Cleanthes.[7] While Butler supplies some of the method for Cleanthes, other authors supply, in some instances, exact words. Hume relied upon the scientific theism of two of Newton's disciples, Dr. George Cheyne and Colin Maclaurin, whose arguments he has employed almost word for word in some places.[8] Preserved Smith suggests that Cleanthes represents John Locke; his key to the identity of the character in the *Dialogues* is at least curious: "Cleanthes, derived from the Greek worlds for 'lock' and 'flower,' is John Locke, the flower of philosophy and the champion of the intellectual argument for the reasonableness of Christianity."[9] Still, another commentator, who has identified Cleanthes as a "follower of Locke," observes that he is actually "Hume's portrait of Bishop [George] Berkeley," and more recently it has been claimed that "the historical personage who most obviously fits the character is . . . [Henry Home,] Lord Kames."[10] Cleanthes' thought, however meager it may be in proportion to Philo's, is certainly respectable; the various viewpoints he reflects certainly imply that he is not a philosophical pantywaist. In fact, a number of commentators have thought Cleanthes to be Hume.[11]

Demea is more of a problem than Cleanthes. His religious principles are a priori ones, and he thinks that religion cannot be validated by empirical arguments—not because of religion's weakness but because its evidence is not conformable to human experience. Joseph Milner, whose reaction to the publication of the *Dialogues* I mentioned in chapter 1, said of Demea, "I have taken no notice of Hume's Demea, because I cannot find a feature of Christianity about him. Dr. [Samuel] Clark's metaphysics and the Gospel, have, I think, no sort of connection."[12] The connection, which Milner disputes, between Demea and Dr. Samuel

Clarke, the well-known intellectualist and rationalistic theologian, is tenuous; nevertheless, it is there.[13]

Hume found Clarke's metaphysical pronouncements just a bit silly, and Demea appears just that, in all his shock and bewilderment at Philo's and Cleanthes' failure to use a priori arguments to prove the existence of God. For a reader to see Demea as Clarke implies some intellectual capability on Demea's part, yet Demea's view has been said to represent that of the common people: "Demea, from the Greek word meaning 'common people' presents the ordinary opinions of the masses."[14] From the mathematical principles which Clarke had attempted to use as a model for his religious rationalism, to the skeptical principles of Pierre Bayle or to the mystical ones of Father Nicholas Malebranche is a long step; however, it has been taken: "'Demea' speaks in the manner of the French thinkers, Pierre Bayle, the skeptic, and the mystical Malebranche."[15] While no one has identified Hume as Demea, I should think the range of difference about Demea's intellectual heritage would suggest that Hume, while treating Demea ironically, did not make him an ignoramus.[16]

The identification of Philo as Hume is easy to make. Philo's skeptical principles, his method of argument, his indifference to threats of eternal damnation, and his unwillingness to acquiesce to the gospels as the final authority in matters of fact, very closely resemble the philosophical positions of David Hume. Preserved Smith has identified Philo as Hume by pointing out that "Philo means 'beloved,' just as 'David' does, and hence may be identified with Hume himself."[17] Hume's nineteenth-century biographer, John Hill Burton, states that Philo appears "first as a materialist of the Spinoza school" and then as a "skeptical demolisher"; he then identifies Cleanthes as Hume.[18] Professor Hendel avers that " 'Philo' seems to be a Francis Bacon, empirically-minded in science but skeptical toward reasoned knowledge in religion."[19]

Despite these identifications—and none of them is unreasonable—modern opinion, as in Hume's time, has generally concluded that Philo is Hume and that Hume would not be comfortable as Cleanthes.[20] Some exceptions have been those who have thought that Hume was the narrator, Pamphilus.[21] As I have suggested, Hume chose the names of his interlocutors carefully, with a view to their classical fittingness. In *De Natura Deorum*, Cotta, the skeptic, speaks of Pamphilus who was a student of Plato and says that Pamphilus was ridiculed by Epicurus. That Hume, whose philosophy was about as anti-Platonic as possible in the eighteenth century, would permit a Platonist, a man whose philosophy he scorned, to pass judgment on the arguments in the *Dialogues* is most unlikely.

I have gone into the intellectual homologues of Hume's characters in some detail because I think we ought to be aware of both the learning and precision that went into the composition of the *Dialogues*. The various, if sometimes conflicting, identifications of the interlocutors imply that a considerable amount of knowledge, history, and tradition lie behind the structure of the *Dialogues*. One reason why this work engages our attention repeatedly lies in its richness, a richness which derives in part from Hume's early and nearly obsessive aversion to religion, joined to his impressive knowledge of the history of philosophy and theology.

The chief concern of the *Dialogues* is an extended analysis of both the phenomenological evidence for the existence and benevolence of God and the proper way in which that evidence can be used. The method of this analysis finds Cleanthes employing the argument from design to establish the existence of a perfect, immutable, and divinely created order in the universe, while Philo raises objections to the logic Cleanthes employs. (Demea's arguments are all a priori and rational.) Hume had taken notice of the design argument in the *Treatise* and there he seemed to accept its validity:

The same imperfection [lack of an impression in the external world] attends our ideas of the Deity; but this can have no effect either on religion or morals. The order of the universe proves an omnipotent mind; that is, a mind whose will is *constantly attended* with the obedience of every creature and being. Nothing is more requisite to give a foundation to all the articles of religion, nor is it necessary we shou'd form a distinct idea of the force and energy of the supreme Being.[22]

Hume's statement differs from others in a century in which obedience to the will of God, or at least that of the Church, and the insignificance of man in comparison to God were parts of the rhetorical style of much philosophical writing. Hume means, by an omnipotent mind, one whose will is constantly obeyed—a definition that conforms to natural laws. To disobey the laws of the universe is patently impossible for man, but he can disobey such things as gospel exhortations; that is, he can ignore the biblical injunction "Thou shalt not kill," but he can hardly ignore the law of gravity. Hume, nevertheless, appears in the above quotation to suggest that our knowledge of natural law is sufficient to underwrite the laws of religion.

One such admission, however, does not make a theology. Hume's other pronouncements in his *Essays* and *Enquiries* all examine the phenomenological evidence adduced in support of some theological principle and find it wanting. Moreover, his Demea illustrates the unpopularity of the design argument with proponents of supernatural, revealed religion. Frequently associated with deism, the design argument was thought to rob religion of its autonomy and authority, if not of its mystery and beauty. After all, if the ways of God were revealed in man's subjective experience of everyday events, how could the experience of life after death be as exciting as the gospels promised?

Part one of the *Dialogues* opens with a few observations about the desirability of impressing early, upon children, the principles of religion; however, almost immediately Philo tries to gain assent about the "narrow Limits of human Reason" in matters of religion. Cleanthes accuses Philo of skepticism, but he accuses him of Pyrrhonism rather than the peculiarly Humean brand of skepticism. In fact, Cleanthes iterates some of the psychological limitations of skepticism in much the same manner Hume had done in the *Treatise*.[23] Philo's skepticism concerns itself both with the adequacy and the nature of the evidence adduced in support of propositions about our conceptions of God. He asks about the justification, if any, for the selection of whatever criteria would make up a theological discussion. Concerned not so much with the traditional question "Does God exist?"—or with any other question that does not lend itself to positive, empirical answers—Philo interrogates Demea and Cleanthes about the methodology to be used in an inquiry into natural religion. The promises of and possibilities in natural religion are not, he points out, the same as those related to commerce or politics; before we can "anatomize" natural religion, we must at the very least wonder about our intellectual suitability for such a task.

At the conclusion of part 1, Philo implicitly questions the ways in which any evidence has been used in the history of religious thought. Remarking on the "strong Symptoms of Priestcraft" in the progress of religious thought, Philo observes that unorthodox religious sentiments arose from "presumptuous questioning of receiv'd Opinions" and from a belief that human reason could solve all problems. In the eighteenth century, however, scholars and divines speak of the reasonableness of Christianity since it suits their purposes better than an appeal to mystery. Religious men have, in other words, sought, by any means, what they believed was a desirable end: "Thus, Sceptics in one Age, Dogmatists in another; which-ever System best suits the Purpose of those reverend Gentlemen, in giving them an Ascendant over Mankind, they are sure to make it their favourite Principle, and establish'd Tenet" (*Dialogues*, 158; *Works*, 2:389).

To this statement Cleanthes retorts that men ought to embrace principles which confute the "Cavils of Atheists, Libertines, and Freethinkers of all Denominations" because such a confutation would be a strong presumption of the truth of the principles. This concession is strategically important for

Philo, for he has made Cleanthes confess that he is really less interested in pursuing truth than in upholding religious doctrine. Yet Philo never reminds Cleanthes of this statement, and its implications escape the notice of both Cleanthes and Demea, but not the reader. As the discussion progresses and as the argument from design wilts under Philo's criticism, Hume's strategy is clear: Cleanthes' principles are more elocutionary than philosophical, more expedient than cogent.

This judgment may seem harsh in view of Cleanthes' abilities, but he is more interested in the empirical establishment of religion than in the means by which that establishment is achieved. True, he does not confine his theology to a posteriori arguments and does not condone the hypotheses of Demea; he never forsakes the design argument, either strategically or in principle. Yet he is unwilling within this area to accept any of Philo's criticisms. He articulates his basic argument in part 2:

Look round the World: Contemplate the Whole and every Part of it: You will find it to be nothing but one great Machine, subdivided into an infinite Number of lesser Machines, which again admit of Subdivisions, to a degree beyond what human Senses and Faculties can trace and explain. All these various Machines, and even their most minute Parts, are adjusted to each other with an Accuracy, which ravishes into Admiration all Men, who have ever contemplated them. The curious adapting of Means to Ends, throughout all Nature, resembles exactly, tho it much exceeds, the Productions of human Contrivance; of human Design, Thought, Wisdom, and Intelligence. Since therefore the Effects resemble each other, we are led to infer, by all the Rules of Analogy, that the Causes also resemble; and that the Author of Nature is somewhat similar to the Mind of Man; tho' possessed of much larger Faculties, proportion'd to the Grandeur of the Work, which he has executed. By this argument *a posteriori,* and by this Argument alone, do we prove at once the Existence of a Deity, and his similarity to human Mind and Intelligence. (*Dialogues,* 161–2; *Works,* 2:392)[24]

Hume's ironic strategy in the *Dialogues* leads him to select Demea, not Philo, to reply to Cleanthes' argument. Demea, astonished at Cleanthes' failure to employ a priori proofs and abstract arguments, approves of neither Cleanthes' conclusion nor his manner of reaching it.

Philo responds to Cleanthes by appearing to agree with Demea about the faults in Cleanthes' *method,* but he actually disagrees with Cleanthes' *reasonings.* Philo points out that when an event that has occurred presents itself again, we draw, without hesitation, the accustomed inference, (e.g., that a rock in the air will fall if unsupported). Strong similarity in a particular series of events assures us of recurrence. Departure from the similarity decreases the probability, and the evidence may so decrease as to produce a very weak analogy. This imperfect analogy is often confuted by additional experience. Continuing his argument, Philo states that the sight of a house leads us to infer a builder, but Cleanthes could not affirm that the universe has such a resemblance to a house, and that such a resemblance would lead us to infer a similar cause with the same certainty as we would in the case of the house. Nor would we have so perfect an analogy.

To strengthen his argument, Philo comes to a more damaging objection: a man is not able, without experience, to determine what is and what is not fact, or what is the actual state of the universe. Being unable to call anything impossible which can be conceived must give every "Chimera of his Fancy" an equal footing; for each would be equally plausible in the absence of experience. The mind will not and cannot supply a cause without experience, and one must allow that "Order, Arrangement, or the Adjustment of final Causes is not, of itself, any Proof of Design" (*Dialogues,* 166; *Works,* 2:395). Matter does not organize itself into something regular and ordered, but the mind organizes matter and material into various coherent units.

Restating his arguments in a more powerful form, Philo points out that Cleanthes is assuming that the universe falls into the same category of causality as houses, ships, and machines, and that the causal connection implying design is different only in degree, not in kind. We cannot, according to Philo, legitimately assume that thought, design, and intelligence are the activating springs and principles of the universe any more than we can say that heat and cold are; nor can we logically assume that what we find causally operative in the world of our experience will be so for the universe as a whole. Our limited experience of what we call "cause and effect" does not establish the origin and existence of nature as a whole; the operations of a part of nature do not allow us to reach any just conclusions about the totality of nature.

Philo then asks Cleanthes if he is not mistaken in assuming that intelligence alone could be the exclusive organizing and designing principle of the universe. Nature, having in her possession numerous manners of operation, would not necessarily rely just on thought or intelligence for her creation. Now Philo bolsters his assertion that the causal connections implying design are different in kind, not just in degree as Cleanthes supposed: "When two *Species* of Objects have always been observ'd to be conjoin'd together, I can *infer,* by Custom, the Existence of one, wherever I *see* the Existence of the other: And this I call an Argument from Experience" (*Dialogues,* 170; *Works,* 2:398). Since we have no experience of the origin of a universe, we have no compelling reason to infer a causal connection between the elements of our experience and the creation of a universe by an omnipotent mind.

To Cleanthes' objection that it is not necessary to have observed the origin of a universe or to be in a position to see the earth move to know that it moves, Philo replies that the movement of other planets and celestial bodies, by virtue of their analogy and resemblance to ours, confirms the Copernican hypothesis. No ground for a distinction between terrestrial and celestial objects exists, and the analogy is valid in comparing the two. The argument from design, however, can appeal to no analogies so valid and consistent as these, nor so certain as those of the Copernican system.

The arguments just outlined, which appear in part 2 of the *Dialogues,* constitute, with a few exceptions, the core of the arguments Hume brings against the argument from design. They are, in a manner of speaking, a "theme and variations": for the same attack appears throughout the *Dialogues* but with significant and informative variations each time. Even the several manners of statement are themselves merely elaborate variations and explanations of Hume's skepticism about the necessity of causal inference between two contiguous events. In essence, Hume asks if there is anything in the universe that logically, necessarily, and inexorably implies its creation by an omnipotent mind. If so, does anything in the nature and arrangement of the universe imply that its creation stems from a benevolent and altruistic Deity, who also thoughtfully arranged that such a universe would have a strict and inescapable eschatology? Although Philo's questions are not rhetorical, he suggests that neither he nor Cleanthes can answer them.

Hereafter, Cleanthes would seem to be on the defensive, but his defense consists largely of a good offense. He is on the defensive only in the sense that he ignores or fails to understand Philo's objections. Part 3 opens with Cleanthes' reply to Philo that his arguments are "absurd," and "no better than abstruse Cavils." He asserts, in a rhetorical question, that "the Similarity of the Works of Nature to those of Art . . . is self-evident and undeniable" (*Dialogues,* 173; *Works,* 2:400). To refute Philo's contentiousness, Cleanthes only needs to describe illustrations and examples of his basic principles because the similarities between any two separate kinds of creation are so great as to overwhelm logic.

Cleanthes employs two examples to refute Philo, again taking advantage of the rhetorical question to imply that Philo is more stubborn than perspicacious. He first asks Philo what his conclusion would be should he hear a voice in the sky, speaking more loudly than any human, and instructing mankind, in the language of each nation, in some sentiment appropriate to a benevolent Deity. Philo could conclude only that the cause of the voice entailed some purpose or design. Of course, Cleanthes agrees, such a thing has never happened; but it is the kind of reasonable analogy that supports the idea of design. The analogy Cleanthes suggests is this: when we hear an articulate voice and do not see the speaker, we assume that the person speaking exists. The voice from the skies, however, is unlike any human voice, but the only experience we have of voices is that they issue from intelligent causes. Therefore, we assume that this voice must issue from an intelligence far greater than ours. (Cleanthes' transition from an empirical to a theoretical analogy transforms the kind of argument he is making and would seem to weaken his argument disastrously.) Cleanthes' second example to refute Philo draws attention to a library containing volumes of "the most refin'd Reason and most exquisite Beauty" (*Dialogues,* 175; *Works,* 2:402). The original causes of these volumes, he argues, must have been intelligence, because we have no experience of books like these arising any other way.

The point of Cleanthes' two examples is that human experience can be projected beyond the mundane to the divine. In essence, Cleanthes' logic here is relational—that is, he is saying X is to Y as X_1 is to Y_1. Substituting Cleanthes' propositions for that logical shorthand, we have the following: our knowledge of mundane events bears the same relation to their cause in the same manner that our knowledge of divine events bears a relation to their cause. Philo attacks this logic by saying that Cleanthes is equating experience with knowledge. Although they have both agreed that knowledge must come from experience and from reasoning in the light of experience, Philo had pointed out in Part 2 that we have had no experience of divine events: "Our Ideas reach no farther than our Experience: We have no Experience of divine Attributes and Operations: I need not conclude my Syllogism: You can draw the Inference for yourself" (*Dialogues,* 161; *Works,* 2:391). Thus, Philo will accept neither a syllogistic nor a relational logic for a proof of God's existence. Cleanthes is asserting a relation between mundane causes and divine causes that is based not upon experience but upon intuition. Philo's syllogism clarifies the intuitional and theoretical character of Cleanthes' logic.

Yet it is not Philo who replies to the arguments of Cleanthes; Hume even has Pamphilus say of Philo that he was "a little embarrass'd and confounded" (*Dialogues,* 178; *Works,* 2:404). Demea replies to Cleanthes' assertions and argues that Cleanthes' proofs of God's existence have a great force because of their familiarity. Insisting that the ways of God are not those of man, Demea develops the earlier implications of his theory of the incomprehensibility of God's attributes. What we experience in nature, he says, is but a small part of God's totality which must remain unknown to our earthly existence. To draw analogies between the mind of God and that of man makes us guilty, according to Demea, of "the grossest and most narrow Partiality" (*Dialogues,* 179; *Works,* 2:404), an observation to which Hume, if not Philo, could readily assent.

Hume's strategy here permits the conservative theologian, exemplified by Demea, to make a more severe criticism than Philo could have without being charged with impiety or infidelity. In a paragraph added to Part 2 when he was revising it (probably in 1775), Hume has Demea elaborate upon Philo's syllogism of part 2. Since our ideas are derived from our senses, Demea says, they must be false and illusionary and cannot therefore originate in divine intelligence. We have no idea of what constitutes divine intelligence, and we cannot compare the human way of thinking to the divine way. The language we use to define human thought cannot be used as a metalanguage for divine thought. Demea's a priori conclusion is one to which Hume could give at least partial assent: "the Infirmities of our Nature do not permit us to reach any Ideas, which in the least correspond to the ineffable Sublimity of the divine Attributes" (*Dialogues,* 180; *Works,* 2:405).

Cleanthes' reply opens part 4 of the *Dialogues.* He is astonished that Demea should join the skeptics and atheists who insist upon the unknowability of God or of the first cause. Demea rightly accuses him of namecalling and implies that he himself could respond in kind by assigning the term "anthropomorphite" to Cleanthes. Stating Hume's concept of the self, Demea asserts both the qualitative and quantitative differences between the selfhood of men and that of God. Cleanthes is not, however, overwhelmed. He makes a lucid and philosophically important reply: "A Mind, whose Acts and Sentiments and Ideas are not distinct and successive; one, that is wholly simple, and totally immutable; is a Mind, which has no Thought, no Reason, no Will, no Sentiment, no Love, no Hatred; or in a Word, is no Mind at all. It is an Abuse of Terms to give it that Appellation; and we may as well speak of limited Extension without Figure, or of Number without Composition" (*Dialogues,* 182–83; *Works,* 2:407).

Cleanthes has used Demea's previous linguistic criticism against him. If we have no words within our language by which God can be appropriately described, then we are hard-pressed to assert any proposition, a priori or a posteriori, about Him. Our mind must bear something more than a perfunctory resemblance to God's mind unless we insist that God's mind is literally unknowable. And if his mind is literally unknowable because it is uniquely different from ours, we would have no criteria for recognizing knowledge of God when it was thrust upon us. Not even divine revelation

an organizing principle spring? Philo could reply to this argument by rees-
tablishing the argument against infinitely regressing causes; instead, he indicates that Demea is begging the question, that he has assumed thought to
be the *only* source of order. In his most famous example of a hypothesis as
valid as Cleanthes' design hypothesis, Philo postulates a world inhabited by
spiders. The Brahmins had asserted that the world was spun from the belly
of an infinite spider. Although this sort of cosmogony appears ridiculous to
human beings, it would not in a world inhabited by spiders. A spider obviously spins out an orderly web, and little imagination is required to see that
order could come from the belly as well as the brain. Cleanthes, astonished
by the fertility of Philo's invention, states that he does not know how to answer all these examples, and he asserts that these whimsical conjectures may
puzzle, but will never convince us.

Philo's inventiveness has indeed overwhelmed Cleanthes, although Philo
ascribes his creativity to the supposition contained in the study of natural
religion. Taking a different tack, Cleanthes questions Philo about the adap-
tability of man to the earth and suggests that the numerous instances of
conveniences afforded man by the world are instances of design—and of a
benevolent one at that. To this inquiry, Philo replies that in all our experience our "Ideas are copy'd from real Objects" (*Dialogues*, 213; *Works*,
2:429). Cleanthes reverses this order and gives thought precedence in the
formation of matter, yet we have never experienced such an order. Thought
cannot order matter, at least so far as we know. The hypothesis of design
runs up against that insuperable barrier.

To conclude his remarks and to end this section of the *Dialogues*, Philo
comments upon the difficulties accompanying all religious systems. The
passage is reminiscent of the conclusion found in "The Natural History of
Religion." While the theologians quarrel with each other, they perform a
service whose value they would surely question: "But all of them, on the
Whole, prepare a compleat Triumph for the *Sceptic*, who tells them, that no
System ought ever to be embrac'd with regard to such Subjects: For this
plain Reason, that no Absurdity ought ever to be assented to with regard to
any Subject. A total Suspence of Judgement is here our only *reasonable* Re-
source" (*Dialogues*, 214; *Works*, 2:430 [my italics]).

At the opening of part 9, Demea agrees with Philo about the difficulties
attending a posteriori arguments and says, for that reason, we ought to accept without question the sublimity of the priori argument. Nothing can
exist without a cause, Demea asserts; to avoid an infinitely regressing series
of causes, we must finally fall back upon some "ultimate Cause, that is *necessarily* existent" (*Dialogues*, 213; *Works*, 2:431). Without a necessarily ex-

istent being, we could attribute probability to any supposition or to the existence of nothing since eternity. We cannot accept a necessarily existent being who is his own reason for existence, and whose nonexistence cannot be imagined without involving ourselves in a contradiction.

Before Philo has a chance to demolish this particular piece of metaphysics, Cleanthes does it for him by pointing out, among other things, that the words "necessary existence" have no ascertainable meaning. Hume's permitting Cleanthes to answer Demea is another instance of his strategic irony. He is now in a position to subvert not only the argument for design, which he has in fact already done, but also to render inefficacious all the ontological or otherwise non-empirical arguments for God's existence. The drama of the *Dialogues,* begun in part 7, is now approaching its climax.

Part 9 of the *Dialogues* concludes with Philo's first manifestation of skepticism about the conviction the a priori argument is supposed to bring. Demea, who makes no reply in the opening paragraph of part 10 to this observation of Philo's, merely asseverates that each man feels within him the vital truth of religion. Philo concurs, for the time being, in Demea's contention that religion is responsible for whatever morality man may have. The interlocutors raise some familiar problems—evil, man's inhumanity to man, the innate goodness or wickedness of man—but little is said to advance a proof of God's existence. Observing that man can surmount animals and all his real enemies, Philo adds that he cannot disencumber himself of his imaginary enemies, those who haunt his imagination and terrify him, yet have no real existence. *Boogy mor, Senta Clause*

Cleanthes, who finds Philo's observations revealing, agrees that, if he can prove mankind to be innately corrupt and miserable, then religion can have no real value. Religion can profit little by establishing the natural attributes of the Deity when his moral attributes can be doubted. To this Demea replies, not yet seeing the vast disagreement between Philo and himself, that life on earth is but a moment in comparison to eternity and implies that all events of nature work toward universal good. Finding Demea guilty of hypothesis building, Cleanthes strongly advocates that the only way one can verify divine benevolence is by denying the "Misery and Wickedness of Men." Philo, too much of an empiricist for this assertion, challenges Cleanthes to prove the nonexistence of misery by reflecting upon the various kinds of pain mankind endures. Philo agrees with Cleanthes that the order of the universe can strike us on occasion with enough force to support the design argument. Regardless of the perspective from which we view mankind, we cannot support a system of universal morality unless we do the greatest violence to logic. Only the "eyes of faith" can perceive the moral attributes of the world.

The analysis of evil develops in part 11 with some impressive insights.[25] It is a measure of Hume's literary art that one of the most compelling discussions in the *Dialogues* coincides with the moment of highest drama. Philo's rhetoric points up the irony of pretending that the blind workings of nature can be called "good," when we are surrounded by so much "evil." His long exposition, however, finally reveals to Demea the vast distance between their views when compared to the paradoxical closeness of their initial procedure. When Philo asserts that evil in the world must have a cause but does not accept Demea's a prior notions of future rewards, Demea is astonished: "Hold! Hold! cry'd *Demea*: Whither does your Imagination hurry you? I join'd in Alliance with you, in order to prove the incomprehensible Nature of the divine Being, and refute the Principles of *Cleanthes,* who wou'd measure every thing by a human Rule and Standard. But I now find you running into all the Topics of the greatest Libertines and Infidels; and betraying that holy Cause, which you seemingly espous'd. Are you secretly, then, a more dangerous enemy than *Cleanthes* himself?" Cleanthes answers for him: "And are you so late in perceiving it . . . ? *Philo,* from the beginning, has been amusing himself at both our Expence; and it must be confessed, that the injudicious Reasoning of our vulgar Theology has given him but too just a handle of Ridicule" (*Dialogues,* 242–43; *Works,* 2:453).

The high point of the drama in the *Dialogues* is now reached as well as the high point of the intellectual debate. Demea is not merely content with the recognition of Philo's purpose; he finds some pretense to leave the company of Cleanthes and Philo. Had he remained, he might have more fully appreciated Philo's strategy. Few will doubt that Philo and Demea could agree on the most important postulate in any discourse about God's existence: that a posteriori proofs can never be convincing because of the failures in logic, and the surest approach to knowledge of God must be an act of faith. To affirm that "God exists" is not an empirical proposition but an act of faith. There, however, the agreement would end; for Demea would want to introduce a priori and abstract arguments for God's existence; and, as Philo earlier implied, these would have cogency only for those who are already convinced or who never really doubted.

Demea's petulant departure thus dramatizes the failure of the a priori theologians to see that they had something in common with the skeptics. Unfortunately, they were too busy calling skeptics "libertines and infidels" to see the ironic correctness of Philo's last words in the *Dialogues:* "To be a philosophical Sceptic is, in a man of Letters, the first and most essential Step towards being a sound, believing Christian" (*Dialogues,* 261; *Works,* 2:467). The second step, the act of faith, is not so essential, but is much harder to make because it is individual, unique, and empirically incomprehensible. I need hardly add that Philo never makes the second step, and Cleanthes does not, unfortunately, ask him about the qualification "in a man of Letters" (this phrase is usually ignored in analyses of this passage). He agrees "*that the Cause or Causes of Order in the Universe probably bear some remote Analogy to human Intelligence,*" but he thinks the ways of God to man would be more amply and aptly illustrated "by affording some more particular Revelation to Mankind, and making Discoveries of the Nature, Attributes, and Operations of the divine Object of our Faith" (*Dialogues,* 261; *Works,* 2:467). Philosophy is not much help to the "haughty Dogmatist" who would erect a system of belief upon the inadequate evidence of our senses. A man sensitive to the "reveal'd Truth" of religion will more readily accept faith, not empiricism and reason, as his guide to religious insight.

So ends Hume's cogent, yet deliberately inconclusive, inquiry into natural religion. The major achievement was to lay to rest any pretense to validity that the argument from design might have had. The drama of dialogue, perhaps, also indicates that Hume thought the excitement of intellectual debate more worthwhile than a fruitless search for ultimate truth. In reading the *Dialogues,* it is useful to keep in mind Hume's comment to Adam Smith about the work only ten days before he died: "On revising them (which I have not done these 15 Years) I find that nothing can be more cautiously and more artfully written" (*HL,* 2:334). Caution and artfulness are not, perhaps, the first two components of writing that would come to mind as natural complements, but the *Dialogues* was Hume's last major attempt at another literary form. In his biography (1931) of Hume, J.Y.T. Greig, writing of the "solemn eloquence" of the *Dialogues,* noted that the work "charms us as much by its balance and fair-mindedness as by its other qualities; and in literature, as constrasted with philosophy, conclusions are of less importance than the means taken to arrive at them."[26] Sixty years later, both literary critics and philosophers might take issue with this assertion. The literary quality as well as the consciously literary form and orientation of the *Dialogues* make its "philosophy" more ambivalently interesting than hard–and–fast conclusions might be, and, as a recent commentator has said, consideration of the work as literary or philosophical is a "question which is internal to the text itself and which a reading of the text can help to illuminate."[27]

After the publication of the *Dialogues,* Hugh Blair wrote to William Strahan, Hume's printer, that he was "surprised that . . . they have made so little noise. They are exceedingly elegant . . . but the principles themselves were all in his former works."[28] Blair is largely correct in saying that the principles in the *Dialogues* can be found in Hume's other works. Why, then, did Hume write another work in which he reiterated ideas he had already presented to the reading public? There are doubtless numerous reasons, some of them recoverable from Hume's historical context, some of them not. In view of the various and frequent observations Hume made about his membership in the "commonwealth of letters," and his affirmation in *My Own Life* that his "Love of literary Fame" was his "ruling Passion," we can regard with new interest Philo's qualification about skepticism being a pre-condition for Christian faith "in a man of Letters."

If being a philosophical skeptic is the first step for a man of letters to become a "sound, believing Christian," what is the first step for someone who is not a man of letters? Presumably businessmen, farmers, craftsmen, even layabouts and the idle rich may want to become Christians. Hume is not, I suggest, implying that only men of letters can become Christians; if he is, then his conclusion is even more ironic and far more deeply and bitterly skeptical than we had hitherto suspected. Men of letters, then, are unusually singled out as needing to raise doubts, ask questions, and carefully examine propositions about life, death, and immortality. If they wish to be sound and believing Christians, they cannot accept testimony that favors the views of the observer, nor can they credulously embrace ideas or opinions that have only the dubious authority of an institution to recommend them. Those who are not men of letters must come to Christian faith by other means, but neither Hume nor Philo seems willing to risk an impertinence in inscribing for others their path to faith.

In retaining Hume's "Step" metaphor, I am aware that Philo/Hume is endorsing a process, not a conclusion. Philosophical skepticism is only the first, and the most essential, step towards becoming a "sound, believing Christian." (Hume's phraseology also invites one to speculate about the nature of unsound, unbelieving Christians.) Philo deliberately avoids saying what the next steps are, and where the path will lead; instead, he turns his philosophical proposition into an educational maxim, one which Pamphilus either ignores or tacitly rejects. By using the infinitive, the present tense, and present participle of the same verb, Hume links skepticism and Christianity syntactically: "To be . . . is . . . being." A skeptical Christian might very well have doubts about this conflation of syntax and logic. Indeed, Pamphilus seems unprepared to adopt Philo's philosophical rubric as an educational guide. Once again, Hume's formulation of an idea or principle teases and perplexes the reader by delivering more than it appears to offer.

The dialogue form is probably the least examined literary genre of the eighteenth century, yet it accounts for over two thousand works. That Hume chose the form at a time of its literary hegemony is a measure of his desire to be integrated into a commonwealth of letters. The dialogue form presented Hume with an opportunity to strengthen the connections between what he had to say and how he said it. Even though the ideas and principles that he enunciates and examines are not radically different from those in his other works, Hume recognized the desirability, if not the necessity, of trying different literary modes as a means of communicating with and to his readers, and he clearly relished his attempts at different modes of expression and his excursions into genres other than the "essay" or the "treatise." One reader has even detected a "comic plot" in the *Dialogues*.[29] Demea is clearly mistaken in thinking that Philo is his ally against Cleanthes. It has seemed to most readers that Cleanthes and Philo are in league against Demea. Demea discovers his error in part 11 and leaves the company. There is indeed a good deal of humor in his embarrassment and petulance. Comedy is also a progression from chaos to order, and one could plausibly argue that Hume's *Dialogues* is a progression from order to chaos, and from certitude to diffidence, a reversal of one of the normal modes of comedy. Hume can also be credited with a narratological innovation: the narrator Pamphilus is more changed and affected by the conversation in Cleanthes' library than the other characters are. Before he begins his recitation of the conversation in Cleanthes' library, he tells Hermippus that his youth had rendered him "a mere Auditor of their Disputes," and attributes to his youthful curiosity the reasons why the disputes had "so deeply imprinted in my Memory the whole Chain and Connexion of their Arguments." After he has recounted to Hermippus, in amazing clarity and detail the whole of a discussion that would require upwards of three or four hours, he is a changed person: "nothing ever made greater Impression on me, than all the Reasonings of that day" (*Dialogues*, 145, 261). Although the conclusion of the *Dialogues* resembles, as I have said, that of Cicero's *De Natura Deorum,* there is no corollary in Cicero's text for this personal reassessment. Fiction and drama exhibit lives changed by events, activities or information; Pamphilus' life is changed by the events and discussion of an afternoon.

Hume's *Dialogues* is a work that generates reflection and speculation; the "ambiguous, at least undefin'd Proposition" that Philo reaches in the penultimate paragraph is a conclusion in which, as in Samuel Johnson's *Rasselas*, "nothing is concluded." Philo's conclusion is also a structural reminder and affirmation of the premise upon which Pamphilus began his

narration of a discussion which united "the two greatest and purest Pleasures of human Life, Study and Society" (*Dialogues*, 144; *Works*, 2:378).
Pamphilus is, of course, the pupil of Cleanthes, and, as he admits, he had
not progressed sufficiently in age and, presumably, his education to be
anything other than an auditor to the discussion. Life has other pleasures,
and philosophy has aims and ambitions other than those of giving pleasure to its practitioners. Hume, as author, seems at the very least to endorse
the pleasure of "Study and Society" as much as, if not more than, he
valorizes a "search for truth." As W. B. Carnochan puts it, "The friendship
of Cleanthes and Philo transcends philosophical disagreements," and
Pamphilus' preference for the views of Cleanthes "bears the marks of courtesy and submission to his tutor, and, hence is in keeping with the mood of
the ending."[30] It would be pleasant to think that students always made
"courtesy and submission" the hallmarks of their relationship with their
tutors, but Pamphilus' comment does seem at odds with the effect on him
of the afternoon's events. Philo probably is, as he says at the beginning of
part 12, "less cautious on the Subject of natural Religion than on any
other," and Hume no doubt believed that "nothing can be more cautiously
and artfully written." This reader is not, however, obliged to be cautious
about concluding that *Dialogues concerning Natural Religion* is one of the
most artful and artistic prose developments in the eighteenth century.

Accepting Hume's reasonings and conclusions, the reader can, as Hume
did, prefer to go no farther than that first step in skepticism. The leap from
skepticism to an act of faith crosses a gulf whose depth and width may not
be immediately apparent when the first step is taken.

Chapter Seven
David Hume: Man of Letters

Since Hume wrote neither fiction nor poetry, he is not often perceived as a "literary" figure, but recent scholarship and criticism has begun to alter that perception. Readers in the eighteenth century thought of him both as a "philosopher" (in the much broader eighteenth-century sense of that term) and as a controversial essayist; nineteenth-century readers regarded him primarily as a historian, and his *History of England* went through approximately ninety editions in the nineteenth century. For much of the twentieth century, readers thought of Hume as a philosopher and were frequently surprised to learn that he wrote a history of England. Scholarly and critical attention to the *History of England* in the past twenty-five years has altered that perception. That some literary critics in the twentieth century chose, for whatever reasons, to exclude philosophical lucidity and historical perspective as two of the defining qualities of literature is perhaps lamentable, but understandable when one remembers that quick (often unthinking) generic classifications simplified the problems of interpretation and evaluation.

A twentieth-century attitude towards Hume is not easily documented, although his omission from college and university classes in English literature and English history could serve as a starting-point. More tangible evidence can be found in reviews of books about Hume. When Professor Mossner produced *The Forgotten Hume* in 1943, he observed, perhaps a bit extravagantly, that "In sober truth, it must be put on the record that with a single important exception, [Samuel] Johnson's imposing literary production did not equal Hume's whether in quality, in scope, or influence. The exception was the *Dictionary*" (195). To almost any eighteenth-century scholar or critic of the time, that statement was an immediate challenge. In reviewing the book, Professor René Wellek took Professor Mossner to task for his assertion by asking in what way Johnson's work was inferior to Hume's and by replying: "Surely not in literary quality, in imagination, in style, in critical ideas on literature, in sheer personality and character. All these are qualities which count for more in *literature* than Hume's philosophical mind, his power of analysis, and even his lucidity of style and skill of exposition."[1] Thus, one of the most important twentieth-century critics placed Hume's achievement in the *realm of thought* and apparently not in *literature*.

Time has at least absolved Hume of one of Professor Wellek's charges in the same review that "The man Hume will remain, except for biographers, the 'forgotten Hume,' however good he might have been." Instead, Hume does elicit a sympathetic response from many modern readers who appreciate his wit, his irony, and his urbanity. Hume studies (including a journal of that title) have flourished in the last twenty-five years. As a result, he is no longer "forgotten"; he is being read as much, if not more, than he was in the eighteenth century, judging from the number of recent reprints of his various works. What, then, may we ask, are the reasons for reading Hume today?

First of all, I am not suggesting that Hume is more interesting as a writer or a stylist than he is as a philosopher. In his excellent literary study of Hume's "suasive art," Mark Box concludes

> It is fitting to end this literary study of Hume with an affirmation of the priority of his philosophical achievements. If his writings were to lose their philosophical importance, if, say, we discovered incontrovertibly that sceptical empiricism is wholly unveridical, undoubtedly most of his works would recede in status to that of Hume's *History,* which, being superseded in content, goes largely unread. Their literary merits, considerable as these are, would not save many of them from becoming mere documents of a dead intellectual movement.[2]

As Box notes, the movement is not, however, a dead one, but it is the basis for literary scholarship. What Hume has to say, what his ideas are, what he was thinking—these matters are perennially interesting and challenging. Even if his style were as turgid and cramped as that of Thomas Hobbes or F. H. Bradley, we would still read him. His philosophical achievements would undoubtedly have been different, and differently perceived, were he not so accessible as author, but the quality of his thought would still take priority.

I think that we read Hume in order to learn something about men's ways of thinking about their environments, their customs, their attitudes, and their limitations. Hume applied his considerable powers of analysis to almost every subject concerned with the life of the mind. His writings are valuable because of his attempts to explain, for example, why tragedy in drama affects us as it does and why it creates pleasurable sensations in us when the "real thing" would disgust or frighten us. His own reasons for writing are, in fact, similar to our reasons for reading him. Like other authors in the eighteenth century, Hume "wrote not to be *fed,* but to be *famous*" (as Laurence Sterne put it), though in Hume's case he had to earn his living by his pen.

Nevertheless, in applying his energies to intellectual problems, he found, in their complexities, enough material for a lifetime of reflection and exposition.

Hume's primary interest was not peculiar to his age: he sought to expand, where practical, the limitations imposed upon philosophical inquiry. Hume however, also sought to fence off those areas (like school metaphysics) that pretended to knowledge but were empty. For every intellectual discipline which engaged his interest, Hume tried to formulate the principles appropriate to its study. In many instances, he discarded old methods of inquiry because of their inherent defects. The new method he proposed was, in almost every instance, guided either by his skepticism or by what he called the "experimental method of reasoning." Where others began inquiries into the "laws of nature" in terms of cause and effect, he questioned the validity of causal imputations. Where others began inquiries into religious matters by assuming the existence of a benevolent Deity, he questioned the evidence for that assumption. In writing historical or expository prose, he joined to his powerful analytical mind an engaging personality which permitted him to be ruthlessly skeptical and thoroughly human at the same time.

We read Hume, then, for exactly those qualities that Professor Wellek described—for style, for literary quality, and for imaginative observations about human nature. While Hume's style is by no means perfect, it is eminently readable; it contains a number of fine pieces of rhetoric that have the same immediate appeal as some of Dr. Johnson's aphorisms and witticisms. In fact, the similarities and differences in the two men's styles are instructive. Both styles rely upon the vocabulary of science; Hume makes metaphorical use of an astonishing number of Newtonian concepts, while Johnson's style is partially derived from writers like Dr. George Cheyne, Dr. John Arbuthnot, and Sir Thomas Browne.[3] Dr. Johnson's prose style is sometimes ironic, often moralistic, almost always didactic. Hume's style is less frequently didactic, less openly moralistic, and more subtly ironic. Johnson's vocabulary is more extensive than Hume's and more ornate, but Hume is given to sentences more complicated than Johnson's. Both exhibited the tendency for the long, involved sentence of their time.

Hume's imaginative use of language can be found in the analogies and metaphors with which he described and defined certain human activities and other phenomena; we saw some examples in chapter 2. More interested in accurate representation or analysis than in the glib phrase, he could nevertheless compound some rhetorically fascinating phrases, of which "Reason is, and ought only to be, etc.," "Whatever *is,* may *not* be," and the conclusion of the first *Enquiry* are good examples. More importantly, his imagination suggested logical alternatives or antitheses in discourses where they had been neither conceived nor conjectured. When analogies were offered in support of natural phenomena, Hume offered another analogy, one just as plausible, which demonstrated the infinite variety of causes which could be invoked to account for any given event. His imagination expressed itself in expository constructs, not in fictionalized or "creative" representations of life or "Nature."

The best sustained examples of Hume's literary skills are the *History of England,* the *Enquiry concerning Human Understanding,* and the *Dialogues concerning Natural Religion.* In the *History,* Hume handles a vast amount of information in an easy manner; indeed, his narrative is a decided improvement over the accumulated verbiage of his predecessors. In the *Dialogues,* a work Hume polished for several years, he presents a number of intricate ideas with grace and energy. We do not consider the *Dialogues* easy reading; we are even likely to miss the subtleties of Hume's thought because of the attractive prose. But these works exhibit, as all his writings (with the exception of the essays he termed "frivolous") do, Hume's enduring qualities: they all have ideas as their logical core. For Hume, meaning is the most important component of any writing. Even in the essays that he withdrew from circulation he invariably attempted some meaningful inquiry in each, however light or easy the tone may have been. He was neither adept at writing frothy and clever essays whose only value lay in momentary diversion, nor was he proficient at cultivating seriousness for its own sake. He recognized the values of irony and raillery, and they were constant companions to his ideas.

Hume's literary achievements are found in the quality of his prose, in the imaginative projections of his skepticism, and in the lucidity of his exposition. Having attempted (so far as we know) neither novels nor poetry,[4] he cannot be labelled an outstanding "literary" figure in the strictest sense of the word. Yet he brought to philosophy, history, and politics many literary qualities with the result that all were mutually improved. He thought of himself as a "man of letters," which is indeed the best way of describing him. Alexander Pope had observed in a famous couplet in his *Essay on Criticism* (297–98) that *"True Wit* is *Nature* to Advantage drest,/What oft was *Thought,* but ne'er so well Exprest."* Hume was thinking what was *not* often thought, and he could not seek new ways of expressing old insights.

Although he falls short of this criterion of Pope's, he easily meets another: that of having ideas as the controlling unity in one's writing. In evaluating Hume's literary significance, then, we would not necessarily think of him as a stylistic innovator or developer, but we find that attention to his imagery give unexpected emphasis to certain ideas and leads us into the "new realms of thought" he was mapping out himself. In assessing anyone's literary achievement I would not want to separate ideas from literature: to do that would advocate a literature that appeals solely to the senses, where no standards exist for proper evaluation. Hume would prefer to think that the standards for writing philosophy or history should not be forgotten when writing poetry; equally, one should not forget the rhetorical demands of poetry when writing philosophy or history, in order to avoid a turgid enumeration of details.

Interest in Hume's rhetorical, linguistic, and literary skills has been a feature of academic commentary on Hume in the last twenty-five years; in addition, the importance of Hume's historical context has been given greater emphasis, and philosophical commentators have been eager to reassess Hume in light of new information about what might loosely be called "his life and times." In a volume of essays on the philosopher as writer, Robert Ginsberg notes that the term "Eighteenth-Century Studies . . . has had currency for about twenty-five years" and that scholars working in this field attend to the "contexts, language, values, and controversies" of the eighteenth century.[5] The key nouns in the titles of Hume's nonhistorical works indicate his own search for a suitable generic term that would both convey his intentions and engage his readers' interests: the "treatise" of 1739–40 gave way to "essays" in 1741, while "dissertations" (1757) and "dialogues" (1779, although Hume was using the word in his early drafts of the *Dialogues concerning Natural Religion*) followed. *Philosophical Essays concerning Human Understanding* became *Enquiries concerning Human Understanding.* Eventually, for his collected works, Hume settled on "essays and treatises" in 1758, and he seems to have been happy with this "user-friendly" generic designation.

Hume's awareness that the severe intellectual constraints in the connotation of such terms as "philosophical" or "metaphysical" might deter readers is best seen, and documented, in Hume's own historical perspective. The initial failure of the *Treatise* to attract readers on a large scale, and the misinterpretations made of the work, led Hume to write his *Abstract* as an explanation of his principles. In 1745, he made a further explanation of the work, in *A Letter from a Gentleman,* which was announced in the *Daily Advertiser* of 11 March 1740, where the subtitle was somewhat more dramatic than the one which eventually appeared: *Wherein the chief Argument and Design of that Book, which has met with such Opposition, and been represented in so Terrifying a Light, is further illustrated and explain'd.* How or why Hume was persuaded to give up this description of the reaction that he had perceived to the *Treatise* is unknown. It is yet further evidence that he had to present his works to a reading public in terms of a genre that might more readily comport itself with his readers' expectations and inclinations.

There is, thus, an argument for seeing Hume, both retrospectively and in his historical context, as the first philosopher writing in English who was openly sensitive to not only what he was saying, but how he was saying it, to whom modes of expression were as important as the expression of modalities.[6] It is certain that Hume attracts more commentary on his literary and stylistic skills than John Locke, George Berkeley, or Adam Smith. Hume's accessibility to literary analysis seems to irritate some of the more dogmatic and historically ignorant philosophical commentators who do not wish to see the rigorous purity of Hume's thought diluted by the readiness with which Hume's texts lend themselves to literary commentary. Writing of the styles of Locke, Berkeley, and Hume, John Richetti comments:

> To some extent, Berkeley treated writing as an obstacle to clarity. . . . Locke's garrulity is a sign of his concession to the limits of thought and reason. . . . Locke and Berkeley are writers who often claim to put writing aside, to subordinate it to thought and sometimes to disparage it. Hume always conceived of his philosophy in literary terms and saw his problems as essentially rhetorical.[7]

Contemporary evidence that Hume's readers were as concerned about style as he was can be found in a copy of the 1772 edition of his *Essays and Treatises*. This copy once belonged to John Milton's biographer, Thomas Newton (1704–1782) as well as another eighteenth–century owner, William Tyson (unidentified). In what appears to be Newton's autograph on page [2] of the second volume is the comment, "This Author's stile is in the main a good one; but He, like the other Scotch writers, very frequently renders his Language perplexed & embarassed [sic], by–*the former* &–*the latter,–the one, &–the other*."[8] The brief life of Newton in *Dictionary of National Biography* tells us that Newton was "disgusted by Gibbon's history" and "shocked" by the "malevolence" in Samuel Johnson's *Lives of the Poets,* so his restraint (if it is his hand–writing) in commenting on Hume's ideas is interesting, as is his identification of a particular "Scotch" style.

The metaphor that Hume used to describe the alterations he was making in the *Treatise* to make his work as inoffensive as possible to Bishop Joseph Butler—"castrating my work, that is, cutting off its nobler parts" (*HL,* 1:25)—is undoubtedly revealing and tells us just how personal a work the *Treatise* was for Hume. Donald Siebert remarks that by studying Hume's "ideas apart from their author's personality, we risk making Hume himself into a philosophical eunuch" and that the *Treatise* "is a very personal work, perhaps more personal than anything else Hume ever published, including his autobiography."[9] Hume was perhaps not aware just how much of himself he had revealed in the *Treatise*. In the first paragraph of the Appendix, which presumably was written after the first three books, Hume is sublimely confident about what he has accomplished: except for one article "he has not yet been so fortunate as to discover any very considerable mistakes in the *reasonings* deliver'd in the preceding volumes" but he has found "by experience, that some of my expressions have not been so well chosen" (*Treatise*, 624; my italics). The modest and moderating skepticism of, for example, the conclusion to book 1 is not on display here; Hume's concern for style leads him to betray a certitude about his "reasonings" that he vigorously opposes elsewhere.

Even in his most densely packed philosophical inquiries, Hume thinks of himself as a "man of letters" and the phrase that he uses to describe the community to which he belongs is the "republic of letters." In 1751, he composed a "little Endeavour at Drollery" that he called "The Bellman's Petition" which displayed "some good pleasantry and Satire." He admits that he wrote it "at an idle hour," but more revealingly he says that "I have frequently had it in my Intentions to write a Supplement to *Gulliver,* containing the Ridicule of Priests" (*HL,* 1:149, 153). His *Account of Stewart* is a broadly satirical treatment of an unjust accusation against a friend, while the pamphlet, *Sister Peg* (1760)[10] has some fairly trenchant satire in it, though it is often too topical to respond to a historically naive reading.

Summary

I have dwelt upon Hume's literary achievements because they tend to be ignored or only vaguely appreciated in any discussion of his philosophy. His ideas are asserted to be "superior" to his prose, but whether one can, or should, make that kind of judgment is at best dubious. Hume's writings endure not because he is so compelling a personality as Dr. Johnson, but because his remarkable ideas were expressed in excellent prose. His most important achievements, however, lie in these fields: epistemology, ethics, history, and religion.

Hume's analysis of induction can be generally regarded as his most important contribution to epistemology. Briefly, Hume argued that a sequence of events to which we have grown accustomed in the past does not logically entail that this sequence will be repeated in the future. Or, to put it more accurately, we cannot assume that, because of the frequency of occurrence of events X belonging to class Y, that the next series of events X will also belong to class Y. Many philosophers have argued that Hume's statement of the problem is unique and that induction cannot be scientifically justified; others have argued that a "probability calculus" can be used to justify induction.[11] Bertrand Russell has observed that this form of inference (induction) "has been considered to be, like the hangman, necessary but unpleasant, and not to be talked of if the subject could possibly be avoided—except by those who, like Hume, refuse to be limited by the canons of good taste."[12] Hume's criticism of the inductive method of inference was neither recognized nor generally appreciated in his own time, with one notable exception. Speaking of the connections between cause and effect, Immanuel Kant remaked, "I openly confess, the suggestion of David Hume was the very thing, which many years ago first interrupted my dogmatic slumbers, and gave my investigations in the field of speculative philosophy quite a new direction."[13] Although Kant recognized the legitimacy of Hume's criticism of induction, he never applied his a priori theories to a solution of the problem.[14] Since Kant's time, Hume's analysis of induction has been the subject of many developments, extrapolations, and refinements.

When Hume remarked in his autobiography that he considered his *Enquiry concerning the Principle of Morals* "incomparably the best" of all his writings, he revealed the predilection of his era for "moral science." His statement or formulation of a naturalistic ethic is often considered the most plausible yet offered,[15] and he would have appreciated the reputation it has achieved. The modern age is particularly intrigued, thanks perhaps to Wittgenstein, by Hume's discussion of the coextensiveness of ethical speculation and the structure of language. Like many eighteenth-century writers, Hume attempted to formulate an ethic which would bridge the gap between the "dignity of human nature" and the indignities of the actions in which it all too frequently engaged. The reader looking for a "moral imperative" in Hume's writings, however, will look in vain. He admits that we owe a duty to ourselves and that a concept of duty is apparent in even the "most vulgar system of morals." Hume will not tell us "You ought to do your duty," but suggests that we will find similarities in the approbation we give to our duty to ourselves and the approbation we give to our duty to society. Individuals are uniquely responsible for their actions, and they should not and cannot expect that responsibility to be assumed by others, or, for that matter, by the state. Man, Hume suggested, is capable of either moral strength or moral weakness, but the decision is exclusively his.

Since Hume was first a philosopher before he was a historian, there is strong inclination to draw parallels between Hume's philosophy and his judgment of events in the *History of England*. Hume's *History* is admittedly philosophical: it exhibits the judgments and discriminations we would find in good philosophical writing. But it is also a *historical* work, and its value as history cannot be overlooked. That it was widely accepted as a "standard" for more than a hundred years testifies to its value as history. While the student reading Hume's *History* today might be misled about the events of English history (because of the scanty information available to Hume regarding certain eras), he would more than make up for this loss by observing Hume's mind at work in an area not always distinguished by intellectual precision. His *History of England* is not only a narrative, it is also a study of history: Hume is consciously aware of history as a process, affected by natural laws and human passions. Hume examines and discusses the ways in which these natural laws interact with human passions to produce the events of history. Thus, if we read Hume's *History* today, we can read it for information; but we can also gain from it an understanding of the process of history, not to mention certain insights into human nature as it reacts to the stress of events. And, in reading it, we will discover a very fine prose style, a quality sometimes missed in other histories of England.

History, having laid down its assessment of Hume's contribution to religious thought, has now begun to reassess the verdict. No less a thinker than Kierkegaard quoted with approval Hume's observation in "Of Miracles" that the Christian religion could not be believed without miracles and that faith was the only foundation for religion.[16] Hume's continuing relevance to the "dismal science" of economics is well–illustrated by an article on 21 February 1989 in *The Wall Street Journal,* where the author, Thomas M. Humphrey, commended Hume for his remarks on the external debt of sovereign nations: "Had modern policy makers and bankers heeded his words, they might have avoided the sorry sequence of overlending, overborrowing, debt mis-management, waste and potential default that he foresaw."

I have suggested elsewhere that Hume's initial religious skepticism was the source of his subsequent discoveries in philosophy.[17] The significance of his religious thought lies in his damaging analyses of almost all anthropomorphic conceptions of the Deity and his works. Hume so undermined the argument from design that it is no longer an intellectually respectable argument for the existence of any god. In doing so, he separated religion from epistemology and ethics and suggested that it was a discipline that would have to survive without appealing to anything but its own internal authority. To the rigidly righteous, Hume's religious thought will seem heretical, blasphemous. But Hume thought it equally heretical to conceive of the Deity as a species of man "writ large." To the religious inquirer, Hume's religious thought may prove to be a prolegomenon to the foundation of any true religion—faith.

Hume's interest in religious matters is indisputable and unavoidable. Until recently, very little was known about his early education and training; biographers and commentators have relied on his autobiography and some early letters to infer as much as they could about Hume's education. Recent scholarship has brought to light information and documents that may materially change the way in which future assessments of Hume are made. In a brilliant piece of literary and historical research, Michael Barfoot has shown that Hume's interest in and competence at science and mathematics was far more comprehensive than Hume scholars had hitherto appreciated. Barfoot's essay is too complex and specialized to be summarized here, but his researches reveal that Hume's acquaintance with mathematics and physics was extensive: "While science affords merely one of the intellectual cultures which impinged upon his development as a metaphysician, moralist, critic, and political theorist, its significance is more profound than most Hume scholars have previously recognized."[18]

Hume is, in large measure, what *The Times Literary Supplement* termed him, in the title to a review of Kemp Smith's edition of the *Dialogues*: an enigma.[19] Many of his contemporaries, or near–contemporaries, were puzzled by the apparent contradictions in his nature. Some fifteen years after his death, Francis Garden, Lord Gardenstone (1721–1793), published this amusing poetical assessment of Hume:

> What better way, to spend a day,
> Than turning over thoughtful Hume;
> For though on priests he broke his jests,
> He fairly rivals Greece and Rome
>
> He did, 'tis true, deny their due
> To Bacon, Shakespeare, Hampden, Brutus;
> But still we know he did not show
> A mean servility to Plutus.
>
> He took his pen, like other men,
> Because he wanted food and fame;
> But then he wrote whate'er he thought,
> Nor courted praise, nor feared blame:

> And since we know he roasts *below*
> For what he said upon the Bible,
> It would be wrong to make our song,
> Like Beattie's bitter book, a Libel.[20]

Because many of his conclusions about human nature were couched in either skeptical or ironic terms, Hume is certainly perceived as enigmatic; the abundant, conflicting assessments and interpretations of his writings, both in his own time and in ours, all too emphatically attest to a degree of incertitude about the man who could be said to have invented and promoted incertitude as a sensible, fail–safe habit of mind. He was not a "character" in either the seventeenth-century sense or in the sense that Boswell's Johnson is, nor was he a stereotypical philosopher. He was a true philosophical skeptic, a man of letters, and above all, a "good man," *le bon David*. Or, as posterity can say for him, "Be a philosopher; but amidst all your philosophy, be still a Humean."

Notes and References

Chapter One

1. J. C. Hilson, "An Early Account of David Hume," *Hume Studies* Vol. 1, no. 2 (November 1975):79.

2. *The Letters of David Hume,* ed. J.Y.T. Greig (Oxford, 1932), 1:13; hereafter cited in the text as *HL,* followed by page volume and number(s).

3. The complete text of this essay is reprinted in Professor Ernest Campbell Mossner's article, "David Hume's 'An Historical Essay on Chivalry and modern Honour,' " *Modern Philology* 45 (1947):54–60.

4. Cf. the first edition of *The History of England from the Invasion of Julius Caesar to the Accession of Henry VII* Vol. 1 (London: John Millar, 1762), 423. Also, *The History of England from the Invasion of Julius Caesar to The Revolution in 1688* Vol. 1 (Indianapolis, Indiana: Liberty Classics, 1983), 486–87.

5. This is the text of that repudiation: "Most of the Principles and Reasonings contained in this Volume, were published in a Work in Three Volumes, intitled, *A Treatise of Human Nature*: a Work, which the Author had projected before he left College, and which he wrote and published not long after. But not finding it successful, he was sensible of his Error in going to the Press too early, and he cast the whole anew in the following Pieces; where some Negligences in his former Reasoning, and more in the Expression, are, he hopes, corrected. Yet several Writers, who have honoured the Author's Philosophy with Answers, have taken care to direct all their Batteries against that juvenile Work, which the Author never acknowledged; and have affected to triumph in any Advantages, which, they imagined, they had obtained over it: a Practice very contrary to all Rules of Candour and Fair-dealing, and a strong Instance of those polemical Artifices, which a bigotted Zeal thinks itself authorised to employ. Henceforth, the Author desires, that the following Pieces may alone be regarded as containing his philosophical Sentiments and Principles." See the article by A. Wayne Colver, "A Variant of Hume's Advertisement Repudiating the *Treatise,*" *Publications of the Bibliographical Society of America* 67 (1973):66–68.

6. *New Letters of David Hume,* ed. Raymond Klibansky and E.C. Mossner (Oxford: Clarendon Press, 1954), 3–4; hereafter cited in the text as *NHL,* followed by page number(s).

7. The letter appears in *HL,* 1:12–18. John Hill Burton, in his nineteenth-century biography of Hume, identified the addressee as Dr. George Cheyne, a conjecture Greig accepts. Professor Mossner has identified the unknown physician as Dr. John Arbuthnot in "Hume's Epistle to Dr. Arbuthnot, 1734: The Biographical Significance," *Huntington Library Quarterly* 7 (1944):135–52.

8. Professor Mossner's explanation and discussion of Hume's recovery is detailed and authoritative; see *Life* 2nd ed. (1980):81–91.

9. Hume is alluding to Alexander Pope's couplet: "All, all but Truth, drops dead–born from the Press,/ Like the last Gazette, or the last Address" in "Epilogue to the Satires, Dialogue 2,":226–27.

10. See E.C. Mossner's article, "The Continental Reception of Hume's *Treatise*, 1739–1741," *Mind*, 56 (1947):31–43. The information and quotations in this paragraph about the reception of Hume's *Treatise* are from this article. The quotation from Tacitus's *Histories* Vol. 1:1: "Rare happiness of our times, that you may think as you will, and speak as you think."

11. See *Life*, 122–23 and 617–18 for Mossner's identification, which has been disputed by R.M. Ryley in "Did Warburton review Hume's *A Treatise of Human Nature?*" in *Notes and Queries* 23 (1976):354–55.

12. *An Abstract of A Treatise of Human Nature 1740, A Pamphlet hitherto unknown* by David Hume, reprinted with an introduction by J.M. Keynes and P. Sraffa (Cambridge: The University Press, 1938). For some time, biographers and scholars thought that Adam Smith was the author of an abstract of Hume's *Treatise*, though no copy had been located. Keynes and Sraffa made the first discovery of the *Abstract* and conclusively identified Hume as the author. See *Life*, 120–28. R.W. Connon provided even more conclusive evidence for Hume's authorship in his "Some Hume MS Alterations on a Copy of the *Abstract*" in *Journal of the History of Philosophy* 14 (1976):353–56.

13. See E.C. Mossner's article, "Hume's 'Of Criticism' " in *Studies in Criticism and Aesthetics, 1660–1800: Essays in Honor of Samuel Holt Monk*, ed. Howard Anderson and John S. Shea (Minneapolis: University of Minnesota Press, 1967), 232–48.

14. See article by Norah Smith, "Hume's 'Rejected' Essays," in *Forum for Modern Language Studies* Vol. 8, no. 4 (October 1972):354–71.

15. For a recent commentary on the intellectual relationship between Butler and Hume see Terence Penelhum, "Butler and Hume," *Hume Studies* Vol. 14, no. 2 (November 1988):251–76.

16. [David Hume]: *A Letter from a Gentleman to His Friend in Edinburgh* (1745), ed. E.C. Mossner and J.V. Price (Edinburgh: The University Press, 1967). The introduction contains a summary of events relevant to Hume's candidacy for the chair.

17. Adam Ferguson attributes some remarks to Cleghorn in a manuscript in Edinburgh University Library, "Dialogue on a Highland Jaunt," which was edited and published by Ernest Campbell Mossner in *Restoration and Eighteenth–Century Literature*, ed. Carroll Camden (Chicago: The University of Chicago Press, 1963), 297–308. Douglas Nobbs, in "The Political Ideas of William Cleghorn, Hume's Academic Rival," *Journal of the History of Ideas* Vol. 24, no. 4 (1965):575–86, draws on a set of notes of Cleghorn's lectures made by a student for information about this elusive figure.

18. In a work generally known as *Descent on the Coast of Brittany,* Hume defended General St. Clair from the ridicule of Voltaire. See Paul H. Meyer, "Voltaire and Hume's 'Descent on the Coast of Brittany,'" *Modern Language Notes* 66 (1951):429–35. The defense is reprinted in *Works,* 4:443–60.

19. Conyers Middleton, *Free Enquiry into the Miraculous Powers which are supposed to have subsisted in the Christian Church from the Earliest Ages throughout several successive Centuries* (London: R. Maney and S. Cox, 1749).

20. C.D. Broad, *Five Types of Ethical Theory* (London: Routledge and Kegan Paul Ltd., 1956), 9.

21. The most thorough discussion of the miracles controversy in the eighteenth century is by R.M. Burns, *The Great Debate on Miracles From Joseph Glanvill to David Hume* (London: Associated University Press, 1981), and the section in J.C.A. Gaskin's book, *Hume's Philosophy of Religion* 2nd ed. (London: Macmillan, 1988), 135–65, is very helpful.

22. Published anonymously in London, 1749, by Andrew Millar. Skelton's biographer records that Hume was actually the reader for the MS; see Samuel Burdy, *Life of the Late Rev. Philip Skelton* (London Baynes, 1824), 2:351; see also *Life,* 232.

23. *Ophiomaches* 2:42–43.

24. Several other polemicists joined the ranks of those attempting to refute "Of Miracles." Many began by answering Hume on philosophical grounds, but often found the ad hominem argument useful, that is, "The remainder of this Essay is little more than a rude insult on the Scriptures and the *Christian* religion" (William Adams, *Essay on Mr. Hume's Essay on Miracles* [London: A. Millar, 1754], 87). Toward the conclusion of his essay, Adams inquires, "And here I ask my reader whether he has anywhere met with either a more sceptical, disputatious turn of mind, or a more imperious, dogmatical style, than in the writings of this author?" (pp. 98–99).

Others summarized Hume's position as if it represented the last outpost of nihilism or solipsism. In 1752, John Douglas, in *The Criterion: Or, Miracles Examined,* asserted that "If no event, however, well attested, be credible, which contradicts experience, then there can be no certain standard of the credibility of facts" without realizing that Hume would probably agree. Douglas goes on to say that Hume's argument is sophistical because he argues that the connection between cause and effect can never be discovered. But religion is in no danger from Hume: "I shall only add, than an author who espouses such opinions [of the most extravagant scepticism], can never be a dangerous enemy to religion. His arguments having novelty, may please for a while; but so opposite are they to every one's settled notions, that their influence cannot be lasting. Sorry I am to say, that the author of the *Philosophical Essays* seems to have a right to this character—a character which must sink the value of his writing, in spite of the most eminent abilities." (John Douglas: *The Criterion* [London: T. Cadell and W. Davies, 1807], pp. 14, 34–5).

25. The first volume of Leland's *View of the Principal Deistical Writers,* which eventually ran to three volumes, was first published by B. Dod in 1754; the

first volume paid no attention to Hume, but this oversight was rectified in a second volume published in 1755. I quote from this 1755 volume; hereafter abbreviated in the text as *View,* followed by page number(s).

26. Hume's letter is in *HL,* 1:360–61; Campbell's answer is found in the MSS of the Royal Society of Edinburgh, now deposited in the National Library of Scotland, RSE, 4:11. See also next note.

27. George Campbell, *A Dissertation on Miracles* (Edinburgh: A. Kincaid . . . [et al], 1762), v–vi; hereafter cited in text as *DM,* followed by page number(s). Although I quote from this text, later editions of Campbell's work, particularly the editions of 1796 and 1797 (both styled "third edition") have interesting supplementary material, including the correspondence by Blair, Campbell, and Hume.

28. See Richard B. Sher, *Church and University in the Scottish Enlightenment: The Moderate Literati of Edinburgh* (Edinburgh: The University Press, 1985), 155–56.

29. See A. Wayne Colver, "The 'First' Edition of Hume's *Essays and Treatises,*" *Papers of the Bibliographical Society of America* 68 (1974):39–44, and W.B. Todd, "David Hume. A Preliminary Bibliography," in *Hume and the Enlightenment: Essays presented to Ernest Campbell Mossner,* ed. William B. Todd (Edinburgh: The University Press; Austin, Texas: The Humanities Research Center, 1974), 194–96, for a discussion of the bibliographical complexities of the first collected edition.

30. The discrepancy between the date of the appearance of the *Political Discourses* given in *Works,* 3:56, and the review, which seems to appear a month earlier, is easily explained. In a letter dated 29 September 1751, Hume wrote to Robert Wallace: "The Discourses are at present in the Press, & will be publish'd as soon as they are printed off & sufficiently dry; which I fancy will require two or three Months" (*NHL,* 30). The work was published by Alexander Kincaid, who also published Hume's *Essays, Moral and Political.* The reviewer for the *Monthly Review* undoubtedly used proof–sheets or early unbound copies of the *Political Discourses* for his review. The first review in the *Monthly Review* dealt with the *Enquiry concerning the Principles of Morals;* the second with the *Political Discourses* might have been published in mid–January; see *HL,* 1:167.

31. Rose's review of the second *Enquiry* appeared in *Monthly Review* 6 (January 1752):1–19; his review of the *Political Discourses* in the same periodical, 19–43, 81–90. The passages quoted are also cited in part in *Life,* 225–26.

32. See the definition in Samuel Johnson's *A Dictionary of the English Language,* ed. the Rev. H.J. Todd (London: Longman, Hurst, Rees, Orme, and Brown, 1818, 1:5Z4^v).

33. The quotation is from *My Own Life.* The *Political Discourses* became Hume's best–known work in Europe. It was translated, by itself and as part of his collected works, into French, German, and Italian during his lifetime. During the 1750s, it contributed to Hume's international reputation more than any of his other works. See *Life,* 227–29.

34. A list of Scotticisms was prefixed to some copies of the first edition of the *Political Discourses*. For Hume's correspondence with Wallace, see *NHL,* 28–35.

35. Smith quotes Hume six times in the *Wealth of Nations* (1776), but the intellectual debt is much more extensive. See Eugene Rotwein; *David Hume: Writings on Economics* (Edinburgh: Nelson, 1955) and, more recently, Knud Haakonssen, *The Science of a Legislator: The Natural Jurisprudence of David Hume and Adam Smith* (Cambridge: The University Press, 1981).

36. See James G. Basker, *Tobias Smollett: Critic and Journalist* (Newark: University of Delaware Press, 1988) for information about Smollett's history.

37. For the complete story of the "Conspiracy of the Booksellers," see E.C. Mossner and Harry Ransom, "Hume and the 'Conspiracy of the booksellers': The Publication and Early Fortunes of the *History of England*," *Texas Studies in English* 29 (1950):162–82.

38. *Diary of Sylvas Nevill, 1767–1788,* ed. Basil Cozens–Hardy (London: Oxford University Press, 1950), 202.

39. For the complete history of the publication of the *Four Dissertations,* see E.C. Mossner, "Hume's *Four Dissertations:* An Essay in Biography and Bibliography," *Modern Philogy* 48 (1950):37–57. See also *Life,* 313–35.

40. For an interpretation of the episode that is favourable to Rousseau, see Jerome Christensen, *Practicing Enlightenment: Hume and the Formation of a Literary Career* (Madison: University of Wisconsin Press, 1987), 243–73.

41. James Beattie, *Essays: On the Nature and Immutability of Truth, in Opposition to Sophistry and Scepticism* (London: Edward and Charles Dilley, 1776), ix–x. See my discussion, "The reading of philosophical literature," in *Books and their Readers in Eighteenth–Century England,* ed. Isabel Rivers (Leicester: Leicester University Press, 1982), 182–86.

42. Beattie, *Essays* 8–9.

43. An account of the composition and publication of the *Dialogues* can be found in my edition of the work (Oxford: Clarendon Press, 1976), 105–28.

44. Hayter, *Remarks on Mr. Hume's Dialogues concerning Natural Religion* (1780), 2. Some other identifications of sources for the ideas in the *Dialogues* are given in chapter 7 and in my edition of the work.

45. Hayter, *Remarks,* 48–49; see *Dialogues,* 254.

46. *Boswell: Laird of Auchinleck, 1778–1782,* edited by Joseph W. Reed and Frederick A. Pottle (New York: McGraw–Hill Book Company, 1977), 173.

47. See *Life,* 620–22 for posthumous controversy over Hume.

Chapter Two

1. H.H. Price, "The Permanent Significance of Hume's Philosophy," *Philosophy* 15 (1940):37. One of the better recent commentaries on Hume's notion of causality is that by Tom L. Beauchamp and Alexander Rosenberg, *Hume and the Problem of Causation* (New York and Oxford: Oxford University Press, 1981).

2. Tadeusz Kozanecki, "Dawida Hume'a Niezane Listy w Zbiorach

Muzeum Czartoryskich (Polska)," *Archiwum Historii Filozofi i Mysli Spolecznej* 9 (1963) (Religie Racjonalne. Studia z filozofi religii xv-xvii w), 133. I am grateful to Dr. Wojciech Nowicki of the Catholic University of Lublin (Katollicki Uniwersytet Lubelski) for providing me with photocopies of the autograph documents and for checking the transcriptions.

    3. Cf. Joseph Butler, chapter 1 of the *Analogy of Religion* in *Works,* ed. W.E. Gladstone (Oxford; Clarendon Press, 1896), 1, 29–30.

    4. Norman Kemp Smith in *The Philosophy of David Hume* (London: Macmillan, 1949) has clearly shown that Hume's philosophy is not an adaptation of Locke and Berkeley, as was commonly thought by many commentators, among them T.H. Green in his long introduction to the *Treatise* in *Works* 1:1–299.

    5. An excellent discussion of Hume's Pyrrhonism can be found in Richard H. Popkin, "David Hume: His Pyrrhonism and his Critique of Pyrrhonism," *The Philosophical Quarterly* 1 (1951):385–407. The best discussion of Hume's "skeptical realism" is John P. Wright's *The Sceptical Realism of David Hume* (Manchester: The University Press, 1983).

    6. In the article mentioned in note 5 above, Professor Popkin has pointed out that Hume's formulation of Pyrrhonian skepticism differs from the standard formulation in Sextus Empiricus and that Hume omits any reference to the methodology by which the Pyrrhonian decides practical matters once he has posited the impossibility of deciding certain questions (p. 386). Hume may be equating Pyrrhonism with the ideas attributed to Pyrrho by Pierre Bayle in his *Dictionnaire.*

    7. Cf. Sextus Empiricus, *Outlines of Pyrrhonism* (London and Cambridge, Massachusetts: Loeb Classical Library, 1961), 1, 17; book 1, secs. 23–24.

    8. In a useful article, "The Self and Perceptions: A Study in Humean Philosophy," *The Philosophical Quarterly* 9 (1959):97–115, Panayot Butcharov has argued that Hume's seeming contradiction on the concept of self is not a contradiction at all: "It amounts to the elimination of the *myself* although it preserves the existence of *selves* (as collections of perceptions)" (p.115).

    9. In the appendix published with the third volume of the *Treatise* in 1741, Hume asserted that one could never perceive self without self having one or more perceptions and that these perceptions formed the self. See *Treatise,* appendix, 604–35.

    10. This viewpoint, which I share, is Kemp Smith's, in *The Philosophy of David Hume,* 160–61.

    11. Kemp Smith's viewpoint "that it was through the gateway of morals that Hume entered into his philosophy, and that, as a consequence of this, books 2 and 3 of the *Treatise* are in date of first composition prior to the working out of the doctrines dealt with in book 1" (p. vi) is not one I share, nor is it shared by many of Hume's other commentators. While no one would wish to denigrate the value of Kemp Smith's studies in Humean philosophy, I find the above assertion a little confusing when compared to his statement that "The least original . . . part of Hume's philosophy, is his ethics" (p. 562).

12. Kemp Smith has made a useful tabulation of the passions (p. 168); I have relied upon it somewhat for my summary.

13. The meaning of this passage, both by itself and in context, is much debated. See Páll S. Ardal, *Passion and Value in Hume's Treatise* (Edinburgh: The University Press, 1966), pp. 106–108.

14. Anthony Ashley Cooper, third earl of Shaftesbury, is usually accounted the founder of the "Moral Sense" school. See particularly his *An Inquiry concerning VIRTUE and MERIT* and *The MORALISTS; a Philosophical Rhapsody* in *Characteristicks of Men, Manners, Opinions, Times* (London: n.p., 1711). For commentaries on Shaftesbury, as well as on Francis Hutcheson and Hume, see James Bonar, *Moral Sense* (London: Allen and Unwin; New York: Macmillan; 1930) and D.D. Raphael, *The Moral Sense* (London: Oxford University Press, 1947), the better of the two books.

15. See A.H. Basson, *David Hume* (London: Penguin, 1958), 88–90.

16. One of the most thoughtful commentaries is that by John Sitter, *Literary Loneliness in Mid–Eighteenth–Century England* (Ithaca and London: Cornell University Press, 1982), 21–49. See also, Donald T. Siebert, "Hume as Philosophical Traveler: From 'Wild Agreeable Prospects' to a 'Very Pretty Machine' " in *Studies in Eighteenth–Century Culture, Volume 18*, ed. John W. Yolton and Leslie Ellen Brown (East Lansing Michigan: Colleagues Press for the American Society for Eighteenth–Century Studies, 1988), 187–198. The writings of Jacques Derrida, among others, have changed attitudes towards tropes and metaphors in philosophical discourse, and philosophical language is often at its most revealing and important when analyzed at the level of tropes and metaphors.

17. John Locke, *An Essay concerning Human Understanding,* ed. P.H. Nidditch (Oxford: Clarendon Press, 1975), 118 (2:i, 25).

18. The most famous example of this metaphor is the Great Chain of Being as in Pope's *Essay on Man.* One scarcely need mention A.O. Lovejoy's book, *The Great Chain of Being* (Cambridge, Massachusetts: Harvard University Press, 1936), which is now a staple of graduate as well as undergraduate reading.

Chapter Three

1. Hume omitted this essay from all future editions of his works, apparently because it was "too frivolous," as he said of several others in a letter to Adam Smith 24 September 1752 (*HL*, 1:168).

2. For a detailed exposition of this essay see Ralph S. Pomeroy, "Hume's Proposed League of the Learned and Conversible Worlds," *Eighteenth–Century Studies* vol. 19, no. 3 (Spring, 1986), 373–94.

3. See R.S. Crane's article "Suggestions towards a Genealogy of the 'Man of Feeling' " *Journal of English Literary History* 1 (1934):205–30.

4. Ralph Cohen, *The Art of Discrimination: Thomson's THE SEASONS and the Language of Criticism* (Berkeley and Los Angeles: University of California Press, 1964).

5. The most cogent discussion of Hume's concept of taste is Ralph Cohen's "David Hume's Experimental Method and the Theory of Taste," *Journal of English Literary History* 25 (1958):270–89. I have, in part, relied upon Professor Cohen's analysis for my understanding of both Hume's concept of taste and other eighteenth–century uses of the term. More recent studies that I have found helpful are those by C.W. Korsmeyer, "Hume and the Foundations of Taste," *Journal of Aesthetics and Art Criticism* 35 (1976):201–15, and Noel Carroll, "Hume's Standard of Taste," *Journal of Aesthetics and Art Criticism* 42 (1984):181–94.

6. *Ibid.*, 278.

7. See Ralph Cohen, "The Transformation of Passion: A Study of Hume's Theories of Tragedy," *Philological Quarterly* 41 (1962):450–64. Professor Cohen has provided us with the best analysis and discussion of Hume's theories of tragedy, with particular emphasis on "Of Tragedy."

8. Shaftesbury's comments about Epicurus in *Miscellaneous Reflections* in volume 3 of the *Characteristicks* exemplify eighteenth-century thought in regard to Epicureanism, namely, "It need not be thought surprizing, that *Religion* it-self shou'd in the account of these Philosophers be reckon'd among those Vices and Disturbances, which it concerns us after this manner to extirpate. If the Idea of *Majesty* and *Beauty* in other inferior Subjects be in reality distracting; it must chiefly prove so, in that *principal Subject*, the Basis and Foundation of this Conceit" (*Characteristicks of Men, Manners, Opinions, Times* [Birmingham: John Baskerville, 1773], 3:35).

9. I have discussed the irony of Hume's presentation and method in *The Ironic Hume* (Austin, Texas: The University of Texas Press, 1965), 22–25.

10. John Laird, *Hume's Philosophy of Human Nature* (London: Methuen, 1932), 245. Robert J. Fogelin, *Hume's Skepticism in the* Treatise of Human Nature (London: Routledge & Kegan Paul, 1985), 118. Fogelin's qualification about tone is important, since the exceptional subtlety of many of Hume's arguments depend on careful scrutiny upon the tone and conduct of the argument. I also am inclined to agree that "The Sceptic" is the most thorough statement of Hume's "position in everything."

11. Indeed the essays contained in Hume's volume of 1752, *Political Discourses,* are primarily devoted to economic subjects. They are discussed later in this chapter.

12. See *Works*, 3:445; *Essays*, 468. Also on this point, see John B. Stewart, *The Moral and Political Philosophy of David Hume* (New York: Columbia University Press, 1963), 156–58.

13. In discussing Hume's notion of the origin of government, David Miller, in *Philosophy and Ideology in Hume's Political Thought* (Oxford: Clarendon Press, 1985) asserts that "Hume is not particularly concerned about the question of origin except in so far as it provides him with more ammunition to fire at the social contract theory" (p. 84).

14. This same position appears in the *History of England,* in chapter 71:

"And it may justly be affirmed, without any danger of exaggeration, that we, in this island, have ever since enjoyed, if not the best system of government, at least the most entire system of liberty, that ever was known amongst mankind" (*History*, 6:531).

15. A valuable study of Hume's treatment of mixed government in Britain is found in Stewart's *The Moral and Political Philosophy of David Hume*, 221–55.

16. Laird, *Hume's Philosophy of Human Nature*, 257. In a useful essay, "The Economic Thought of David Hume," *Hume Studies*, vol. 15, no. 1 (April 1989): 184–204, Robert W. McGee concludes with this comment: "Had Hume devoted as much time to economics as had Adam Smith, we might now be referring to Hume as the father of modern economics rather than Smith."

17. See Eugene Rotwein, *David Hume: Writings on Economics* (Edinburgh, 1955), xxxii. Professor Rotwein's discussion of Hume's economic thought is exemplary, and I have relied on it to some extent for my discussion here.

18. Ibid., iv.

19. See, however, Robert W. McGee, "The Economic Thought of David Hume," *Hume Studies* vol. 15, no. 1 (April 1989):190: "Hume's version of the quantity theory is the later, sophisticated theory, not the original, crude theory."

20. Rotwein, *David Hume*, Liv–Lvii.

Chapter Four

1. Selby–Bigge's editions of Hume's *Treatise* and *Enquiries* were first published in 1888 and 1894, respectively. Professor P.H. Nidditch revised the text of the *Treatise* for a new edition for the Clarendon Press in 1978. He had earlier revised the text of the two *Enquiries* in 1975. My quotations from the *Enquiries* in this chapter are from Nidditch's revised 1975 text.

2. This attitude is adopted for a cogent book on Hume by Antony Flew, *Hume's Philosophy of Belief* (London: Routledge & Kegan Paul, 1961). My discussion in this chapter owes much to Professor Flew's arguments and insights; his book is by all odds the best work written on Hume's first *Enquiry*. I ought to remind the reader here that the *Enquiry concerning Human Understanding* acquired that title only in the 1758 edition of the *Essays and Treatises on Several Subjects*; it was originally published in 1748 as *Philosophical essays concerning Human Understanding*.

3. This quotation acts as a subtitle and unifying theme in Professor Mossner's *Life*. The idea permeates all of Hume's writings, from the political essays to the *History of England* and must be a part of any evaluation of Hume's philosophy. See, for example, Flew, *Hume's Philosophy of Belief*, 9.

4. See the article by Norah Smith, "Hume's 'Rejected' Essays," in *Forum for Modern Language Studies* vol. 7, no. 4 (October 1972):354–71 for a discussion of the Addisonian flavor of Hume's essays.

5. This method of inquiry apparently has always been popular with philosophers, and Hume records in his letters his questions to the blind poet Blacklock

(*HL*, 1:201, 209): Blacklock could form no idea of color, but he formed certain associations with words whose origin in perception was unknown to him.

6. "Of Miracles" and "Of a Particular Providence and a Future State," sections 10 and 11 respectively, constitute more of an appendix than anything else—but they are nonetheless the most devastating part of the *Enquiry*.

7. Flew, *Hume's Philosophy*, 53.

8. Cf. Flew, *Hume's Philosophy*, 108–9. Flew has described the methodology for Hume's approach to the problems of causality and necessary connection as "psychogenetic."

9. The reader who is interested in a more extensive discussion of section 8 can consult Flew, *Hume's Philosophy*, 140–65.

10. In the first and second editions of the *Enquiry concerning Human Understanding*, Hume began his sentence even more strongly: "Upon the whole, then, it appears, that no testimony for any kind of miracle can ever possibly amount to a probability."

11. Bertrand Russell, *Why I Am Not a Christian* (New York: Simon and Schuster, 1957), v.

12. See A.E. Taylor, *David Hume and the Miraculous* (Cambridge: University Press, 1927), 53–54.

13. Cf. *HL*, 11:154: "What Danger can ever come from ingenious Reasoning & Enquiry?" Hume's irony here, and in the quotation, is many–layered and not easily "unpacked," but it allows him to suggest to the attentive reader a wealth of possibilities.

14. David Norton, in *David Hume: Common–Sense Moralist, Sceptical Metaphysician* (Princeton: Princeton University Press, 1982), has argued persuasively, though not without some vigorous dissent, that Hume is incorrectly described as a naturalist.

15. Isaac Newton, *Optics*, 3:i, 31; cf. Flew, 269.

16. See Flew, *Hume's Philosophy*, 271–72.

17. These ideas are found in a passage omitted in the authorized editions of Hume's works published after 1760; cf. *Works*, 4:173n. Yet the same import of the ideas remains in the *Enquiry concerning the Principles of Morals*.

18. Hume's use of the concept of self–love is only one of very many in the Restoration and eighteenth century; the term is peculiarly associated with eighteenth–century thought (see James Hastings, *Encyclopaedia of Religion and Ethics* [Edinburgh: J. and T. Clark, 1958], 11:359). Famous examples can be found in Alexander Pope's *An Essay on Man* (1733–34) and Joseph Butler's *Sermons* (1726; numerous reprints). In 1815, the Aberdonian philosophical writer, John Duncan, in his *The Philosophy of Human Nature*, asserted in his chapter on self–love that it "forms the only complete theory on that subject with which the Author is acquainted" (p. iv).

19. Hume's good friend and fellow Scotsman/philosopher, Adam Smith, in his own book on moral theory commented that "The cause too, why utility pleases,

has of late been assigned by an ingenious and agreeable philosopher [i.e., Hume], who joins the greatest depth of thought to the greatest elegance of of expression, and possesses the singular and happy talent of treating the abstrusest subjects not only with the most perfect perspicuity, but with the most lively eloquence" (*Theory of Moral Sentiments,* ed. D.D. Raphael and A.L. Macfie [Oxford: Clarendon Press, 1976], 179). Smith's *Theory* was first published in 1759.

20. Many of Butler's sermons are concerned with the difficulties of reconciling the seemingly opposite qualities of benevolence and self–love. See his *Works,* ed. by the Right Hon. W.E. Gladstone (Oxford: Clarendon–Press 1896), 2:21–28, 185–229.

21. This is not Hume's example but an extrapolation. Hume apparently had some second thoughts about the principle of universality in discourses about ethics. Cf. *A Dialogue* published along with the first edition of the *Enquiry concerning the Principles of Morals;* there Hume outlines some ideas in antiquity which would cause revulsion or disapproval in eighteenth–century people but which were acceptable and even praiseworthy in antiquity.

Chapter Five

1. See E.C. Mossner, "An Apology for David Hume, Historian," *Publications of the Modern Language Association* 56 (1941):675–76, for a list of the manuscript sources documenting Hume's early interest in and plans for writing a history of England. Mossner thoroughly demolishes the once popular notion that Hume's *History* was neither scholarly nor careful. Hume had at his command useful and sometimes unique resources, and he used them painstakingly.

2. Manuscript notes for the *History of England* are now in the archives of the National Library of Scotland (MSS 733–34) and the Huntington Library in San Marino, California (MS HM 12263). See *Life,* 301.

3. Ralph's work may also be exhaustive, but I have been able to read only part of its two volumes. Each volume is about the size of a demy folio, contains over a thousand pages, and is elaborately annotated.

4. (James Ralph), *The History of England: during the Reigns of K. William, O. Ann, and K. George I, with an Introductory Review of the Reigns of the Royal Brothers, Charles and James; in which are to be found the Seeds of the Revolution* (London, 1744), 1:1. Ralph published the work anonymously; the title–page pronounces the work to be *By a Lover of Truth and Liberty.* It is amusing, if not instructive, to compare Ralph's comment to one written after the histories of Hume and Smollett had achieved profitability and success. Edward Seymour, in his *Complete History of England* (London, 1764), wrote in his introduction, "let us remember, that, as the excellence of History centers in a circumstantial and well–digested recital of matters of fact, independent of the prejudice of education, and uninfluenced by the bias of interest; he who writes last, if possessed of equal abilities with those who have preceded him, must write best; because he has the greatest scope from which to collect materials, for the due execution of the task he has undertaken"

(p.v). Perhaps a re–assessment of Seymour's abilities is necessary, since his history seems to have disappeared from sight.

5. Ralph, *History of England*, 1:1.

6. Fraser was an acquaintance of Hume, who parodied his rabid Jacobitism in a pamphlet, never published, entitled *To the Right Honble the Lord–Chief-Justice Reason, and the Honble the Judges, Discretion, Prudence, Reserve, and Deliberation, The Petition of the Patients of Westminster against James Fraser, apothecary.* Printed in *HL*, 2:340–42. Cf. *HL*, 1:146–48.

7. John Bennett Black, *The Art of History* (London: Methuen, 1926), 85.

8. Ibid., 90.

9. These quotations and others similar are cited by those who consider Hume's concept of history as "antihistorical," for example, R.G. Collingwood in *The Idea of History* (Oxford: Clarendon Press, 1962). See, in contrast, Donald W. Livingston's article, "Hume's Historical Theory of Meaning" in *Hume: A Re–Evaluation* (New York: Fordham University Press, 1976), 213–38, and the discussion in his first–rate book, *Hume's Philosophy of Common Life* (Chicago and London: University of Chicago Press, 1984), 235–46.

10. Duncan Forbes, *Hume's Philosophical Politics* (Cambridge: Cambridge University Press, 1975), 188–89.

11. In 1773, Dr. Johnson had not yet read Hume's *History*. See James Boswell, *Life of Johnson,* ed. Hill and Powell (Oxford: Clarendon Press 1934–50), 2:236–37.

12. This point has been re–emphasized by Nicholas Phillipson in his *Hume* (London: Weidenfeld & Nicolson, 1989 [the Historians on Historians series]; see, for example, 134–35.

13. Donald Livingston's comments in *Hume's Philosophy of Common Life,* 235–46 are particularly apt on this point.

14. W.E.H. Lecky, *A History of England in the Eighteenth Century* (London: Longmans, 1925), 1:329–30. For a thorough discussion of the Naturalisation Bill, see Cecil Roth, *A History of the Jews in England* (Oxford: Clarendon Press 1949), 215–21.

15. For Hume's sympathetic attitude, if a bit tinged with irony, towards Jews, see *HL,* 1:423–24.

16. Two useful articles on Hume's style, particularly with regard to sentiment and sentimentality, in *The History of England,* are J.C. Hilson, "Hume: The Historian as Man of Feeling," in *Augustan Worlds,* ed. J.C. Hilson, M.M.B. Jones and J.R. Watson (Leicester University Press, 1978), 205–22, and Donald T. Siebert, "The Sentimental Sublime in Hume's *History of England, The Review of English Studies* vol.40 no. 159 (August 1989), 352–72.

17. I have discussed Hume's concept of civil and individual liberty in "Hume's Concept of Liberty and *The History of England,*" *Studies in Romanticism* 5 (1966):139–57. A recent book on the subject is that edited by N. Capaldi and

D.W. Livingston, *Liberty in Hume's* 'History of England' (Dordrecht: Kluwer Academic Publishers, 1990).

18. See his column for 22 October 1964, "Nonsense about Anti-Intellectualism."

Chapter Six

1. When *Four Dissertations,* containing "The Natural History of Religion," appeared in February 1757, Warburton made good his earlier threat to publish a "refutation" of Hume; accordingly, he published the work described in the following note. For additional information, see *Life,* 326.

2. *A Selection from Unpublished Papers of the Right Reverend William Warburton,* ed. Francis Kilvert (London, 1841), 309–10. Warburton published a reply to "The Natural History of Religion," under circumstances which made clear that he did not want to be identified as the author. Warburton's tract was called *Remarks on Mr. David Hume's Essay on the Natural History of Religion: Addressed to the Rev. Dr. Warburton* (London, 1757). The book was actually a culling of marginal remarks in his copy of Hume's essay. Writing to Richard Hurd in early 1757, Warburton said the reply should "bear something like this title, *Remarks on Mr. Hume's late Essay, called the Natural History of Religion, by a Gentleman of Cambridge, in a Letter to the Rev. Dr. W.* I propose the address should be with the dryness and reserve of a stranger, who likes the method of the letters on Bol[ingbroke]'s Philosophy, and follows it here against the same sort of writer, inculcating the same impiety, naturalism, and employing the same kind of arguments. The address will remove it from me: the author, a *Gentleman of Cambridge,* from you; and the secrecy in printing from us both." (*Letters from a Late Eminent Prelate to One of his Friends* [Kidderminster T. Caddell and W. Davies, 1808], 176.) Why Warburton, who had never been shy about his "triumphs" over skepticism, should want to publish this work in secrecy is a mystery. The abusiveness of the contents may be the reason.

3. E.C. Mossner in "The Enigma of Hume," *Mind* 14 (1936):334–49 makes the estimate based on the page count given in J.Y.T. Greig's *David Hume* (London: Jonathan Cape, 1931), 236 and n.

4. For a discussion of Hume's irony in general, see my *Ironic Hume.* Chapter 4 contains an analysis of the irony in the *Dialogues.*

5. See my two articles, "Empirical Theists in Cicero and Hume," *Texas Studies in Literature and Language* 5 (1963):255–64, and "Sceptics in Cicero and Hume," *Journal of the History of Ideas* 25 (1964):97–106. Also, Christine Battersby, "The *Dialogues* as Original Imitation: Cicero and the Nature of Hume's Skepticism," in *McGill Hume Studies,* ed. David Fate Norton, Nicholas Capaldi, Wade L. Robison (San Diego, California: Austin Hill Press, Inc., 1976), 239–52.

6. I have deliberately quoted from an eighteenth-century translation of *De Natura Deorum,* published by Thomas Francklin (London, 1741), 268, since eighteenth-century attitudes towards translation of the classics were different from

modern ones. (This translation, incidentally, is usually attributed to Thomas Francklin, but David Berman has persuasively attributed it to Anthony Collins: "Hume and Collins on Miracles," *Hume Studies* vol. 6, no. 2 [November 1980]: 150–54.) Compare an anonymous translation of 1683: "This having Pass'd, we gave our *Opinions*. *Velleius* lookt upon *Cotta*'s Dispute to be *Truer* than *Balbus*'s; but, to *me*, *Balbus*'s *Argument* seem'd of a *Nearer Resemblance* to *truth*" (Cicero: *Cicero's Three Books Touching the Nature of the Gods; Done into English* [London, 1683], 252). Finally, Cicero's Latin text, in the Loeb edition, is as follows: "Haec cum essent dicta, ita dicessimus ut Velleio Cottae disputatio verior, mihi Balbi ad vertatis similitudinem videretur esse proprensior" (Cicero, *De Natura Deorum,* trans. H. Rackham [Cambridge: Loeb Classical Library, 1956], 383).

7. Mossner, "The Enigma of Hume," 314–47.

8. See R.H. Hurlbutt III, "David Hume and Scientific Theism," *Journal of the History of Ideas* 17 (1956):493–96. Also, my edition of the *Dialogues,* 162, 177, 179, 261.

9. Preserved Smith, *A History of Modern Culture* (New York: Macmillan, 1962), 2:448.

10. C.W. Hendel, *Studies in the Philosophy of David Hume* (Indianapolis, Indiana: Bobbs-Merrill, 1963), 278. M.A. Stewart, "Hume and the 'Metaphysical Argument *a priori*' " in *Philosophy, its History and Historiography,* ed. A.J. Holland (Dordrecht: D. Reidel Publishing Company, 1985), 262. The "obviousness" of this identification of the character of Cleanthes with Henry Home, Lord Kames has escaped notice for over two centuries.

11. See Norman Kemp Smith's list in his edition of *Dialogues* 2nd ed. (Indianapolis, Indiana: Bobbs-Merrill, 1947), 58–59 and n.

12. Milner, *op. cit.,* 221.

13. Mossner, "The Enigma of Hume," 336. I note several parallels between Demea's words and the writings of Samuel Clarke in my edition of the *Dialogues,* and Martin Bell in his edition of the *Dialogues* (Harmondsworth: Penguin, 1990) has noted others.

14. Smith, *History of Modern Culture,* 2:448.

15. Hendel, *Studies,* 278.

16. M.A. Stewart, in the article cited in footnote 10, points out that the Rev. George Anderson (1676–1756), was a "declared opponent of Kames (and Hume) and was writing in defence of Clarke" (p. 266), but it is unclear to what extent Stewart wishes to associate the characterization of Demea with Anderson.

17. Smith, *History of Modern Culture,* 2:448.

18. John Hill Burton, *Life and Correspondence of David Hume* (Edinburgh, 1846), 328, 330.

19. Hendel, *Studies,* 278.

20. Cf. Mossner, "The Enigma of Hume," 334; Also Kemp Smith's introduction to *Dialogues* and 59–75. For recent suggestions that Philo cannot be conclusively or exclusively identified with Hume, see Terence Penelhum, "Natural

Belief and Religious Belief in Hume's Philosophy," *Philosophical Quarterly* 33 (1983):166–81, and R.H. Hurlbutt, "The Careless Skeptic: The 'Pamphilian' Ironies in Hume's *Dialogues*," *Hume Studies* vol. 14, no.2 (November 1988):207–50.

21. Hendel, *Studies,* 271–72.

22. This passage is a footnote to a paragraph Hume added in the appendix affixed to volume 2 of the first edition of the *Treatise.* See *Treatise,* 1:iii, 14; also *Works,* 1:445–56 and n.

23. Cf. *Dialogues,* 132–33 and *Treatise,* 1:iv, 7.

24. Compare Pope, *Essay on Man,* 3:7–14:

> Look round our World; behold the chain of Love
> Combining all below and all above.
> See plastic Nature working to this end,
> The single atoms each to other tend,
> Attract, attracted to, the next in place
> Form'd and impell'd its neighbour to embrace.
> See Matter next, with various life endn'd,
> Press to one center still, the gen'ral Good.

25. In the past twenty–five years, critics, philosophers, and scholars have had much to say about the problem of evil as presented in the *Dialogues.* For a typical analysis of the moral problems of evil discussed in parts 10 and 11 of the *Dialogues,* see Nelson Pike, "Hume on Evil," *The Philosophical Review* 72 (1963) :180–97. See also his edition of the *Dialogues* (Indianapolis, Indiana: Bobbs–Merrill, 1970), 183–204.

26. J.Y.T. Greig, *David Hume* (London, 1931), pp. 231, 235.

27. Gary Shapiro, "The Man of Letters and the Author of Nature: Hume on Philosophical Discourse," *The Eighteenth Century: Theory and Interpretation,* vol. 26, no. 2 (Spring 1985):133.

28. Edinburgh University Library, Ms. Dc. 2. 76[10]. Cited in *Dialogues,* 121.

29. W.B. Carnochan, "The Comic Plot of Hume's *Dialogues*," *Modern Philology* vol. 85, no. 4 (May, 1988):514–22.

30. W.B. Carnochan, "The Comic Plot of Hume's *Dialogues*," 522.

Chapter Seven

1. René Wellek, review of *The Forgotten Hume, Philological Quarterly* 23 (1944):169; the italics are Wellek's.

2. Mark Box, *The Suasive Art of David Hume* (Princeton: Princeton University Press, 1990), 255.

3. See the two books by Professor W.K. Wimsatt, Jr., on Johnson's prose style, *The Prose Style of Samuel Johnson* (New Haven and London: Yale University

Press 1941), chapter 8; also *Philosophic Words: A Study of Style and Meaning in the "Rambler" and "Dictionary" of Samuel Johnson* (New Haven: Yale University Press, 1948).

4. In his *Life and Correspondence of David Hume* (Edinburgh: William Tait, 1846) John Hill Burton prints (1:228–31) some poems in Hume's handwriting from manuscripts in the Royal Society of Edinburgh. They appear to be originals, but Hume does not mention them in his letters, and of course, they were never published.

5. Robert Ginsberg, ed., *The Philosopher as Writer: The Eighteenth Century* (Selinsgrove: Susquehanna University Press; London and Toronto: Associated University Press, 1987), 11.

6. John Locke's *Essay concerning Human Understanding* (1790) is certainly in a style different from previous philosophical treatises in English, but Locke did not make quite so conscientious an effort as Hume did to adapt his style to the demands of the reading public. Moreover, Locke's *Essay* was popular and widely read from its first publication. See John J. Richetti, *Philosophical Writing: Locke, Berkeley, Hume* (Cambridge, Massachusetts: Harvard University Press, 1983), 32–36.

7. Ibid., 184.

8. I am grateful to the owner of this copy, who wishes to remain anonymous, for permission to quote this comment.

9. Donald T. Siebert, " 'Ardor of Youth': The Manner of Hume's *Treatise*," in Ginsberg, *The Philosopher as Writer*, 180.

10. *Sister Peg: A Pamphlet Hitherto Unknown by David Hume,* ed. David R. Raynor (Cambridge: Cambridge University Press, 1982). This work has usually been attributed to Adam Ferguson, but Raynor's case for admitting it into the Hume canon is convincing.

11. See Hans Reichenbach, *The Theory of Probability* (Berkeley and Los Angeles: University of California Press 1949), vii–ix, 469–82.

12. Bertrand Russell, *Human Knowledge: Its Scope and Limits* (London: Allen and Unwin, 1956), 451.

13. Immanuel Kant, *Prolegomena to any Future Metaphysics,* ed. Paul Carus (Chicago, 1949), 7.

14. This circumstance led Bertrand Russell to remark, "After mediating for twelve years, he produced his great work, the *Critique of Pure Reason*; seven years later, at the age of sixty-four, he produced the *Critique of Practical Reason,* in which he resumed his dogmatic slumbers after nearly twenty years of uncomfortable wakefulness." *Unpopular Essays* (New York: Simon and Schuster, 1950), 51.

15. H.H. Price, *op. cit.,* 36.

16. Walter Lowrie, *A Short Life of Kierkegaard* (Princeton: Princeton University Press, 1942), 108.

17. *The Ironic Hume,* 146–52.

18. Michael Barfoot, "Hume and the Culture of Science in the Early Eight-

eenth Century" in *Studies in the Philosophy of the Scottish Enlightenment,* ed. M.A. Stewart (Oxford: Clarendon Press, 1990), 190.

19. See the November 2, 1935 issue; also E.C. Mossner's article with the same title, "The Enigma of Hume."

20. Francis Garden, Lord Gardenstone, *Miscellanies in Prose and Verse* 2nd ed. (Edinburgh: J Robertson, 1792), 96.

Selected Bibliography

PRIMARY WORKS

The following texts were consulted for quotations from Hume's writings.

An Abstract of a Treatise of Human Nature (1740): *A Pamphlet hitherto unknown by David Hume.* Reprinted with introduction by J.M. Keynes and P. Sraffa. Cambridge: University Press, 1938. (Cited as *Abstract.*)

Dialogues concerning Natural Religion, ed. by John Valdimir Price. Oxford: Clarendon Press, 1976. (Cited as *Dialogues.*) [With Colver: *Natural History of Religion,* below.]

An Enquiry concerning Human Understanding, ed. by L.A. Selby–Bigge, revised by P.H. Nidditch. Oxford: Clarendon Press, 1975; 3rd ed. (Cited as *ECHU.*)

An Enquiry concerning the Principles of Morals, ed. by L.A. Selby–Bigge, revised by P.H. Nidditch. Oxford: Clarendon Press, 1975; 3rd ed. (Cited as *ECPM.*)

The History of England, from the Invasion of Julius Caesar to the Revolution in 1688. Indianapolis, Indiana: Liberty *Classics,* 1983; 6 vols. (Cited as *History*).

A Letter from a Gentleman to his friend in Edinburgh, ed. E.C. Mossner and J.V. Price. Edinburgh: Edinburgh University Press, 1967. Reprints, with introduction, a unique copy of this pamphlet now in the National Library of Scotland.

The Letters of David Hume, ed. by J.Y.T. Greig. Oxford: Clarendon Press, 1932; 2 vols. (Cited as *HL.*)

New Letters of David Hume, ed. by Raymond Klibansky and E.C. Mossner. Oxford: Clarendon Press, 1954. (Cited as *NHL.*)

The Natural History of Religion, ed. by A. Wayne Colver. Oxford: Clarendon Press, 1976. (Cited as *NHR.*) [With Price: *Dialogues,* above.]

The Philosophical Works of David Hume, ed. by T.H. Green and T.H. Grose. London: Longmans, Green, and Co., 1874–75; 4 vols. (Contains all of Hume's works, except the *History,* the *Bellmen's Petition,* and the *Account of Stewart*: Cited as *Works.*)

Sister Peg: A pamphlet hitherto unknown by David Hume, ed. David R. Raynor. Cambridge: Cambridge University Press, 1982. Attributes to Hume a pamphlet hitherto attributed to Adam Ferguson.

A Treatise of Human Nature, ed. by L.A. Selby–Bigge, revised P.H. Nidditch. Oxford: Clarendon Press, 1978; 2nd ed. (Cited as *Treatise*.)

SECONDARY WORKS

The following items supplement books referred to in the notes and may also be consulted for more detailed commentaries on Hume's life and writings.

Basson, A.H. *David Hume.* London: Penguin Books, 1958. Introductory book devoted mostly to Hume's principles of knowledge, morality and religion. Reissued in 1968 (New York: Dover) with the author named as A.P. Cavendish.

Becker, Carl L. *The Heavenly City of the Eighteenth Century Philosophers.* New Haven: Yale University Press, 1960. Contains some interesting misunderstandings of Hume.

Box, M.A., *The Suasive Art of David Hume.* Princeton: Princeton University Press, 1989. One of very few books to study Hume's literary career, and a very good one at that. Highly recommended.

Brunius, Teddy. *David Hume on Criticism.* (Figura: Studies edited by the Institute of Art History, University of Uppsala, No. 2) Stockholm: Almqvist and Wiksell, 1952. Only book–length study of Hume's critical principles, but not, alas, very good.

Capaldi, Nicholas. *David Hume: The Newtonian Philosopher.* Boston: G.K. Hall & Co., 1975. An important book for the historical and scientific context of Hume's philosophy.

Cohen, Ralph. "David Hume's Experimental Method and the Theory of Taste," *Journal of English Literary History* 25 (1958): 270–89. Thorough and penetrating analysis of Hume's concept of taste; valuable historical information.

―――――― "The Transformation of Passion: A Study of Hume's Theories of Tragedy," *Philological Quarterly* 41 (1962):450–64. Excellent study of the development of Hume's theories of tragedy.

Flew, Antony. *Hume's Philosophy of Belief: A Study of his First Inquiry.* London: Routledge and Kegan Paul. New York: Humanities Press, 1961. Devoted exclusively to the *Enquiry concerning Human Understanding.* Very useful.

―――――― *David Hume: Philosopher of Moral Science.* Oxford: Blackwell, 1986. Excellent general introduction.

Gaskin, J.C.A. *Hume's Philosophy of Religion.* London: Macmillan, 1978; 2nd ed., 1988. Easily the best discussion of its topic and a good introduction to Hume.

Hall, Roland. *Fifty Years of Hume Scholarship: A Bibliographical Guide.*

Edinburgh: Edinburgh University Press, 1978. Covers Hume scholarship from 1927 to 1976; updated from time to time in the journal *Hume Studies.*

Hendel, Charles William, Jr. *Studies in the Philosophy of David Hume.* New York: Liberal Arts Press, 1963. Contains a review of Hume scholarship since 1925, mostly concerned with interpretations of Hume by various modern philosophers.

Huxley, Thomas H. *Hume, With Helps to the Study of Berkeley.* New York: Appleton, 1897. Great agnostic writes about great skeptic, with some interesting results.

Jessop, T.E. *A Bibliography of David Hume and of Scottish Philosophy from Francis Hutcheson to Lord Balfour.* London: A. Brown & Sons, 1938.

Laird, John. *Hume's Philosophy of Human Nature.* London: Methuen & Co., 1932. Good general study of Hume's philosophy.

Leroy, Andre. *La Critique et la Religion chez David Hume.* Paris: F. Alcan, 1930. Lengthy study of Hume's religious thought.

McGilvary, E.B. "Altruism in Hume's *Treatise,*" *Philosophical Review* 12 (1903):272–98. Argues that Hume admits the existence of an original altruism in the *Treatise.*

MacNabb, D.G.C. *David Hume: His Theory of Knowledge and Morality.* London: Hutchinson's University Library, 1951. Contains useful exegeses of Hume's theories of understanding.

Mossner, Ernest Campbell. "An Apology for David Hume, Historian," *PMLA* 56 (1941):657–90. Valuable information about the composition and structure of the *History.*

———— "The Enigma of Hume," *Mind,* XIV (1936), 334–49. Concerned with he identity of the participants in the *Dialogues.*

———— *The Forgotten Hume: Le bon David.* New York: Columbia University Press, 1943. Discusses Hume's relations with various eighteenth-century literary figures.

———— *The Life of David Hume.* Austin: University of Texas Press; London and Edinburgh: Thomas Nelson & Sons, 1954; 2nd ed., 1980. The standard biography, not likely to be excelled. (Cited as *Life.*)

———— (ed.). "New Hume Letters to Lord Elibank," *Texas Studies in Literature and Language* 4 (1962):431–60. Additional Hume letters.

Norton, David Fate and **Popkin, Richard H.** (eds.). *David Hume: Philosophical Historian.* New York: The Library of Liberal Arts (The Bobs–Merrill Company), 1965. Selection from Hume's works of items bearing on his position as a historian; Professor Norton has contributed an essay on "History and Philosophy in Hume's Thought" and Professor Popkin on "Skepticism and the Study of History."

Noxon, James. *Hume's Philosophical Development: A Study of his Methods.* Oxford: Clarendon Press, 1973. One of the more interesting and important books published on Hume in recent years.

Popkin, Richard H. "David Hume: his Pyrrhonism and his Critique of Pyrrhonism," *Philosophical Quarterly* 1 (1951):385–407. Excellent commentary on Hume's Pyrrhonistic skepticism.

Price, H.H. "The Permanent Significance of Hume's Philosophy," *Philosophy* 15 (1940):7–37. Sensible appraisal of the value of Hume's contributions to philosophical discourse.

Price, John Valdimir. *The Ironic Hume.* Austin: University of Texas Press, 1965. Study of the ironic structure of Hume's language and thought; reprints Hume's *Bellmen's Petition* and *Account of Stewart.*

Rotwein, Eugene. *David Hume: Writings on Economics.* Edinburgh: Thomas Nelson & Sons, 1955. Reprints Hume's economic essays with elaborate introduction and commentary.

Siebert, Donald T. *The Moral Animus of David Hume.* University of Delaware Press, 1990. Lucid and persuasive study of Hume as practical and practising moralist. Siebert's attention to the importance of *The History of England* in assessing Hume's ideas makes this one of the most valuable contemporary studies of Hume.

Smith, Norman Kemp. *The Philosophy of David Hume: A Critical Study of Its Origins and Central Doctrines.* London: Macmillan & Co., 1949. Best general study of Hume's philosophy. Detailed and authoritative.

Stewart, John B. *The Moral and Political Philosophy of David Hume.* New York and London: Columbia University Press, 1963. Excellent and valuable discussion, superior in many ways to Kemp Smith's.

Todd, William B. "David Hume. A Preliminary Bibliography" in *Hume and the Enlightenment: Essays Presented to Ernest Campbell Mossner.* Edinburgh: The University Press; Austin, Texas: University of Texas Humanities Research Center, 1974, 189–205.

Index

The index covers significant references in Chapters 1–7 and the notes and references (not the preface or the bibliography). Works by Hume are listed under: Hume, David, Works. Titles of works are printed in italic type, e.g. *Four Dissertations*. References to notes are indicated by n followed by the note number, e.g. 141n24 represents page 141, note 24. Where there are several page references for a heading, the principal ones are shown in italic.

Adams, William, comments on *Of Miracles*, 141n24
aesthetics, 39–42
anatomist metaphor, 38
Anderson, Rev. George (opponent of Hume), 152n16
Arbuthnot, Dr. John (physician), 139n7

Beattie, James: *An Essay on . . . Truth*, 18–19
Bedford, John, Duke of, example of Whig politics, 85
belief, 27–28
Blacklock (blind poet), 147–48n5
Blair, Rev. Hugh (friend of Hume), comments on *Dialogues concerning Natural Religion*, 19–20; letter from Hume on history, 92; letter to William Strahan about *Dialogues concerning Natural Religion*, 123–24; sends Hume ms. of Campbell's *Dissertation on Miracles*, 11
Boswell, James, comment on *Dialogues concerning Natural Religion*, 22–23
Boufflers, Comtesse de, correspondence with Hume, 18
Briggs, Henry (mathematician), overlooked by Hume in favor of Napier, 96
Bruce, Robert (king of Scotland), 93–94
Burton, John Hill (biographer of Hume), 111
Butler, Dr. Joseph (bishop), *The Analogy of Religion*, 6; Hume amends *Treatise* to avoid offense to, 9, 132; ideas supported by Hume's comments on self-

love, 78; source of arguments in *Dialogues concerning Natural Religion*, 110

Campbell, Dr. George: *A Dissertation on Miracles*, 10–11
causality, *27–28*, 30, 69–70, 143n1
chain metaphor, 35–36
Cheyne, Dr. George, 110, 139n7
Cicero, source for *Dialogues concerning Natural Religion*, 109–10, 125
Clarke, Dr. Samuel, source for *Dialogues concerning Natural Religion*, 110–11
Cleghorn, William (professor of philosophy), 7
Clephane, John (friend of Hume), 15, 84–85
combat metaphor, 36–37
commerce, 59
commonwealth metaphor, 34
Cooper, Anthony Ashley, Earl of Shaftesbury, founder of "Moral Sense" School, 145n14

dialogue form, 125
dissertations, 17
divorce, 47–48
Douglas, John, comments on *Of Miracles*, 141n24

economics, 58–61
Elliott, Sir Gilbert (friend of Hume), 1, 19
eloquence, 43–44
emotion, 39–45
Epicureanism, 48–49, 50

epistemology, 25, 133–34
essay writing, 39
ethics, 30, 75–82, 134
evil, 122

fabric metaphor, 32
Ferguson, Adam (reputed author of *Sister Peg*), 154n10
Fraser, James (Jacobite acquaintance of Hume), 85
freedom of the press, 56

gaming metaphor, 37
Garden, Francis, Lord Gardenstone, poem on Hume, 136
government, 53–58
Green, Prof. T. H. (editor and commentator, Hume's philosophical work), 62
Greig, J. Y. T. (biographer of Hume), 123

Hamilton, Gavin (publisher), 16
Hayter, Thomas: *Remarks on Mr. Hume's Dialogues...* , 20–21
heap metaphor, 31–32
history, 86
Home, Henry, Lord Kames (friend of Hume), anecdote about Hume, 17; letter from Hume about *Essays, Moral and Political*, 6; letters from Hume about *Treatise*, 2, 9; possible characterization in *Dialogues concerning Natural Religion*, 110; publishes Hume's defense of *Treatise*, 7
human understanding, 62–75
Hume, David, application for chair of ethics, Edinburgh University, 7; chronology, xi–xiii; death, 23; education, 1; employment, 7–8, 18; health, 3, 20; status as man of letters, 127–37

WORKS:
Abstract of ... A Treatise of Human Nature ... , An, 5
Account of Stewart, 133
Bellman's Petition, The, 133
Dialogues concerning Natural Religion, 19–23, 108–26, 130

Enquiry concerning Human Understanding, An, 12, 62–75, 130
Enquiry concerning the Principles of Morals, An, 8, 12, 53, 75–82, 134
Essays, Moral and Political, 6–8, 39–61
Essays and Treatises on Several Subjects, 2, 12, 86
Four Dissertations, 17, 143n39
Historical Essay on Chivalry and modern Honour, An, 1
History of England, The, 15–17, 83–105, 130, 135
Idea of a Perfect Commonwealth, The, 57, 58
Natural History of Religion, The, 106–8
Of the Balance of Trade, 60–61
Of Commerce, 58–59, 61
Of the Delicacy of Taste and Passion, 39
Of the Dignity or Meanness of Human Nature, 45
Of Eloquence, 43
Of Essay Writing, 39
Of the First Principles of Government, 53
Of the Jealousy of Trade, 61
Of the Liberty of the Press, 56
Of Miracles, 9–13
Of National Characters, 46–47
Of the Original Contract, 54
Of the Origin of Government, 55
Of Polygamy and Divorces, 47
Of the Populousness of Antient Nations, 14, 57
Of Public Credit, 60
Of the Rise and Progress of the Arts and Sciences, 44
Of the Standard of Taste, 40
Of the Study of History, 86
Of Tragedy, 42
Philosophical Essays concerning Human Understanding. See *Enquiry concerning Human Understanding*
Political Discourses, 8, 13–15
Sceptic, The, 48, 51–52
Sister Peg, 133, 154n10
Stoic, The, 48
That Politics may be Reduced to a Science, 53

Three Essays, Moral and Political see Essays, Moral and Political
Treatise of Human Nature, A, 1–6, 24–38, 62
Whether the British Government inclines more to Absolute Monarchy, or to a Republic, 56
poems, 154n4

Hume, David (nephew), 20, 22, 57
Hume's Fork, 65
hunting metaphor, 37
hypocrisy, religious, 98–104

ideas, 25, 63–65
identity, personal, 28–29
imagery in *Treatise...*, 31–38
Independents (sect), 103–4
induction, 24, 27–28, 133–34
irony, 49, 70, 109, 148n13, 150n15

jealousy, 47–48
Jews, Hume's attitude to treatment of, 100–102
Johnson, Dr. Samuel, moral judgments similar to Hume's, 97–98; style compared with Hume's, 129

Kames, Lord. *See* Home, Henry
Kant, Immanuel, comment on Hume's analysis of induction, 134
Kierkegaard, Soren, comment on '*Of Miracles*', 135
Kincaid, Alexander (publisher), 6, 142n30

labor, 59
language, 46
Leland, John: *View of the Principal Deistical Writers,* 10
Leland, Thomas: *History of the Life and Reign of Philip, King of Macedon,* 90
liberty, 55–56, 150–51n17
literature, 39–45
Locke, John: *Letter concerning Toleration,*

98–99; style, compared with Hume, 132

Maclaurin, Colin, arguments used by Hume in *Dialogues concerning Natural Religion,* 110
marriage, 47–48
master-slave metaphor, 30, 36
metaphor in *Treatise...*, 31–38
metaphysics, 2–3
Millar, Andrew (publisher): *Enquiry concerning the Principles of Morals,* 12; *Four Dissertations,* 17; *History of England,* 16; letter from Hume about Ralph's *History of England,* 84; *Natural History of Religion,* 106; *Philosophical Essays concerning Human Understanding,* 8
Milner, Joseph: *Gibbon's Account of Christianity considered...*, 21–22, 110
mind, 31–38
miracles, 9–13, 70–73
monarchy, 56–57
money, 59–61
morals, moral sciences, 30–31, 39–61, 75–82, 134
"Moral Sense" school, 145n14
Mure of Caldwell, William, Baron, comment on Hume, 1; letter from Hume about American revolution, 57

Napier, John (inventor of logarithms), 96
national character, 46–47
national debt, 60
naturalism, 74
Newton, Sir Isaac, regarded by Hume as genius, 95–96
Newton, Thomas, comment on Hume's style, 132

original contract, 54

passion(s), 28–30, 32–33, 36, 37, 59; delicacy of, 39–40; *see also* self love
personal identity, 28–29
Platonism, 50–51
politics, 53–58

polygamy, 47–48
power, religious, 98–104
press, liberty, 56
probability, 35, 67–68
propositions, 65–66
public debt, 60
Pyrrhonian skepticism, 26–27

Ralph, James: *History of England, 83–84,* 90
Ramsay, Andrew Michael (Chevalier), 24
Ramsay, Michael (friend of Hume), 24
reasoning, inductive, 24, *27–28,* 133–34
Rapin (Rapin-Thoyras), Paul de, history of England, 15, 83
Relations of Ideas, 65–66
religious power and hypocrisy, 98–104
religious skepticism, 106–26, 135–36
republicanism, 56–57
republic metaphor, 34
rhetoric, 39–45
Robertson, William (historian), 90, 92
Rose, William (reviewer), 13–14
Rousseau, Jean-Jacques, relationship with Hume, 18
Russell, Bertrand, on induction, 134; on miracles, 72

St. Clair, General James, Hume as secretary, 8
Scotticisms, 14
Selby-Bigge, L. A. (editor), 62
self, 28–29
self-love, 75–82
sentiment and sentimentality, 39, 150n16
Sextus Empiricus (skeptic), 26
Shaftesbury, Earl of. *See* Cooper, Anthony Ashley
Skelton, Rev. Philip, 9–10

skepticism, *26–27,* 36, *51–52,* 74, 81; religious, 106–26, 135–36
Smith, Adam (friend of Hume), comment on Hume's life and death, 23; discussion with Hume about *Dialogues concerning Natural Religion,* 19, 123; ideas on economics, compared with Hume, 15, 58; moral theory, 148–49n19; mss. left to S. by Hume, 20; reputed author of *Abstract,* 5
Smollett, Tobias: *Complete History of England,* 15–16
social contract, 54
step metaphor, 124
Stoicism, 49–50
Strahan, William (printer), correspondence and discussions with Hume about *History of England,* 16, 84, 92; inauguration of association with Hume, 8; letter from Hugh Blair about *Dialogues concerning Natural Religion,* 123–24; letter from Hume about *Dialogues concerning Natural Religion,* 20
sympathy theory, 42

taste, 39–42
theatre metaphor, 33–34
trade, 61
tragedy, 42
tyranny, 100–102

Voltaire, ridicule of General St. Clair, 141n18

Wallace, Rev. Robert, 14, 142n30
Wallace, Sir William (patriot), 93
Warburton, Rev. William, 4, 106
women, marriage and divorce, 47–48

The Author

Born in 1937, John Valdimir Price, a native of Texas, received his Ph.D. from the University of Texas in 1962. He taught in California for three years before taking a position in the Department of English Literature at the University of Edinburgh in 1965. In 1988, he was named honorary fellow there.

Dr. Price is the author of *The Ironic Hume* (1965). His edition of Hume's *Dialogues concerning Natural Religion* was published by Clarendon Press in 1976. He has written a number of articles on Hume, and has edited several of Hume's letters. Other publications of his include a monograph on Tobias Smollett's novel, *Humphry Clinker,* as well as essays on Henry Fielding, Alexander Pope, the eighteenth-century novel, and the history of ideas in the eighteenth century. He is currently continuing his research on Hume's literary career and working on a study of English literature in the Scottish Enlightenment.